HOW TO
PROGRAM
COMPUTERS
IN
COBOL

ALSO BY MORTON D. BLUESTONE

Accounting

HOW TO
PROGRAM
COMPUTERS
IN
COBOL

Morton D. Bluestone

AND

Richard Mautner

COLLIER BOOKS

A Division of Macmillan Publishing Co., Inc.

New York

COLLIER MACMILLAN PUBLISHERS

London

ACKNOWLEDGMENT

The following acknowledgment is reproduced at the request of the American National Standards Institute as it appears in their publication X3.23-1968, approved August 23, 1968, by the American National Standards Institute, and approved as a Federal Information Processing Standard by the Office of Management and Budget on January 28, 1972:

Any organization interested in using the COBOL specifications as the basis for an instructional manual or for any other purpose is free to do so. However, all such organizations are requested to reproduce this section as part of the introduction to the document. Those using a short passage, as in a book review, are requested to mention "COBOL" in acknowledgment of the source, but need not quote this entire section.

COBOL is an industry language and is not the property of any company or group of companies, or of any organization or group of organizations.

No warranty, expressed or implied, is made by any contributor or by the COBOL Committee as to the accuracy and functioning of the programming system and language. Moreover, no responsibility is assumed by any contributor, or by the committee, in connection therewith.

Procedures have been established for the maintenance of COBOL. Inquiries concerning the procedures for proposing changes should be directed to the Executive Committee of the Conference on Data Systems Languages.

The authors and copyright holders of the copyrighted material used herein
FLOW-MATIC (Trademark of Sperry Rand Corporation, Programming for the UNIVAC® I and II, Data Automation Systems), copyrighted 1958, 1959, by Sperry Rand Corporation; IBM Commercial Translator Form No. F28–8013, copyrighted 1959 by IBM; FACT, DSI 27A 5260–2760, copyrighted 1960 by Minneapolis–Honeywell.
have specifically authorized the use of this material in whole, or in part, in the COBOL specifications. Such authorization extends to the reproduction and use of COBOL specifications in programming manuals or similar publications.

Macmillan Publishing Co., Inc.
866 Third Avenue, New York, N.Y. 10022
Collier-Macmillan Canada Ltd.

How to Program Computers in COBOL is published in a hardcover edition by Macmillan Publishing Co., Inc.

FIRST COLLIER BOOKS EDITION 1974

Printed in the United States of America

Library of Congress Cataloging in Publication Data

Bluestone, Morton D
  How to program computers in COBOL.

  1. COBOL (Computer program language) 2. Electronic digital computers—Programming. I. Mautner, Richard, 1933–   joint author. II. Title.
QA76.73.C25B58 1974   001.6′424   74–6061
ISBN 0–02–008080–8

CONTENTS

PART B
Environment: Current Logical
Tools

2   FLOWCHARTING AS A PROGRAMMING AID   23

PART C
COBOL as a Logical Tool
in the Environment

3   THE STRUCTURE OF COBOL   37

4   THE DIVISIONS OF A COBOL PROGRAM   47

PART D
Some Additional
Perspectives

14 SYSTEMS AND PROGRAMMING CONTROLS 145

15 CONCEPTS AND TECHNIQUES FOR FURTHER STUDY 154

Introduction

The intended uses of this textbook are two:

1. As a tool of instruction in a college or programming school course in COBOL programming.
2. As a means of self-instruction for anyone literate in the English language who desires to acquire a basic working knowledge of how to program computers for business use.

Both of these uses presume that the student will write source programs based on the sample specifications provided in the text and will have access to keypunch and computer equipment to permit compilation and testing with adequate test data. In a formal course, this equipment is usually available through the educational institution; the self-instructing student assumes the burdens of, first, locating a computer operation whose management will permit the necessary access to equipment, and, second, familiarizing himself with the variations of specific instructions as required by the particular computer manufacturer's subset of ANSI COBOL.

Since the primary objective of this book is to provide a base for learning how to program computers for business purposes rather than a specific model or type of computer, it was necessary to settle upon the only current business programming language that is basically independent of any particular computer and is capable of being used most generally. At present, COBOL is the only business programming language that is available on almost all digital computers for general business

purposes. The basic procedural logic of COBOL is the same for all computers for which COBOL subsets are available; computer "hardware" for performing specific functions varies among computers. Consequently, certain COBOL statements involving the "hardware" environment will vary. In the course of textual presentation, the points of variation are made known, and representative examples of differences are cited so that the student may be aware of the statements in a COBOL program which must be varied depending on the computer being used.

To best fulfill the main textual objective for both uses, a specific general plan is used, intended for adaptability to needs of students at different stages. Sequentially, the text is in three phases:

1. A brief history of the development of business-oriented computers and programming languages for them. The student who has no background at all in these areas must be supplied with enough information to obtain a clear perspective of the uses of computers and understand how and why machine-oriented languages and "problem-oriented" (really subject-oriented) languages such as COBOL were developed. The college student who has taken an overview course in computer history, concepts, and functions prior to a programming course may need this section only as a "reminder" review of background.

2. A brief treatment of flowcharting logic as a necessity for defining problems and outlining action

for orderly solution, both generally and as applied to computer programming. The necessity of flowcharting as a preliminary step to writing all but the simplest of computer programs cannot be overemphasized as a time-saver in both the writing of the source program and testing with "live" data after compilation. If the college student has had a prior course which included flowcharting principles, the general principles will be mere review, but those relating principally to computer programming should be useful; the student with no initial background should find both the general and specific portions of value.

3. The main body of text specifically concerning COBOL programming attempts to develop knowledge of the basic statements in the context of a complete program wherever possible. COBOL and other "problem-oriented" languages were evolved to simplify the writing of *programs*; the aim here is to show how each basic instruction or language rule fits into a *program* perspective. Variations and exceptions for individual statements can be discussed with meaning after the place of each statement in relationship to others in a whole program has been established. For example, such concepts as comparing a record's code number to the code number stored from the preceding record, or the use of page headings, or, even more essential, the sequence of routines to accumulate and print sequential data-group totals at various levels of inclusiveness must be established by demonstrating their function in a complete program. Discussion of the concept or principle, no matter how detailed or inclusive of variations or exceptions, may establish the theory, but it does not demonstrate *how to program*. We have attempted here to show first how principles fit into specific objectives of a complete program, believing that subsequent development of a principle's variations and exceptions will have more meaning once the basic idea has been put to use in writing a program in which the new principle has been meshed with the use of others. We have, in a sense, sacrificed the neatness of discussing all aspects of a particular COBOL verb or statement in one place to showing the functional use of several types of statements or verbs combined to produce a specific basic type of program. Reinforcement of knowledge by exercise of a principle in various examples of typical basic programs provides

a sound basis for later detailed theoretical discussion organized along more catalogued lines, and is more practical than an initially "complete" discussion of theory illustrated with entries and routines, which are at best only fragments of programs. Having put together a program, the student will be better able to perceive what part of one a fragment represents.

All three phases of this book are intended to be geared to the outlook of problem-oriented programming languages—how to use a tool, the computer, in a relatively specific range of applications. The acknowledged base of ANSI COBOL specifications, rather than any specific computer subset, is the foundation for the technique of applying the tool to the "problem." Variations of the tool that require marginal alterations of technique are placed in perspective as incidental; possible differences between computers producing verbiage variations of specific computer subsets from the ANSI COBOL specifications are identified as such. Responsibility of textbook-writer to student requires that some forewarning be provided the student of those areas in COBOL which are still, at least in part, computer-dependent. Too much confusion has resulted from textbooks that fail to clearly indicate that a described routine is applicable only in a particular COBOL subset applying to one type of computer, or represent as an ANSI COBOL reserved word list one which contains implementor names and even verbs that occur only in a particular manufacturer's subset.

Some final words of caution should precede the body of any computer programming text: Computers as information-handling tools and programming languages as techniques in using the tools are both very recent additions to our technology. In the next decade or two the programming techniques described here may acquire even greater acceptance and be more tightly standardized, or they may be replaced rather completely by others, different or similar, for better or for worse. It is too early in this particular technological area to determine what will happen. Currently, however, COBOL is the most nearly universal of business programming languages for computers and provides the most practical basis for learning existing computer control techniques and establishing a point of departure for evaluation of new ones that may have to be learned.

PART A

Environment: History, Hardware, and Functions

1

HISTORY AND FUNCTIONS
OF COMPUTERS

WHAT IS A COMPUTER?

The term "computer" in today's world is at best loose and misleading. Probably the most accurate use of the word is in its reference to the pocketsize or desk-used machines that contain electronically controlled (*a*) components to do arithmetical operations, (*b*) "storage" areas for holding data to be accumulated or referenced in performing the arithmetic, and (*c*) areas for display of results, usually on an illuminated registration line. These are true computers, whose only function other than the computing process is to make the results visible to the user. "Programming" is limited to the pressing of keys related to specific arithmetical processes in the sequence required for a specific type of computation and is done while operating the computer. Though this type of machine (as well as its forerunners, the desk-type electric and mechanical calculators) is strictly a computer, it is not what most people have in mind when they use the term. Most people are referring to the fairly large, electrically-powered electronic computers used for scientific and/or commercial purposes in government, business, and a variety of scientific and engineering applications. There is often a vague idea expressed that one generic type of "computer" is used for all of these applications, and that all applications require the same type of programming knowledge. A brief review of the kinds of computers used in these areas should indicate the major differences, as well as the types to which COBOL programming is relevant.

Computers can be classified as either analog or digital. An analog computer works by comparison (analogy) to known quantities (such as pressure, temperature, or electric current) registered in some indicator on the computer, and by combining representations of these quantities mathematically to provide informative results. The slide rule, which expresses mathematical relationships based on length, is essentially an analog computer. Modern electronic analog computers are typically used for "real-time" applications, processes in which data received by the computer during part of the process are analyzed and the results used (either by the computer itself or with some manual aid) to control further steps in the process. Most processes to which analog computers are applicable are in the areas of research, simulation, and engineering. However, in the vast majority of applications involving "real-time," such as for specialized industrial processing, special digital computers must be used in combination with analog devices to convert the analog-originated data to usable form. Both analog and special-purpose digital computers, however, are programmed and controlled in a significantly different manner from computers used for business purposes, and are outside of the scope of this book. In addition, many of the general-purpose commercial computers are designed to handle scientific data, but the programming languages used are not generally those used for business applications. These computers are also outside the scope of this book.

FORERUNNERS OF PRESENT DIGITAL COMPUTERS

Present business purposes require the use of digital-type computers. Though machines that can be logically described as digital computers have been in business use for many years, they have normally been referred to as "adding machines" or "calculators." The first Comptometer, a key-driven machine operated with no other source of power than human fingers, was patented in 1887. By the 1920s and 1930s, this machine, as well as similar ones (such as Burroughs') were widely used for desk calculations involving addition, subtraction, multiplication, and division. Results produced on a visible register on the machine had to be hand-copied to documents. The introduction of electrified machines (such as the Monroe, Marchant, and Friden calculators) eliminated repeated key depressions for multiplying and dividing but, until after World War II, these machines provided no printed output on paper. Adding machines that listed and printed totals on a roll of paper tape about two inches wide were produced as early as 1889 by Felt (originator of the Comptometer) and 1892 by Burroughs. The simplified ten-key adding machine was produced by the Sundstrands in 1914, also with printout capability.

The principles of adding machine printout and typewriter capabilities were combined to a limited extent in the "posting," "bookkeeping," and billing machines of the era between World Wars I and II. These machines performed a partial computer function, but were, as were the desk calculators and adding machines, controlled by the operator on each item of input data. Meanwhile, punched-card techniques (initiated by Dr. Herman Hollerith for the 1890 United States census) had developed to the extent that such business operations as sales analysis and portions of accounting operations subject to code-numbering for identification were typical uses for punched-card electric machine accounting. Computing, however, was limited to addition and subtraction; and until the very late 1930s, such machines had no alphabetic printing capabilities. Combination of machine printouts with the use of addressograph plates, typewriting, or even handwriting, was a frequent makeshift. Introduction of alphabetic printing capability widened the scope of applicability of punched-card machines to most business areas; they soon became competitive to key-driven billing and posting machines in such activities as accounts payable and receivable bookkeeping and payroll accounting.

The ability to multiply and divide did not fully become a part of punched-card machine facilities until after World War II; in fact, the "first-generation" (electronic vacuum-tube) computers were just coming into use in the period (about 1945–58) when adequate punched-card calculating equipment was being made functional in the United States by IBM and Remington–Rand (later Sperry–Rand). Essentially, the full complement of punched-card data-processing operations, with the development of an electronic calculator as the last machine in a diverse group, was established simultaneously with the development of early large- and medium-scale "computers," which do most of the same work faster and in a somewhat different manner.

PUNCHED-CARD ACCOUNTING: BRIDGE TO THE COMPUTER WORLD OF THE 1950s

Punched-card equipment in the mid-1950s, whether by IBM or Remington–Rand, was characterized by several types of machines, each performing a specific function or functions in an inter-related series.[1] A typical configuration of equipment would consist of one or more of each of the following machines:[2]

Keypunch: This machine has a typewriter-like keyboard enabling the operator to record an alphabetic, numeric, or special character as one, two, or three holes punched in any column of an eighty-column card. A printing mechanism to record on the face of the card, along the top edge, each character punched is a frequent feature; this enables reading of the punched data without deciphering the punched holes. The keypunch operates at the typing speed of the operator.

Verifier: Although almost identical in appearance to a keypunch, the verifier does not punch. It is used ordinarily by an operator who has not punched the batch of cards being verified. The verifier operator checks the keypunch operator's work by using the same source data and simulating the punching of each original card as it is fed into the verifier. The verifying mechanism compares the verifier operator's

---

1. Even in the 1950s, IBM's "share of the market" in the United States was far greater than 50 percent; Remington–Rand was the only significant competitor.

2. The characteristics of the machines are described as they existed at the indicated time. Present capabilities of those still in use are described on pp. 14–15.

keystrokes individually to each punched-card column. When there is a difference, the verifier stops, requiring the operator to repeat the keystroke; if the keystroke is still different from the original punching, the machine notches the top edge of the column in error and enables the operator to continue verifying. The notched cards are later replaced by the keypunch operator with correct ones.

Sorter: Each card in a file normally contains a code number (such as employee, account, or department). Commonly, it is desirable that the cards be sequenced in ascending order of code number. Such a file is said to be sorted on the code number. This is done on the machine called a "sorter," which sorts the file of cards by processing it once for each digit in the code number. By processing large or small volumes of cards (at a then-typical rate of 650 cards per minute) on each column of a given code area, or field, from the units position leftward, a sorter operator places cards in specific sequences required for further use, such as collating or report preparation.

Collator: Sorted cards often require matching or interfiling, or a combination of both, with another set of cards already in the same sequence on a common code field. The collator, a machine with two card-input feed hoppers and then four (later five) card-output stackers, can then simultaneously process about 400 cards per minute from each feed hopper. In the processing, the code sequence of the cards in one feed can be checked; and matching, interfiling, or selecting cards from either feed into specified output stackers can be done. The operator's wiring of a plugboard-type removable control panel governs the selection of the card fields to be compared and the filing and selection conditions for the processing.

Line printer: Called by IBM an "electric accounting machine," the line printer is able to "read" data from punched cards, add, subtract, accumulate group totals, and print out individual card data or group totals a line at a time. By the early 1950s, the ability to store a small amount of data had also been developed. The fastest machine (IBM's 407) could print 150 lines per minute, each line containing a maximum of 120 alphabetic and/or numeric and special characters. On other printers, the typical speed was about 100 lines per minute. Controlled by a removable plugboard panel (on IBM printers, wired by user personnel, on Remington–Rand's, prewired by manufacturer for user's needs on specific reports), these machines were communicators of card-processing results to various areas of the user business. Typical printouts might be checks paying employees or suppliers, invoices or statements to be sent customers, various types of sales analyses, inventory movement reports, and many others.[3]

Automatic punching equipment: By the mid-1950s the need for reproducing (transferring punched data from one set of cards to another matched set), gang-punching (punching information from a single card into numerous other cards following it), and summary-punching (punching group total data generated by the printer into a single card per group by having the punching equipment and printer connected by a cable) was served by machines which processed up to 100 cards a minute. All these machines were controlled by plugboard panels. IBM's equipment was of two types: a summary-punch which could also be used as a gangpunch, and a reproducing punch which could, in addition to these operations, perform its named function. Remington–Rand's reproducing operation was performed by its collator; the summary punch was another piece of equipment; and gang-punching could be performed on its keypunch machine as an automated operation.

Interpreters: Reproduced or summarized cards were often used by areas outside the punched-card operations, to be returned with marking as new documents; but the automatic punching equipment producing these cards had no printing facility to interpret the punched holes as readable letters and numbers. To make cards readable before release to outside areas, interpreting machines (which do not punch), usually processing about sixty cards a minute, performed printing of the punched data across a line area of the card not occupied by punching. Printing, controlled

---

3. It should be noted here that what was probably the first use of the term "program" as applied to data-processing machine operations was in connection with the wiring of IBM "electric accounting machines." The process of these machines in accumulating totals for sequential groups and subgroups of cards containing the same identifying code numbers was referred to as a "program." Recognition, through plugboard wiring, of the last card of a common-coded group and the beginning of the next initiated a "program start" and permitted further wiring to cause totals for a group of cards to print following reading of the last card in the group. Sockets (hubs) on printer plugboards were available for "programs" on IBM equipment prior to World War II. This enabled printing of identifications of three levels of groups and subgroups of cards within a report batch, as well as totals of data at the group levels.

by wiring of a plugboard panel, could be in a form not restricted by the sequence of punching in the card.

Calculating punches: Electronic calculating punches were developed almost simultaneously with first-generation electronic computers. Reference to them as computers seems to have been rather rigorously avoided, yet they were, properly speaking, more essentially computers than are current "computers," which typically perform numerous functions in addition to computing. Utilizing comparatively small capacities for computations and storage, vacuum-tube calculators such as IBM's 604 and 607 and, a little later, Remington–Rand's Univac 60 and 120 could make relatively elaborate calculations and punch the results in up to 100 cards a minute. User-wired plugboard panels controlled the card-reading, arithmetical, and card-punching operations.

Essentially, in the 1950s, punched-card machines could be used to originate data at typewriter speed, verify its accuracy manually at about the same speed, sort it into a desired sequence at perhaps thirty to fifty times manual speed, interfile sorted data with perhaps the same time advantage, both print and summarize data at about fifty times the speed of typewriting, and perform calculations at a rate which could sometimes yield an even greater time advantage. Cost of machines, personnel, and overhead for such organization of data-processing activities still did not necessarily run lower than that of manual activities aided by simpler machinery.

The chief advantage of punched-card equipment, particularly after the introduction of vacuum-tube calculators, was the ability to do jobs successfully that would not be undertaken at all on a manual basis because of prohibitive cost or time limitations. Normally such types of work involved data analysis in *multiple* ways in a relatively short time, so short as to require a prohibitively large manual task force to do the work. In such cases, as long as preparation of source data by keypunching and verifying were feasible, and time limits permitted completion of the high-speed machine processing, the activity became a practical punched-card application even if not less costly than the amount of manual processing that could not be coordinated to meet the time deadlines. Conversely, the keypunching and verifying of even a large volume of data for a *single* processing through various punched-card machines often cost more in *both* time and money than manual processing. Multiple uses of the same data became an important determinant of the time (if not cost) advantage of punched-card equipment over manual techniques.

EARLY MODERN COMPUTERS: "FIRST-GENERATION" VACUUM-TUBE TYPES

The large-scale computers that were first developed in the 1940s were not originally designed to meet general business needs. Such pioneer vacuum-tube-type computers of the 1940s as the Mark I and ENIAC were constructed to produce mathematical data and solve problems for physicists, mathematicians, engineers, and meteorologists. Punched cards were the input and output media. The ENIAC could perform 300 multiplications per second as compared to one per second for an efficient contemporary electromechanical calculator. The punched-card input to and output from the first computers, however, were at the speeds of the then-existing punched-card equipment (such as a somewhat altered reproducing or gangpunch machine) which had to be connected to the computer itself. Moreover, these early computers had no facilities of their own for rearranging data (sorting or collating) in *external* files or printing out results. The EDVAC (1945) for which Dr. John von Neumann wrote the first sorting program, performed internal rearrangement of data in numeric sequence. Sorting data internally, however, made costly demands on computer storage areas.

The first electronic "computer" eventually adapted to business purposes was the UNIVAC (designed by John Mauchly and J. Presper Eckert, the developers of the ENIAC). The first UNIVAC was used in 1951 at the United States Bureau of the Census. The UNIVAC and such large-scale machines as IBM's 701 and 702 and medium-scale ones such as the IBM RAMAC and 650 and Remington–Rand's UNIVAC File Computer were among those which soon were being promoted for general use by businesses large enough to benefit from their use. The sole function of extremely rapid computing, however, was not enough to meet general business needs. IBM's early 650, for example, the most widely used medium-scale computer, read and punched cards with equipment similar to IBM's 519 reproducer, at precisely the same speed, 100 cards per minute. Internal storage (memory) of large-scale computers, while vast for some purposes, was not convenient for file retention or updating; and sorting of internally stored data was of limited practicality. Printout was confined to the 100- or 150-line-per-minute equipment available for conventional punched-card processing. The lightning speeds of internal computation were bottlenecked by slow input and output processing and lack of storage facilities which would permit rapid rearrangement and communication of "computed" data. A major problem was that the computer's internal capacity was being used not only to store processing instructions (programs) but whole files of data as well.

By the middle and late 1950s, however, some notable advances had been made in "peripheral" devices for the vacuum-tube machines now referred to as "first-generation" computers. The use of magnetic tape as an external data-storage medium was introduced, bringing with it the development of programmed techniques for sorting the externally-stored data. Substantial increases in card-reading and line-printing speeds were also being developed in the few years before the appearance of the "second-generation" computers.

"SECOND-GENERATION" (TRANSISTORIZED) COMPUTERS

Transistorized (solid state) internal components had, at the end of the 1950s, begun the "second generation" of computers, which replaced the vacuum-tube type. This change in internal "hardware" vastly reduced both the size of a computer's operating units and the air-conditioning capacity requirements for maintenance and moderate operating temperatures in the computer area. By this time, much progress had also been made in introducing faster input and output devices and providing more practical means of rearranging data through use of external storage devices. Large-scale computers had card-input feeds capable of processing 800 to 1000 cards per minute; a typical card-reading speed for medium- and small-sized computers was 400 cards per minute. Printers of up to 500- or 600-line-a-minute speeds were beginning to be available, to be supplemented or replaced in the early 1960s by ones with 1,000 to 1,200 lines per minute capability. One of several changes that most affected the nature of computers, begun toward the end of the first generation, was, however, the shift of emphasis from internal to external file storage. A second change was simultaneous reading, "writing," and internal processing, which enabled time-saving by overlapping of the three operations. A third change introduced in second-generation computers was the development of operating-system and programming language techniques that made possible, among other things, "blocking" of records on output devices. These features will be discussed a little later.

As already suggested, the use of internal "memory" areas of the computer for data-file storage was awkward and costly. Even the "first-generation" computers processed data internally many times faster than read-in, print-out, or punch-out speed; and in spite of a four- to ten-fold increase in the input–output speeds for "second-generation" computers, internal processing still took place at a far faster rate. Updating of data files in internal memory often taxed computer operational capacity, caused problems of sequencing or data rearrangement, and sometimes necessitated read-in and read-out at costly lower-than-internal speeds in order to make internal storage available for storing of a new data file. Development of rapidly accessible external storage devices to an operational stage in the late 1950s released computer storage areas for program control capabilities. Effectively, the computer became the central control device monitoring not only input–output functions but the intermediate functions of file sorting, collating, and reproducing, all of which had been performed by separate single-function machines in the days when electric punched-card machines predominated. Two new names were now added to the data-processing vocabulary: *unit-record*, to identify strictly punched-card techniques; and *EDP* (electronic data processing), to refer to computer-controlled operations involving mass-storage devices, on which "unit records" were *not* manually reachable individually.

The two chief types of mass-storage devices external to a computer that are still in use are the magnetic tape unit and the magnetic disk "pack." The former is more truly external; the disk is, in a sense, an extension of internal storage. Computer magnetic tape is essentially the same as used on recording devices, except that for readability of the far more microscopic electronic "bit" patterns that must be read and written by a computer, far more rigid manufacturer's quality testing must be made to assure accurate reproduction. A disk pack resembles a "juke box" in construction and operating principle; it is essentially a stack of records on which files of data can be stored and, under control of a computer program, has a specific area selected almost immediately in connection with a required computer operation in the program. Sorting of data on magnetic tape reels or disk packs is accomplished by combinations of repeated copying of data onto other reels or packs in resequenced groups. Disk sorting in most (but *not* all) cases is faster than tape sorting; disk storage, however, takes up more physical space at a higher cost. The chief advantage of disk storage over tape, however, is that any part of an entire disk-stored file of data is available for immediate reference; with tape, only one record at a time is sequentially available. Input data related to a disk-stored file can be read into the computer in no order at all, and the related file data immediately located for each input data record; this is known as *random access*. Tape storage requires that the stored data be in sequence by some numeric or alphabetic code, and related input data must be in the same sequence as the stored data for efficient processing. Unsequenced input data would create the necessity for processing the stored file either backward or forward for each input record, making not only unpredictable but impractically long the amount of time required for any volume operation.

Although some early computers (notably IBM's RAMAC) employed disk storage and some smaller second-generation computers were available at relatively low cost with disk storage, tape storage was probably more widely used during the 1960s. Currently, disk storage appears to be returning to favor, as the technique of storing major segments of programs on disk has been developed to enable smaller computers to make use of voluminous programs, which formerly required the internal storage capacity available only on much larger computers.[4]

These developments of computers for business purposes, gradually adding external devices to perform most (but not quite all) of the functions of the older "unit-record" electrical equipment have changed the computer's functional nature so that actually the time the typical computer is used for sorting (which includes no real computing), file updating (which sometimes involves computing, but frequently is only collating), and printout not involving concurrent computing, far exceeds the time for which the computer is used strictly *as a computer*. As a configuration of equipment with a "central processor," capable of internally storing instructions and large but limited volumes of data and performing various types of operations, connected to various *input* and *output devices*, the computer is really a multifunction arsenal of data-processing "hardware," not just a computer. These changes in computer functions over the last quarter-century have also changed the nature and proportions of the programming function, or at least the business concepts of it.

WHAT IS A PROGRAMMER?

Neither first-generation nor present computers perform arithmetic in the "base-ten" operational framework. Various other methods, most frequently binary, hexadecimal, and octal, are built into the "hardware" as a more efficient means for the computer of interpreting data characters and performing arithmetic. Results are then translated within the computer into our alphabetic and decimal-numeric characters for the purpose of creating readable printout.

When the first-generation computers were made, each computer manufacturer created its own sets of symbols to identify specific computer operating func-

tions and areas, and these symbols (usually alphabetic and sometimes mnemonic) constituted the vocabulary of a "machine language" in which a program of instructions to the computer had to be written. Much of the programming and testing of the programs necessitated reference to the arithmetical system in which the computer operated; moreover, the first computers were intended for "higher" mathematical operations than typically occur in business applications. Hence it was somewhat expectable that in the middle and late 1950s there was almost an insistence that persons interested in becoming programmers must have a good background in mathematics, preferably at college level. Occasionally, exceptions were made for unit-record operating personnel with demonstrated ability to wire accounting machine and calculator control panels. This attitude persisted until at least the mid-1960s, when a trend set in to accept as programmer trainees *any* college graduates (usually after taking specialized aptitude tests to indicate probable adaptability to computer programming). But even while first-generation vacuum-tube computers were in use, problems arose in connection with machine-language programming and computer manufacturers' substitutes for it.

Machine-language programming was quite tedious for the programmer. In essence, it required the programmer to allocate data and instructions to computer storage areas in the program and refer in program instructions to the allocated areas to perform specific computer operations. This meant, in effect, that in writing a relatively complicated program, the programmer needed to maintain in some way a memorandum running reference between each data field and the computer area to which it was allocated. Fairly early in the first-generation computer era, computer manufacturers initiated a means of simplifying this tedious side effect of programming in machine language. An "assembly language" was originated by the computer manufacturer which permitted the programmer to identify the data fields and operations to be performed without concerning himself with their allocation to specific computer areas. Sometimes the assembly language would contain codes which could be used to combine two or more operations in one instruction. The programmer using assembly language would write a "source program" rather than a program of instructions to be used directly by the computer on input data. The source program would be keypunched as a set of cards. The computer manufacturer furnished a standard "assembly program" (assembler) which (usually as a set of cards, later on magnetic tape), read into the computer ahead of the source program, would translate the assembly language into machine-language instructions, allocate the required computer storage areas, and

---

4. This technique is one of the uses of a capacity rather confusingly named *virtual storage*, which makes use of disk storage in lieu of internal storage.

produce an "object program," typically as punched-card output, in machine language. The object program, fed into the computer ahead of data input, would be stored in the computer and supply the instructions to the computer for processing of the data. The burden of detail for the programmer was lightened; but a problem remained for the first and largest user of computers—the Federal government.

The Federal government was, in the late 1950s, the largest customer in the computer market; and within the Federal government, the largest user of computers was the Department of Defense. Faced with the necessity of competitive bidding on contracts for computer rental or purchase, the Department of Defense found distressingly costly and chaotic the resulting need for training programmers not only in one assembly language, but in as many of them as there were computer manufacturers who were successful contract bidders. In addition, if the new computer was to be a replacement for an existing one, and used a different programming language, all continuing computer applications would require reprogramming in the language of the new computer.

In 1959, at a series of meetings promoted by the Department of Defense and attended by representatives from computer manufacturers, business and government computer users, and other interested groups, the desirability and feasibility of establishing a common programming language for computers in business-type usage was agreed upon and implementation begun. Out of this Conference on Data Systems Languages (CODASYL) was evolved a *co*mmon *b*usiness-*o*riented *l*anguage (COBOL) for computer programming. Some "problem-oriented" languages had already been developed to enable programming to be done in terms of instructions logical to the type of problem to be handled (as opposed to terms of internal operation of the computer); but these were rather specialized mathematical languages, such as FORTRAN. This type of program writing required a "compiler," itself a program which equated the programmer's language terms with "machine-language" terms, and produced the object program in a somewhat different, and usually slower, manner than did an "assembler." COBOL was to do, using general "English-language" terms, what FORTRAN did in mathematical terms. Any computer manufacturer claiming COBOL capability for his machine would now have to develop a compiler program to translate COBOL terminology to his computer's "machine language."

By 1962, bidders to sell or rent computers for Department of Defense use were required to offer a computer that could be programmed in COBOL. Outside of Federal government areas, acceptance of COBOL was neither immediate, widespread, nor enthusiastic. A majority of computer manufacturers (including the largest) continued to emphasize to their nongovernment customers the virtues of their own assembly languages or of compiler languages they developed as substitutes for COBOL (such as IBM's PL–1) or complements to assembly and compiler languages (such as IBM's RPG). Nevertheless, the Department of Defense's position did not change; and some computer manufacturers (such as Honeywell) developed, in addition to the full-scale CODASYL COBOL, abbreviated versions of COBOL for smaller computers—with considerable success. Now, early in the second decade of COBOL history, the only business programming language available on practically all large and many medium-sized and small computers is COBOL. In addition, two "minicomputers" (IBM's System 3 and Honeywell's Model 58) are programmable in the smallest versions of COBOL to date. Any other business computer languages, whether assembly (machine-oriented) or compiler (problem-oriented), are special to the computers for which they were created, and cannot be used for programming other computers. It is probable that COBOL is used by the largest number of programmers, even considering the dominance of IBM in the computer market and the fact that such languages as BAL (*B*asic *A*ssembly *L*anguage) and RPG (*R*eport *P*rogram *G*enerator) have been very widely used.

The development of assembly and compiler languages, particularly the latter, has minimized the programmer's need for advanced mathematical background; and as a result, the insistence of business organizations on four-year college degrees for trainee programmers has largely subsided in favor of training in specific programming languages at computer schools, two-year colleges, or programming courses given at four-year colleges and universities or by computer manufacturers. The primary function of a programmer is to translate specified requirements for a data-processing application into a logical series of computer-processable instructions so that the results from the computer will be usable in the specified format. The programmer's function can be broken down into the following steps:

1. Analyze the specifications for the program application to make sure that he or she understands the requirements. What is the form and content of the input data? the required output data? What specific computer operations must be performed? What conditional tests must be made? Are any checks to be made by the computer for detection of possible errors in data input? If so, how are such errors to be identified, and are they to be processed or rejected? Are there any seeming inconsistencies between the specifications for the program's operations and the format of the

results to be obtained? Is test data (see Step 6) being supplied, or is the programmer to formulate it?

2. Review the specifications with the personnel supplying them to clarify any areas of uncertainty created in the programmer's attempt to answer the above questions.

3. Define the programming requirements, preferably by constructing a logic flowchart, showing the sequential logical paths and subpaths required. For certain types of programs, a decision table may be desirable as either a supplement to or substitute for the flowchart.

4. Using the flowchart and/or decision table, write the source program of instructions in the coding format required by the programming language being used. Have the program keypunched.

5. Have the keypunched source program compiled (processed by the computer, using the compiler program to produce the object program). At this stage, a computer printout of the source program occurs. Errors made (by either programmer or keypuncher) that are misuses of the programming language will be identified on the printout; these identifications are known as "diagnostics." The programmer must now do his preliminary "debugging"—correction of these technical errors so that the corrected source program may be compiled into a workable object program (except, of course, in the rather rare instance of successful compilation without error on the first attempt, or whenever error-free compilation occurs).

6. Test the object program, using test data for which correct results have been determined independently of program or computer. If the results from the object program disagree, the programmer must now do his final "debugging," this time not being concerned with the technical use of the programming language as much as with the correctness of the logic used in writing the program. Here the flowchart or decision table is of almost immediate aid. The type of error in the test results suggests an error in a specific part or parts of the program. Do the program instructions follow the flowchart logic? Is the logic of the flowchart itself a misinterpretation of the specifications? Or, everything else being correct, are the predetermined results of the test data themselves incorrect? Where disagreement with predetermined results is not clearly confined to programming error, the programmer must review his results with the supplier of the specifications for possible differences in understanding of them.

7. Once final corrections have been made to the source program and an object program has been compiled and successfully tested, the programmer's final responsibility is often to supply documentation to the computer operating organization. At a minimum, this includes turning over to operations personnel the source and object programs, a source program listing, and a "run sheet" or similar paperwork. The run sheet, prepared either by the programmer or the systems personnel supplying the specifications for the program, is a set of instructions indicating what data input is to be used and how frequently, what output the computer is to generate, and what special procedures are to be followed in preparation of the input data, in computer processing, and in disposition of computer output.

Steps 1 and 7 in particular are ones where the programmer's function is sometimes not too clearly defined by an organization (whether business or government) making use of a computer on its premises. While the area of computerized data processing can be neatly divided into three parts—systems, programming, and operations—the first two are sharply separated by some businesses and combined by others. Where they are separated, the programmer will normally receive his specifications for a program from a systems analyst, with whom the reviews at Steps 2 and 6 will be conducted; and in some organizations, the systems analyst, rather than the programmer, will be responsible for constructing test data to accompany the specifications for the program and for the documentation described in Step 7. Where the systems and programming functions are joined in one department, a senior programmer assumes systems functions as well as programming, and may be aided by a junior programmer who performs only the programming function at the earlier stages of his employment. Viewpoints differ as to the desirability of combining or separating the systems and programming functions; but without passing judgment on relative superiority, it should be noted that both practices seem to be evident almost equally. It should also be noted that the systems *function* involves such responsibilities as collecting information concerning the requirements of the activities to be "computerized"; organizing the information into a proposal for a computerized system; setting up (after proposal approval) the detailed specifications for forms, programs, and movements of paperwork; and, as the system is made operational, monitoring the data-processing procedure until both the activity areas served and the computer operating area are able to coordinate without benefit of systems personnel serving as liaison or coordinator.

Another, perhaps less frequent, practice is to combine programming and operations in one department, with the systems organization acting as liaison between the organizations being served and the computer operating area. In such a framework, the programmer is usually closer to operations and may be expected to be familiar with computer operation, though not necessarily to operate the computer. In this organizational environment, the programmer is usually responsible for the internal operating instructions in the computer area as far as use of programs is concerned, and may have some responsibility for maintenance of program and data-file "libraries." Normally he will have *no* responsibilities in other computer-operations functions, such as data preparation (largely keypunching), clerical control over incoming source data, computer scheduling or operation, and checking out and making ready for using areas the results of computer output.

Regardless of his environmental organization, the programmer's work will involve not only the computer but numerous related machines with whose functions he should be familiar. In addition, the form and system in which data is "read" by computers and related equipment and stored in disk, tape, and punched-card files often requires specific programmer familiarity. A brief description of equipment and these interpretive techniques follows.

TODAY'S COMPUTERS AND THEIR DATA FORMATS

Today's computers (those of the early 1970s) are known variously as third- and fourth-generation machines. In addition to containing transistors rather than vacuum tubes, their internal construction may contain other types of circuitry and "hardware" coordinated with the transistorized system; both the third- and fourth-generation computers are often referred to as possessing "integrated circuitry." The changes in internal construction have not changed the basic components of a computer, however. "Computing" occurs internally; but the basis for it must be "read" by the computer, first in the form of a set of instructions (the object program) to be stored and referred to as, second, the input data are read in and worked on according to the instructions in the stored program. In addition, the results of the operation of the program instructions on the input data must be recorded somewhere for eventual communication to the users of the data; the recording may be on disk, tape, punched cards or paper printout. A basic computer, then, must have input and output devices in addition to its computing capability.

Input Devices and Media

An input device is any piece of equipment capable of transmitting data directly into the processing component of a computer, and is either a part of the computer itself or connected to it. Input devices are not to be confused with data-preparation equipment, which is used to put data into a form that can be processed in computer input devices. Currently, input devices can be placed in about seven groups, some of them for general, others for special, use:

Card readers: These are the oldest and still most generally used input components of computers. Almost all card readers are designed for processing eighty-column cards.[5] On smaller computers, typical speeds range from 300 to 500 cards per minute; on larger ones, 800 to 1,300.

Magnetic tape units: Connected to a computer as potentially either input or output devices, these have the capability of having their recorded data contents transferred to and from a computer processing unit at rates in the tens of thousands of digits per second. Until the late 1960s, magnetic tape records had to be computer-created from other types of input data (usually cards) prior to being used as computer input in subsequent operations; now data-preparation devices make possible the creation of magnetic tape records prior to their use as computer input, as will be indicated shortly.

Magnetic disk units: Like magnetic tapes, these can be used as either input or output devices in much the same manner. Data-preparation devices to transmit data to disks without computer involvement followed similar devices for magnetic tape record-writing by only a few years. Processing speeds for disk input-output are in roughly the same ranges as for tape.

Punched paper-tape readers: The use of punched paper tape is somewhat specialized. It is usually associated with the collection of fairly low-volume data prepared at each of many locations remote from a centralized computer area. Typical examples are branch office billing and payroll data, prepared on typewriters or billing machines with special attachments to generate punched paper tape as a by-product of the invoice or paycheck data output. The compactness of punched paper tape is convenient for mailing in ordinary envelopes. Reading devices used as computer input components transmit the punched data at a typical rate of several hundred characters per second. This relatively slow speed normally results in use of punched paper tape only with small computers, but an occasional large one may be equipped with a paper-tape reader as an input device.

---

5. The current exception is IBM's System 3, which makes use of a "minicard" requiring a special keypunch and sorter.

Character-reading devices: While based on the one principle of reading characters printed on paper directly into a computer, at present there are two main types of character readers. *Magnetic ink character recognition* (MICR) currently requires numeric and special character printing in magnetic ink on the document to be processed. It is confined largely to banking use, and appears to be gaining almost universal acceptance in banking circles. Checkbooks are made up with bank and account numbers preprinted on the checks; and in the bank or clearinghouse a machine operator records in magnetic ink the amount on each check being cleared, in a predetermined position on the check. The MIC reader is also a sorter which can rearrange the checks by bank and account numbers and, when a "read" switch is turned on, transmit the magnetic ink characters on each check to a computer equipped to accept the information.

Optical character readers (OCR) are special input devices available on some computers. They depend on preparation of input by typewriters with slightly different character styles from standard ones. An OCR can be used to scan an entire page of such typewriting or parts of one in a selected format. Applications of the OCR are limited only by the necessity of preparing the data input on typewriters employing the special type font. About a decade old, OCR is not yet a typical input technique.

Remote terminal devices: These include various key-driven machines, usually with basic typewriter keyboards, which are programmed to transmit data through telephone lines to a computer in another locality; the computer is mutually programmed both to process the data for immediate and later computer results, and to transmit the immediate results by the same telephone line through the remote terminal keyboard, which operates at typewriter speed. In a sense, the remote terminal is both an input and an output device. The computer's function for immediate output is usually to perform calculations and supply names for coded data. The former is time-saving; the latter standardizes print-out and relieves the machine operator of typing, but gains little, if any, time. During the automated typing time, the terminal operator is expected to check the source document to make sure that the code number keyed in resulted in transmittal back of the desired name data.

A growing use of this technique involves "small" businesses that use manually operated billing or bookkeeping machines or typewriters for such operations as billing, payroll, or accounts payable or receivable, and have a large enough data volume for efficient computer use, but find the cost of a computer operation of their own beyond their budget. A data-processing service with a large enough computer having disk storage may be able to serve a number of businesses in different nearby localities, each with its own remote terminal. Through efficient program and storage device use, a number of terminals (each in a different locality and each doing a different operation) may be able to communicate with the same computer simultaneously and independently. For clarity, a brief description of the function for a single user is needed.

For a functional remote-terminal operation, data files related to the operation (such as vendor, customer, or payroll master records, or inventory item data) are first stored as disk record files in the computer area. Through the mutual programming of computer and terminal, the computer assists the terminal operator as described above in preparing business documents, and usually updates disk record files in the process. In billing, for example, the terminal operator, by keying in a customer code number, gets the related name and address automatically typed as the computer transmits it to the terminal; by keying in an inventory item number and quantity shipped, the operator receives a typed line showing item name, price, and extended value. The computer meanwhile, has accumulated the extended value toward an invoice total and, if so programmed, has reduced the inventory item balance for the item billed. If the remote operation is confined to daytime hours, during those hours when remote-terminal connections are switched off, the same computer may be available for processing daily sales journals, updated inventory reports, and accounts receivable data from the files created or updated during the remote operation. Such reports are available to the user the next day. In some cases, reports may be transmitted back through the remote terminal; this is usually confined to low-volume operations, because of the slow (typewriter) speed of the terminal.

The Central Processing Unit of the Computer

The central processing unit (CPU), sometimes referred to as the "main frame," of the computer has three internal functions and the internal "hardware" to perform them. These are storage (memory), logic (decisions and arithmetic), and control. The storage area, normally comprising most of the physical bulk of the CPU, receives and holds the program during its use in processing the input data and, as required by the program, receives and holds input data, both as it is read in and in its intermediate stages while being changed to be produced as output data. The logic area performs the arithmetical and decisional operations upon the data; the control area functions as the timing and coordinating monitor among the other functions and physical components of the computer. In programming the early computers, using machine language, a programmer had to be aware of the specific storage and logic areas and concern himself with instructions which moved data from a storage area to a "register" or "accumulator" and vice versa. Compiler languages, such as COBOL, shift this function to the compiler, a standardized program that takes a programmer's source program instructions and translates them into a machine-language object program in which the instructions refer to the necessary functional locations specifically.

In addition to the internal control devices, any computer must have some external controls that enable the computer operator to start and stop the computer, perform special instructions, and obtain information from the computer about the status of the data being processed when anticipated or unexpected conditions arise. Accordingly, every computer has some type of "console," the external control device for operator use.

Output Devices

Three relatively standard forms of computer input are also forms of output—cards, disk records, and magnetic tape records. Disk records that contain data input may, after processing, contain the same data (somewhat altered) in the same disk areas. Magnetic tape input data is left intact during processing, but it is also read into the computer and, when processed as tape output, is "written" onto another reel of magnetic tape, providing the ability to retain the input data for other uses. Disk-to-disk processing can also be done in this manner, as well as disk-to-tape, and tape-to-disk. If disk or tape data are to be sorted, multiple units are desirable for disk and necessary for tape, since sorting using either of these devices requires repeated copying and sequence-rearranging of the data records. A typical minimal disk operation requires two or three disk packs; a tape-oriented computer will usually require a minimum of four tape "drives" or units for data-sorting.[6]

To obtain punched-card output, a punch unit with a typical output of 100 cards per minute, (or sometimes 300 to 400 cards per minute on large computers) is an almost-standard output device. Sometimes this unit will be separate from, other times a part of, the card reader input device. Some card readers (basically IBM's original 1402) are equipped to permit placing

cards containing some punched data in the punch feed, having them "read" by the computer, and punching additional data in them as output.

None of the three output devices just mentioned produces immediately readable results for *people*. The basic output device for this purpose is the line printer, of which there are many variations. The speed of mini-computer printers may be in the range of 100 to 150 lines a minute; on small computers 300; and, as already indicated on page 7, from 500 to 1,200 lines a minute on medium and large computers.

In the mid-1960s printouts at 1,000 or more lines a minute seemingly became so voluminous that by the end of the decade a refuge had been found—COM (*computer output microfilming*). Even at 1,000 lines a minute, however, computer printout was then, as now, far slower than computer writeout on magnetic tape. If the computer program formats the tape output as it would appear in a printed report, equipment available since 1970 can translate the tape characters to printed character lines on microfilm; and later-developed equipment is capable of translating directly from computer storage. In either case, speeds far exceed line printer capabilities, and space requirements for record maintenance are far less; but some types of output (such as checks and invoices) are not yet practical subjects for microfilming. The line printer has, almost needless to say, survived the rather minor inroads made by microfilm usage, even though inexpensive microfilm readers have been developed.

Special Optional Devices

Although disk and tape are generally-available input/output data storage devices, some *external mass-storage devices* are available with only specific manufacturers' computers. One is the magnetic drum storage device; another is IBM's data-cell. A third, perhaps more accurately described as an internal storage device, is NCR's CRAM (*card random access memory*) magnetic storage technique.

Many EDP organizations find it necessary or convenient to have one or more communication aids, either in the computer area or between it and the organizations serviced. One device used in the computer room is the *console typewriter*. Equipped with a continuous paper feed and used as a supplement to the computer console, the typewriter console enables the computer operator to type instructions and inquiries to the computer and receive replies from it automatically on the typewriter keyboard; in addition, it serves to provide an automatic log of all activities performed on the computer in the chronological sequence of perform-

---

6. A fairly well-known exception is the three-tape sort available on some of the Honeywell 200 "family" of computers.

ance. It should not be confused with data-input devices; its functions as a supplementary console are inquiry, control, operator-generated instruction, and historian.

A partially similar device, but usually employed as a remote terminal, is the CRT (*cathode ray tube*), basically a television picture tube, equipped with a typewriter keyboard. The keyboard permits inquiry to the computer; responses from computer storage areas are transmitted to the CRT, appearing in illuminated readable character format. While technically both an input and output device, the CRT-keyboard combination performs primarily a single-inquiry-displayed-response function and is not normally used for batch-processing of input or output. Where computers are used to record inventory movements, process airline ticket reservations, and the like, this method of direct inquiry to computer provides quick response.

Remote typewriter terminals also provide inquiry-response and brief problem-solving applications in a variety of situations that involve some form of time-sharing. These applications are frequently mathematical, scientific, or educational rather than commercial and, again, usually do not involve processing of substantial volumes of input or output data. They may range from engineering problems to efforts of high school students to solve mathematical problems in FORTRAN.

Perhaps two other special output devices or techniques should be noted, each connected with different occupational tasks. By far the older is the computer-controlled "plotter," basically a pen positioned over a continuous paper supply and controlled in its movement by instructions in a computer program and data governed by the instructions. Drawings, plans, and even art work can be produced in this manner. A newer and perhaps more workday application is a programming technique which, by using specially positioned special characters in the data, can produce uniquely formatted magnetic tape output, which is in turn employed to control automated typesetting. The special characters are used to control the use of capital and small letters and indicate where changes in type font are to be made in the taped data to be typeset.

Data-Preparation Hardware

Most *original* data going into computers is manually prepared, using some device with a typewriter keyboard, at approximately typewriting speed or slightly slower. *Keypunches* for cards are the oldest form of data-preparation equipment, and are substantially older than computers. At present, only two manufacturers (IBM and Sperry-Rand) market keypunches for eighty-column cards. IBM's 026 and 029 keypunches punch a

column as each keystroke is made; the Sperry-Rand VIP and IBM's 129 simply set up a die on each keystroke, and when the operator has completed keying in the data for one card, another stroke causes the entire card to be punched. This delayed punching feature also permits the operator to backspace and reset the character for a column in which an error is detected before punching takes place. Sperry-Rand's VIP and IBM's 129 can also be equipped to be used as a verifier (see page 4). *Key-tape* equipment and, more recently, *key-to-disk* equipment have appeared within the last several years to eliminate one computer reading step, that of converting card data to tape or disk records. Operation of these machines is basically the same as keypunching for cards, but typically it is supplemented by some display mechanism that makes the data punched readable by the keypunch operator as a means of minimizing or avoiding independent key verification.

The use of punched cards as *original* input may seem to be declining as compared with direct keying to tape and disk. Nevertheless, the tangible unit-record nature of the punched card makes it highly useful as a "turnaround document" which, when punched as computer output or by a reproducing punch, and "interpreted," can be used for a specific purpose and returned to the computer area as input data. The punched card is still widely used in customer accounting areas. Sent out as a supplement to a public-utility bill, telephone bill, or mortgage payment or insurance premium notice, or perhaps to some type of invoice, its return with payment minimizes both paperwork and keypunching in computer processing of cash receipts from customers. Since card punching is one of the slowest computer operations, and reproducing punch monthly rentals are equal at most to only a few hours' use of a computer, *reproducing punches* may be used to generate new cards from old ones where computer processing is not required to punch individually calculated changes in data. Current reproducing punches are substantially the same as in the early computer era, punching 100 cards per minute.

Whether a reproducer or computer punches out the cards to be used as turnaround documents, neither machine prints information on the cards while punching. This is done by somewhat updated versions of precomputer era *interpreters*, which can print information on cards by reading their punched columns at 100 cards per minute. The readable card output from an interpreter is ready for transmittal to outside people or businesses. The mass-punched and *interpreted* card should not be mistaken for computer-*printed* cards, which contain a minimum of punching. These are originally continuous forms, prepunched and printed with a minimum of consecutive coding, where it is possible to have computer input data records in a precise sequence and the computer creates tape or disk records with coding matching that on the cards printed out by the computer.

Another still-surviving precomputer machine is the card sorter. Particularly when card- or tape-oriented computers are used, and data volume is substantial, a card sorter may still be found in computer areas. IBM's 083 and 084 sorters have speeds of 1,000 and 2,000 cards per minute respectively. Since each column of a code field must be sorted separately, this means that a five-column numeric code sort of 1,000 cards would take five minutes of machine time on an 083.

Much less frequently, but still occasionally found in computer areas is the collator. The last models of IBM collators (such as the 088) were substantial improvements over their forerunners, featuring processing speeds of 800 cards per minute and the ability to check the sequence of input cards to both input feeds.

The survival of sorters and collators into the computer era of the 1970s is conditioned by the nature of the computer used: (1) A strictly card-oriented computer requires input card data to be in report sequence; this usually requires sorting detail cards and frequently also collating them with master cards maintained in the same sequence. Typically, after a computer-run report, the master and detail cards are separated into two groups by a pass through the sorter.[7] (2) With a tape-oriented computer in use, the storage of master files on tape might eliminate the need for a collator;

the need for a sorter might be dependent on the amount and frequency of available computer time, as well as on cost and time trade-off considerations. Card detail in random order can be computer-processed into magnetic tape records and then sorted into sequence; but if computer usage and volume of card input are both high, the slower process of card sorting may cost less than increasing the computer capacity and operating speeds. There are even a few instances, where medium or small tape-oriented computers have slow card readers and tape units, in which card-sorting saves time as well as cost. (3) When a disk-oriented computer is used, the need for sorters and collators is at a minimum, if existent at all, because of the random-access capability. Collators are almost never needed; and sorters are needed only when the nature of the processing is such that the time difference between sequential and random-order input is significant for saving of computer time or cost.

Computer Processing Media and Their Reading Formats

Except for paper tape, the only visually readable computer processing medium is the punched card. Though the character configurations (which represent numbers, letters, and special characters on tape and disk records) are not visible to the human eye, a programmer must at times be familiar with the character formats in which such records are stored.

The standard eighty-column IBM (Hollerith) punched card is shown in Figure 1–1. Note the following: Each column contains twelve possible punching positions; a single character is punched per column;

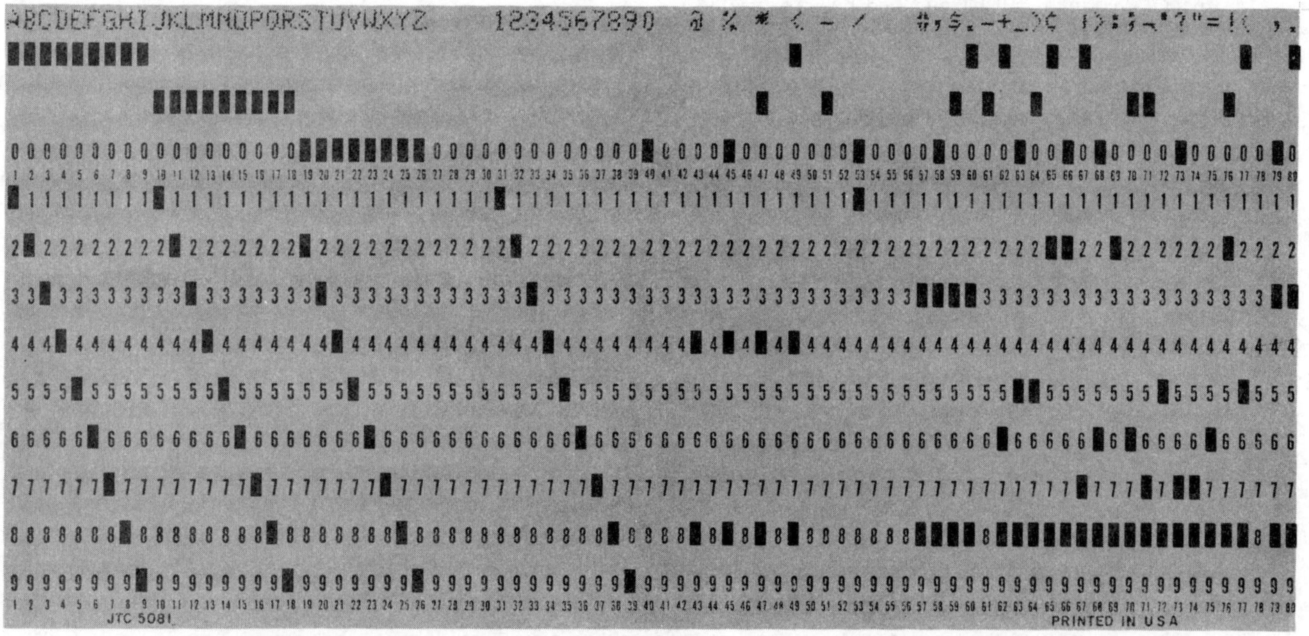

---

7. The card-oriented version of IBM's 360/20 computer featured a unique auxiliary machine known as MFCM (multi-function card machine) which had a collating as well as input-card-reading capacity and could do a limited amount of sorting.

Figure 1–1. A standard eighty-column card, punched to show sixty-three different characters.

and any character can be punched in any of the eighty columns. A numeric character is a single punch on its own numbered level. Alphabetic and special characters register as either one, two, or three punches per column, though only one keypunch stroke is required for any one character. Some alphabetic and special character key strokes punch holes at one or the other of the two unnumbered levels above the zero level. The topmost punching level is referred to as the Y or 12-zone, the level immediately below it as the X or 11-zone. A letter of the alphabet is represented by two punches, one numeric in the 1-through-9 range and the other either a 12-, 11-, or zero-punch. Letters A through I have a 12-punch, J through R an 11-punch, and S through Z a zero-punch. The numeric digit punched as part of a letter represents the letter's sequence in its range; A is 12–1, B is 12–2, and so on. An exception is in the range S–Z, where S, the first letter in the range, is 0–2, T is 0–3, etc. In addition to the twenty-six letters and ten numeric digits (0 through 9), current keypunches (such as IBM's 029 and 129) typically have keys which will punch twenty-five other characters, shown toward the right of the card in Figure 1–1. Special character recognition on current computers (such as IBM's 370) includes thirty-five graphically different characters on computer printout. Two working considerations should be noted, however, concerning special characters:

1. Older keypunches may not have keys for all of the special characters. This can be somewhat awkwardly overcome by using the multipunch key, which permits separately keying the punches required for a two- or three-hole character into a single column. On a printing punch, each keystroke will cause the individual punches to be overprinted on each other; the special character will be punched but not printed.

2. As between a manufacturer's computers of different generations and between computers of different manufacturers, a given special character as keypunched may be read, and printed by the computer's line printer, as some other special character. ANSI (the *A*merican *N*ational *S*tandards *I*nstitute) has attempted, with the cooperation of computer users and manufacturers, to simplify inter-computer data communication by development of ASCII (the *A*merican *N*ational *S*tandard *C*ode for *I*nformation *I*nterchange). Until the ASCII character pattern has been uniformly adopted, keyed-in special characters must be in the format required for the specific computer used. When cards produced on a keypunch with a modified set of special characters are the computer input, some of the special characters may print on the card as the character indicated by the key even though the

punches may be recognized by the specific computer as representing a different special character.

Punched cards were used by machines which preceded computers by more than a quarter-century and "read" cards in a different manner. Adding and subtracting was done by the same method used in adding machines—the internal counter wheel which moved to any one of ten positions (0 through 9) equidistant around its rim based on the numeric information brought to it. When adding two numbers which required movement past 9, the counter wheel tripped the wheel to its left to move one position as it moved the necessary remaining number of positions. Present computers are designed to add electronically rather than mechanically; their internal speeds are limited only by the length of time taken to pass electrical current to, from, and through minute areas which can be magnetized in one of two directions by the direction of flow of the current through them. The requirement of ten positions for recognition of a single numeric digit in one of them, or an additional twenty-six positions for the inclusion of alphabetic characters, would result in many more magnetic areas for recognition of a single character than do the present configurations which are based on the yes-no, 1-or-zero principle of binary choice.

The basic magnetic component of character identity in a computer storage area is known as a "bit," a term condensed from the words "*bi*nary dig*it*." If an internal computer position for storing a character contains four magnetizable areas or bits, the lowest-order valued as a 1 and the other three (in ascending order) powers of two, any number from 0 to 15 can be identified by a magnetizing pattern. Consider a four-bit area having bits representing 8, 4, 2, and 1 respectively. On the binary basis of yes or no for each bit, digits 0 through 9 would appear as follows:

```
0 _ _ _ _        5 _ 4 _ 1
1 _ _ _ 1        6 _ 4 2 _
2 _ _ 2 _        7 _ 4 2 1
3 _ _ 2 1        8 8 _ _ _
4 _ 4 _ _        9 8 _ _ 1
```

And the number 15 would be represented by the complete 8-4-2-1 combination. Although second-generation computers typically used the four-bit configurations to identify numbers in the 0 through 9 range, an internal-arithmetic technique based on the 16-digit (0 through 15) or *hexadecimal* capability of the four-bit area is now quite common in current computers. This, of course, requires conversion after read-in of data, since in practice a *number* greater than 9 would not be represented in a single position of keypunched input data.

To represent alphabetic and special characters, two additional rows of "bits" must be used; these are usually referred to as *A* and *B* bits. Punched-card characters having a 12-punch are translated in a typical second-generation computer as having *both* A and B bits; 11-punch characters as having a *B* bit only; zero-punched characters as having an A bit only. The numeric punch associated with a given character is translated into the four-bit pattern above. Thus:

Letter	Card-punched	Computerized
A	12–1	B A _ _ _ 1
B	12–2	B A _ _ 2 _
E	12–5	B A _ 4 _ 1
H	12–8	B A 8 _ _ _
J	11–1	B _ _ _ _ 1
M	11–4	B _ _ 4 _ _
P	11–7	B _ _ 4 2 1
S	0–2	_ A _ _ 2 _
W	0–6	_ A _ 4 2 _
$	11–3–8	B _ 8 _ 2 1

Note that a configuration of six bits is at least enough to represent any of the characters punched on the eighty-column card (Figure 1–1). One working consideration, however, led to typical computers having a seven-bit pattern—the matter of checking the accuracy of the computer's internal transfer of data read into it. A computer may be equipped to check always for an odd number of bits for each character stored or always for an even number. Obviously, some characters will have an odd number of bits, others an even number. If *all* must have an odd number for checking purposes, then a character like J, P, S, or $ must be supplied with an additional bit. The seventh position, the C- or check-bit, is provided for this purpose. In a computer which checks for an odd number of bits per character, the translation code for the letter J would be C B _ _ _ _ 1; for P, C B _ _ 4 2 1; while the code for such characters as A, B, H would contain no C-bit since each already contains an odd number of bits. Similarly, numeric digits like 0, 3, 5, 6, and 9 (each having an even number of numeric bits) would be supplied a check-bit; while digits 1, 2, 4, 7, and 8 would not since each already has an odd number of bits. The "parity-check" (a count of the number of bits and determination of whether the number satisfies the requirement—in this case, of being odd) is made as each character is "moved" from a computer storage area to other storage areas, whether for internal processing or for output. Some computers make a test for "odd parity" as above. The computers which test for "even parity" use translation codes that supply a

C-bit to the characters which have an odd number of bits in the other six positions, and omit the C-bit for those already having an even number of bits.

The operations described seem time-consuming and laborious, but it must be remembered that they are taking place at essentially the speed of light, so that in traveling short distances *within* the computer, operations may be completed on a given piece of data within microseconds (millionths of a second) or nanoseconds (billionths of a second). The internal speeds of a computer, however, are not to be confused with operations of external devices such as disk and tape drives, printers, readers, and punches, in which transmission of data is limited by electro*mechanical* capabilities of moving parts.

The six-bit (plus check-bit) per character representation just described is referred to as a BCD (*binary-coded decimal*) system. It is employed in numerous second- and third-generation computers, requires a seven-bit core structure internally, and "seven-track" or "seven-channel" output records on tape or disk. Apparently looking toward expansion of character coding to permit use of such features as upper- and lower-case characters, more special characters, and machine-instruction codes, an eight-bit code has been developed, permitting identification of a possible 256 characters in any one storage position. Known as EBCDIC (*Extended Binary-Coded Decimal Interchange Code*), it is one of two systems available for IBM's 360 and 370 and is the internal coding structure for IBM's System 3. An eight-bit expansion of ASCII (referred to by IBM as ASCII–8) is also available in the System 370. Where eight-bit codes are in use, employment of a parity-check-bit results in use of nine-track records in external storage devices.

The eight-bit storage position affords future capacity for an expanded number of characters that can be represented in computer processing. Since a bit is a binary digit, it can represent either 1 or 0. A combination of two bits has four possible combinations and can be used to represent four characters. Each additional bit in a storage position, then, doubles the number of combinations. A three-bit storage position would provide eight combinations of 1 and 0; and as already described, a four-bit combination provides sixteen combinations, which could be assigned values of 0 through 15. Five bits provide thirty-two combinations and six bits provide sixty-four. The six-bit storage position will permit recognition of numeric, alphabetic, and twenty-eight special characters, but leaves little room for expansion. The eight-bit storage position raises the number of combinations to 256. This makes available such possibilities as the use of lower-case alphabetic characters (already in use on some computers), more special characters for print purposes, and the use of special bit combinations to represent machine instructions for processing.

A second effect of the eight-bit storage position is to permit more efficient use of internal storage for arithmetic. Since the use of four bits permits recognition of sixteen different characters, numeric data require only half of a storage position for each numeric digit. This makes possible the use of hexadecimal (sixteen-based) arithmetic through the separation of each storage position into two four-bit areas for location of numeric data. For printout of reports, conversion from the internal arithmetic technique to the generally accepted decimal representation must take place. Since this is an internal technique, and input data is in decimal representation, the programming language must contain some signal for this to be done by the "hardware"; as will be indicated in Chapter 11, the COBOL word-signal is COMPUTATIONAL. Though not universal in current computers, the nine-track record and split-storage-position arithmetic seem to be prevailing in hardware techniques.

The advent of IBM's System 3 brought with it a new punched-card format, the minicard (Figure 1–2), physically about one-third the size of the standard eighty-column card, but containing instead ninety-six columns arranged in three tiers of thirty-two columns each. Usable only on IBM's System 3 family of computers at present, it is originated by use of a special keypunch and can be sorted only with a special sorter, small enough to be placed on a table. Though the System 3 employs an eight-bit code internally, the keypunched holes in the card are in the six-bit BCD representation described above, with the sole exception of the zero representation, a single punch in the A-bit position.

Punched paper tape as an input medium may be available in either the five-channel or the so-called eight-channel format. Because of the limitations of the five-channel format, some letters have the same format as the numeric digits 0 through 9, necessitating the separation of alphabetic and numeric data and requiring a special four-hole punch to indicate that numeric data follow and a five-hole punch to indicate that alphabetic data follow. Eight-channel tape actually employs seven rows of holes in the six-bit-plus-check-bit BCD format. The eighth row, or channel, is employed to indicate by presence of a single punched hole the end of a record (such as a line of billing data, pay data for one employee on a payroll, etc.).

Although in current second- to fourth-generation computers, records written in external output devices such as tape or disk are essentially either seven- or nine-track records (based on six- or eight-bit BCD

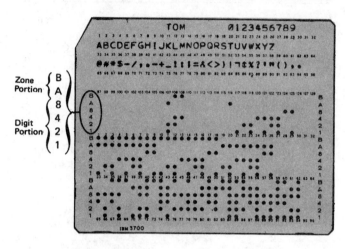

Figure 1–2. A ninety-six-column "minicard" for use in an IBM System 3 computer.

formats plus a check-bit), only those employing the nine-track format can make use of the split-storage technique for arithmetic. The eight-bit storage position is commonly referred to as a *byte*; an area which is a combination of four bytes is typically referred to as a *word*, a term which should not be confused with the COBOL usage of the term. Computers making use of the hexadecimal arithmetic technique typically provide printouts of program compilations and data "dumps" of storage contents, which frequently show certain arithmetic information in hexadecimal terms, with the numbers 10 through 15 expressed as A through F. To interpret such numeric data in base-ten (decimal) terms normally requires the use of a hexadecimal-to-decimal conversion table.

CURRENT USES OF COMPUTERS

The use of computers in the world of business and government (inclusive of the private and public educational fields) ranges from daily applications occurring in all enterprises (such as payroll processing and accounting) to such specialized activities as ticket reservation systems for airlines. The areas in which a "problem-oriented" programming language like COBOL can be put to use can be classified into two or three categories, going from the general to the specialized.

General business applications for computer systems, independent of the nature of the business, include most of the areas of general and cost accounting. Payroll, accounts payable, accounts receivable, general ledger preparation, and preparation of financial statements are areas in which a variety of almost standardized computer processing systems have been developed, varied only by difference in viewpoint or in actual needs among the businesses making use of them.

Two business applications whose use has wide variation are production planning and scheduling (which is a manufacturing function) and inventory reporting (which is useful in manufacturing, wholesaling, and retailing operations). Inventory reporting may be part of a production scheduling or planning system in a manufacturing business, part of a cost accounting system, or a random-access, "on-line" inquiry system involving control over shipping and billing in any type of business selling goods rather than services.

Two other business functions where computers can be efficiently employed are market research analysis, in which very specific techniques of statistical analysis have been developed, and an activity rather indefinitely described as management information systems (typically referred to as MIS). No one has yet defined "management information system" in specific descriptive terms. It may be a set of reports containing data extracted for executive use from other computerized data made available to lower levels of management in different format for day-to-day purposes; it may be a system of supplying information of some desired type not contained in any other computerized files; or it may even be a reorganization and coordination of existing computerized activities so that information supplied at executive or management level can be used for planning and control purposes as well as historical reporting of already accomplished fact. As yet, there is not even a general pattern which MIS follows.

Special business requirements are often found which computer systems are particularly useful in filling. Among these are:

1. Subscription fulfillment—the operations connected with updating the records of data concerning subscribers to periodical publications, and billing and mailing of publications to the subscribers.

2. Savings bank account operations—which include computer-generated interest computations.

3. Airline reservation systems—already mentioned in connection with remote terminal operations.

4. Computer-aided typesetting, mentioned in connection with special optional devices.

5. Computer-aided engineering design—frequently supplemented by use of the computer-controlled plotter already mentioned as a special device.

In addition, certain governmental and educational functions have been computerized with considerable success at various levels. In local government applications, property tax billing, licensing, and various court functions (particularly those related to automobile traffic violations) are frequent areas of computer usage; and in the fields of secondary and higher education, assignment of student course schedules, grading, and preparation of transcripts of student academic performance are frequently computerized. At state and Federal government levels, various taxing, registration, and licensing functions have been computerized, as well as social security, unemployment insurance, and government employee pension system data.

There are numerous types of computer systems and techniques which have a wide variety of applications in areas that are sometimes commercial, and at other times have research, engineering, educational, or almost unique applications. For example, the technique of storing large volumes of file data in random-access devices, and employing a specific type of inquiry to extract or process data held in such a file, has many forms, though always known as *information storage and retrieval*. The principle is applied in airline reservation systems, where inquiry and retrieval are performed by the ticket clerk; in subscription fulfillment operations, where the subscriber file is accessed in the computer room as part of the operations of billing, cancelations, and mailing label printing; and, most typically, an inventory item file accessed by remote-terminal inquiry to determine whether billing or shipment can take place, and to perform the billing or generate the shipping instructions. In areas tending to involve use of mathematical languages rather than COBOL, *statistical computing* and *linear programming* may be used in a wide variety of applications.[8] These may occur in market research, scientific projections, financial planning, and many governmental activities, including those of the Census Bureau, birthplace of punched-card data processing and first customer for a commercial computer.

REVIEW MATERIAL

Terms

Analog computer	Assembly	Compiler
Sorting	language	Documentation
Interpreting	Compiler	Input
Computer	language	Output
memory	Source program	Time-sharing
Mass storage	Object Program	Random access
Programming	Information	Bit
Machine	storage and	Byte
language	retrieval	

---

8. A number of the generic applications discussed in this section are described briefly but in considerable detail in *Computer Usage/Applications*, Computer Usage Company, Inc., Eric A. Weiss, Editor, McGraw-Hill Book Company, 1970.

Questions

Describe the functions of the verifier, the sorter, and the line printer.

Contrast the first-, second- and third-generation computers.

What are the functions of a programmer?

Describe a remote-terminal operation.

Contrast magnetic tape and disk as storage media. What are the data-processing implications associated with the use of each?

What are the most time-consuming computer functions in business data processing?

What were the disadvantages with machine language and assembly language programming that led the Department of Defense to advocate the development of a new language for computers?

In what forms can data be recorded for input to the computer?

In what forms can data be output from computers?

What are the advantages and limitations of MICR and OCR as means of data input?

What are the functions of the central processing unit?

Describe the standard IBM eighty-column punched card.

What is the function of the parity check bit?

Name some common business applications for computers.

True-or-False Statements

Analog computers are normally used for standard business data-processing applications.

The keypunch is used to record data on punched cards.

Punched-card equipment is not capable of performing calculations.

Disk storage allows a piece of data to be accessed immediately, while magnetic tape requires sequential access.

A computer's program is stored in its memory while it is operating.

COBOL is a standard language available on most computers.

A diagnostic indicates an error in programming logic.

Once a COBOL program has been successfully compiled, it can be put into operation with no further testing necessary.

Data recorded on magnetic tape or disk can be read by machines but not by people.

The standard punched card can contain up to eighty characters of information.

Data in the computer's memory is recorded in binary form.

The parity check helps determine whether the program was correctly written.

PART B

Environment:
Current
Logical
Tools

2

FLOWCHARTING AS A PROGRAMMING AID

FLOWCHARTING FUNCTIONS

A flowchart is a sequential diagram of how a job is done. The job may be one phase in a series of machine or manual operations, or it may be an entire series of operations comprising a system. A flowchart describes the job in single steps, basically as either decisions or operations, so that the job is defined in "picture" form. Flowcharting can be used to describe any job procedure in a manner that will aid analysis. As an example, Figure 2–1 describes the work of an accounts payable clerk in processing a supplier's invoice to schedule it for payment. The flowchart shows all decisions made, operations performed, and possible dispositions made of the invoice as a result of this clerical phase. The value of a flowchart in pinpointing the necessity of making decisions and performing operations in a required sequence should be evident.

Flowcharting for business purposes has two main stages of use: (1) in planning the system or program prior to system implementation or writing program instructions, and (2) as documentation for later reference made by operations personnel in doing processing, and by systems and programming personnel in making changes in system or program. Both stages are essential; and if the flowcharting is done at the first stage, its value at the later stage is likely to be increased. The flowchart function is essentially that of a route map; if prepared before the first trip is taken, the first trip should be easier, and if any modifications are required, the necessary notations can be made as relatively minor changes on a set of already-existing instructions (the flowchart itself). The complete and correct instructions are then available not only as guides for repetitions of the trip, but as reference if and when the route must be altered.

Flowcharting, if looked upon as an essential step in these two separate phases of data processing, should always be a time- and labor-saving technique. If flowcharting is regarded by management as merely delay to getting systems and programming commenced, its absence will result in excessive reliance on specific personnel in systems, programming, or operations for getting a job done; and their absence or memory failures may cause long and unnecessary delays in both processing and in systems or programming original completions or revisions. If flowcharting is formally required by management, but there is no followup to make sure of its use at the planning stages of systems and programming work, there is sometimes a tendency to avoid its use at the time when it is most needed; then when documentation of the completed systems and programs is being prepared, flowcharts are prepared in a rather perfunctory manner as an obligatory compliance with management ritual. When this is done, flowcharts often tend to be superficial, and are of use only for later reference purposes, having lost their real function as guides and checkpoints for their authors in the develop-

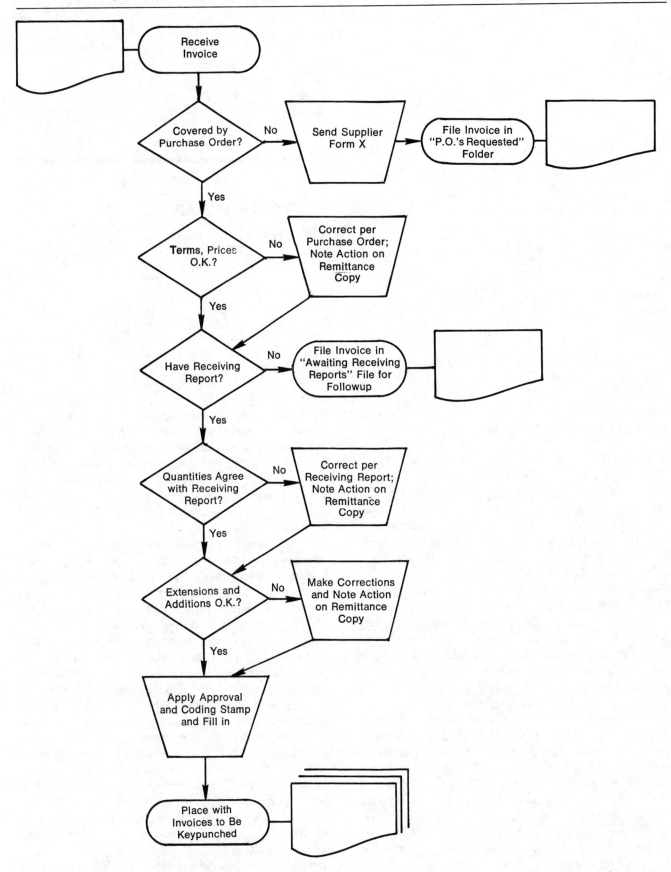

Figure 2–1. Flowchart of clerical steps in reviewing an invoice for payment approval.

ment and completion of their own systems and programming assignments.

The "language" (symbols) of both systems and program flowcharting has undergone such constant and varied change that a programmer or systems analyst trained in the early 1970s would find considerable difficulty in reading either a systems flowchart or logic (programming) flowchart prepared with symbols used in the late 1950s. Computer manufacturers tended to develop their own language of symbols and furnish templates containing the symbols to users for one or both types of flowchart preparation. Differences were numerous and often basic. In recent years, user and professional organizations have been active in developing a common symbolic vocabulary, with the result that two major standards agree on symbol usage. *The International Organization for Standardization (ISO) Recommendation R1028, Flowchart Symbols for Information Processing* agrees with the *ANSI Flowchart Symbols and Their Usage in Information Processing (X3.5–1970).* Templates supplied by computer manufacturers now tend toward conformity with these standard symbols.

Standard flowcharting symbols for information processing refer to logic processes, machine processes and devices, and data forms. A programmer's flowchart, since it is concerned with mapping out the logic processes to be used in his program, will employ mostly the logic-process symbols with rather occasional reference to the others. Systems personnel, in flowcharting systems paths, will use primarily symbols for machine processes and devices, with only occasional reference to logic symbols. A small number of the standard symbols, regarded as being in none of the three specific categories, are considered basic to any type of information processing flowchart and are used with almost equal frequency by systems and programming personnel.

FLOWCHARTING SYMBOL VOCABULARY

The following descriptive listing of the standard symbols is fairly comprehensive. Those symbols used primarily for systems flowcharting are included for several reasons. In the first place, programmers do use them, even if infrequently. Second, they reflect both the hardware and processing environments in which any program will be executed; the programmer may sometimes be supplied with a system flowchart to provide him with better understanding of the function of his program within the system, and he should be able to read such flowcharts and readily comprehend the references to machine devices and processing. Third, as a practical function, current flowcharting templates tend to contain the various types of symbols but do not always thoroughly identify usages; for effective communication and interpretation, the programmer should be reasonably familiar with the proper use of all the standard information processing symbols.

In typical flowchart format, main processing paths are vertical, and short branching paths are shown perpendicular to the main paths. If a return from a short subpath to a main path takes place, a diagonal direction may be justified. Sometimes a possible multiple branch may generate several possible paths, which may be shown as parallel to the main one. The relative number of operational steps and symbols on main and subpaths will help determine which path levels should be horizontal and which should be vertical; rules for the use of flow lines and arrows indicating their direction aid in keeping the flowchart readable. Symbols (below) considered basic to standard flowcharting include the following:[1]

---

1. An asterisk (*) is used here to indicate symbols that are either only parts of or combinations of symbols as they appear on a flowchart symbol template.

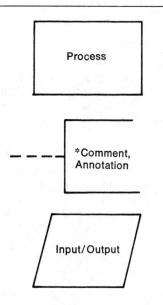

Process	This symbol refers to any processing function. The named process may be one causing change in value, form, or location of information. The symbol is normally used to identify general computer operations in systems flowcharts and strictly internal computer operations (as distinguished from input/output) in programming flowcharts.
*Comment, Annotation	This processing symbol modification is connected by the dotted line to any other symbols when it is necessary or desirable to add description, clarification, or comment to promote readability or understanding of the flowchart.
Input/Output	This symbol refers to bringing information into the processing flow or producing information in its output form. In programming flowcharts, it is used largely to identify reading operations (input to computer) and writing operations (output to tape, disk, or printed report).

Connector

This symbol designates a point of exit to, or entry from, another part of the flowchart. It is used when necessary to break up a chart into groups of numbered subpaths and provide numbered points of return to the main processing. When used as an exit from the main process, the connector contains the path number shown in another connector used as a heading for the subpath. When used as entry identification, the entry point number appears in a connector at the return point and in a connector used as an exit from the subpath.

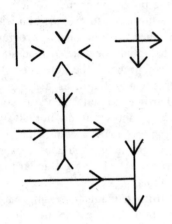

Flowlines must be shown to establish the path of processing from one symbol to the next. The place and frequency of using directional arrows is a matter of opinion; in general, the use should be the minimum necessary to make the flow direction clear and unmistakable. Note that it is permissible to have unrelated flowlines cross each other (though it is advisable to avoid this practice if possible); but where two or more paths form a junction and continue as a single path, directional arrows are necessary to distinguish this situation from the incidental crossing of unrelated flowlines on the chart. In general, flowlines should be top-to-bottom or left-to-right; departures from these general directions should carry directional arrows.

Symbols used almost exclusively by programmers include:

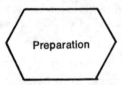

Decision

Although referred to as a decision, this symbol usually notes the question or condition on whose answer or existence the choice of alternative paths depends. Normally, the alternative flowlines proceeding from the right and bottom corners of the decision symbol are marked Yes and No.

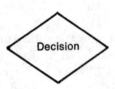

Preparation

More technical than logical, this symbol indicates some preparatory program step prior to a processing step or series of steps. In general terms, it is described as an instruction modification to change program, and is used to indicate such actions as initializing a routine, setting a switch, or modifying an index register.

*Predefined
Process

Note that this symbol is a modification of the process symbol, and is used to indicate the performance of a step or series of steps specified in another part of the flowchart or in another set of flowcharts. It is used when the same operations may occur under several conditions in the same program, and presentation is improved by a single detailed specification in one place and this reference to it in others.

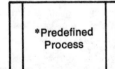

Terminal,
Interrupt

This symbol indicates a terminal point (either beginning or end point) within the flowchart—not necessarily the beginning or end of the program. It may be used to indicate start, stop, halt, delay, or interrupt, or an exit from a closed subroutine.

Systems symbols are almost self-identifying:

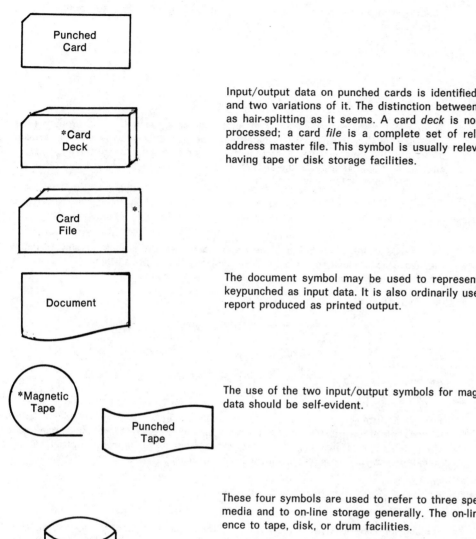

Input/output data on punched cards is identified by the symbol for a punched card and two variations of it. The distinction between a card *deck* and a card *file* is not as hair-splitting as it seems. A card *deck* is normally a batch of detail data to be processed; a card *file* is a complete set of related records, such as a name-and-address master file. This symbol is usually relevant only for smaller computers not having tape or disk storage facilities.

The document symbol may be used to represent source data on documents to be keypunched as input data. It is also ordinarily used to refer to a computer-generated report produced as printed output.

The use of the two input/output symbols for magnetic tape and punched paper tape data should be self-evident.

These four symbols are used to refer to three specific types of input/output storage media and to on-line storage generally. The on-line storage symbol may be a reference to tape, disk, or drum facilities.

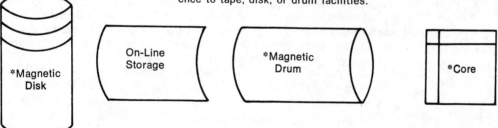

A series of five triangular symbols or combinations of them represent various types of file manipulation, including collating, sorting, and off-line storage. Specifically:

Merge refers to combining two or more sets or files of data into one set.

Extract means removal of one or more specific sets or types of data items from a set or file. This may mean either leaving the original data intact and simply copying the items desired onto another storage medium, or printing a report of the "extracted" items; it may mean copying a tape file and deleting the extracted records so that they do not appear in the new file; or it may mean blanking out records on a disk file. It may also mean simply copying one file's contents into two new and separate files having mutually exclusive data.

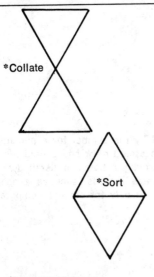

*Collate

*Sort

*Off-line
Storage

Display

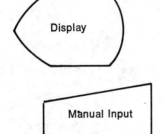

Manual Input

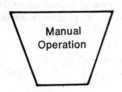

Manual
Operation

Auxiliary
Operation

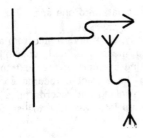

Collating is a combination of merging and extracting; it refers to forming two or more sets or files of items from two or more other sets.

Sorting is the rearrangement of a set or file of data records into a predetermined sequence. In this process, the original data set or file, if on tape or disk, remains intact and the new sequential arrangement is created on other disks or tapes. In card-file sorting, the original data are placed in a new sequence; the original sequence, if any, can be restored only by additional sorting.

The *off-line storage* symbol indicates storage without reference to any particular medium. This is usually a symbol used to indicate disposition of input or output data, and the type of data will indicate what the storage medium is.

Although used chiefly in systems flowcharts, the *display* and *manual input* symbols may occasionally appear in programming flowcharts in connection with the *display* and *accept* statements (see Chapter 12). In systems flowcharting, display may refer to on-line display devices other than a console typewriter, such as video (CRT) devices, plotters, etc. *Manual input* may refer, in either systems or program flowcharting, to special input devices or to console typewriter or control panel key-ins, or external switch settings, or punched-card insertions in the reader.

The *manual operation* symbol refers to completely manual procedures, as distinguished from the machine-aided *manual input*. A *manual operation* is normally some checking stage, usually of computer printout to some predetermined control condition, and may occasionally appear on a program flowchart if some early stages of program execution require checking to controls before proceeding further. In a systems flowchart, it usually indicates checking report totals to controls after one report in a series is completed and before the next is begun.

Auxiliary operation indicates off-line (independent) operations on equipment not under the direct control of the computer's central processing unit. Examples include the use of unit-record equipment to reproduce or interpret cards punched as output from the computer punch unit.

Communication links are shown by zigzag lines, normally with at least one directional arrow. Although primarily used in systems flowcharts to indicate transmission of input and/or output data between computer and a remote point by telecommunication facilities, these symbols may be used to indicate the manner of receiving input data, transmitting output data, or doing both (in an inquiry-and-response type of operation). The bi-directional arrows might be required to describe this last situation.

FLOWCHARTING AS PROBLEM-SOLVING LOGIC

As already suggested, the systems flowchart and program logic flowchart are different in approach and execution. The systems flowchart is concerned primarily with the sequence of clerical and machine processing of data, while the program flowchart is typically concerned with the internal logic involved in what amounts to one computer processing as shown on the systems flowchart. The systems flowchart is, in a sense, a map of the results of analysis which has determined the optimum sequence of a series of clerical and machine operations to produce the desired organization of data input and output. The programmer's flowchart is the outline of the logic required to produce results in the form of organized data at one of those machine-operational steps.

The function of the flowchart, then, is to state the problems involved in the program and the logical steps to be taken to obtain correct solutions. Preparing the flowchart is the first step in programming; the second step is writing the program instructions that will give proper effect to the logic of the flowchart. Since COBOL is a *problem-oriented* language, the writing of the program will be in terms more closely corresponding to flowchart logic than would machine-language instructions. The flowchart, however, should not be regarded as an advance outline of programming instructions; it represents problem definition and orderly arrangement of logic sequence for solution. A program cannot be written unless the programmer understands the "problem" (the subject-matter to be programmed) and establishes the logical steps needed to produce the results desired. The flowchart is the guide for writing the programming instructions; the program is based on and depends on the flowchart, rather than vice versa. A large part of the reason for discussing flowcharting before getting into the details of programming language is to emphasize the independence of the flowchart from the program and the dependence of the program on the flowchart. One need not understand a programming language to draw an adequate flowchart; but a programmer who cannot state problems and logic for solutions in a flowchart is likely to have considerable difficulty and to spend more time in writing a workable program than one who understands the logical processes to be performed and has to search for and select the instructions that will execute those processes. The remaining portion of this chapter will be concerned with the organization of logical statements in flowchart form, using the symbols described, to show how data are to be processed to obtain specified results. In this presentation, it may develop that questions arising when preparing the flowchart can assist in filling logical gaps in specifications furnished to the programmer.

Let us assume that punched cards will be supplied each week, one card per employee, showing hours worked during the week just ended, and that a program is to be written to compute each employee's gross pay for the week, federal income tax, FICA (social security), and union dues deductions, arriving at net pay. The specifications indicate that the only information punched on each card is employee number and name, and regular hours and overtime hours worked. They also indicate that these cards will be processed against a magnetic tape file which contains, in the same sequence as the cards, a master record for each of the employees being paid, and no others. This record for each employee contains employee number and name, year-to-date earnings and deductions, a code S or M (single or married) to determine which of two applicable income tax tables to use for tax calculation, number of income tax exemptions, the hourly rate of pay for the employee, and a code (1, 2, or X) indicating which of two unions or no union is to receive dues. The programmer is told that income tax table data will be supplied later, but meanwhile to plan a program based on union dues being $1.50 for code 1 and $2.00 for code 2; that the FICA deduction in one year cannot exceed X dollars and is at rate Y; that regular hours, which cannot be greater than forty, are to be multiplied by the employee's hourly rate, and overtime hours are to be multiplied by the hourly rate times 1.5. One line of printing of the current earnings, deductions, and net pay data is to be produced for each employee, and a current earnings record containing the same data as printed for each employee is to be written on an output tape. No tests need be made of the master records for absence of codes or rates; the file has previously been edited.

At this point, we have not demonstrated a single programming instruction. To a great degree, this does not affect the ability to flowchart the pay computation problem. The purpose of the flowchart is to state the problem and its solution so that a programmer may use it as a specification for writing all the necessary instructions, which he will select depending on the way the steps in the flowchart are described. Let us list the known elements that can be flowcharted, making note of conditions, not mentioned in the specifications, which should be investigated for possible inclusion.

1. The basic processing is to read a "pair" of records (one card and one input tape record), do the necessary calculations, print the line of results, write the output tape record, and repeat the operation on the next pair of records. Should we assume an always-perfect match, or provide for the possibility of an extra or missing item on either side? Let us start off by reading one card and one master tape record,

posing the decision question: Do employee numbers match? We then proceed on the Yes path, leaving a No path open to be completed when we find out what action should be taken under this condition.[2]

2. Our first processing step is to calculate regular pay (card regular hours times master tape hourly rate) if regular hours are not more than forty. We must leave open, for the time being, what kind of error routine is to be followed if more than forty hours are shown.

3. Overtime pay must be calculated next: Card overtime hours times master hourly rates times 1.5. (If there are no overtime hours, the result is zero.)

4. Add regular pay and overtime pay to obtain total gross pay.

5. The next step should be the income tax calculation. Here we have only a partial specification; we know there is a decision to be made about which of two tables to use based on a code of S or M in the master record. We know, however, that in either case, a tax calculation, which may involve several steps, must be made. If we indicate this as a separate "subroutine," we can chart it later.

6. The FICA calculation is simply total gross pay times rate Y, but we are not to make this calculation at all if year-to-date maximum X appears in the master record as the amount previously deducted during the year. Suppose, however, that the current calculation is an amount which, when added to the already-accumulated year-to-date FICA, will cause the maximum, X, to be exceeded? The arithmetic to be performed in this case includes several steps. For flowcharting convenience and readability, charting of only the main decision should be shown, and the calculation possibilities set up as a separate subroutine.

7. A decision based on the union code precedes the assignment of a specific amount as union dues.

8. The three deductions must be subtracted from total gross pay to determine net pay.

9. A line of employee pay and deduction data must be printed, a current output tape record written containing the same data, and then reading of the next employee's card and tape record will begin the cycle again.

The reader should not be disappointed by the partly incomplete description above, nor by the similarly incomplete flowchart shown as Figure 2–2. One very

---

2. A specific set of possibilities in this type of matching is outlined in the program flowchart in Chapter 8. As indicated a little later in *this* chapter, in the present case the important matter is the raising of the *question* as a result of using the flowchart approach.

good reason for preparing a logic flowchart before programming is that, in preparing it, conditions may practically present themselves that have not been covered by the specifications given the programmer. This is particularly true if a programmer persuades himself to "think binary" in preparing the flowchart—as if, in essence, there were a possibility of another condition existing instead of the stated one. Numerous possibilities of this sort were forestalled by the specification that previous master file editing had established that no tests were needed for absence of codes or rates from the master records. But a second condition, though mentioned, specified no alternative: regular hours may not be more than forty; but what to do if they were was not stated. And one possibility, that either card or tape file might contain an unmatched record, was not considered at all. It is not at all unusual that such omissions go unnoticed through the first two functional programming steps of programmer analysis of specifications and review of them with their supplier. The flowchart (or decision table) preparation step provides a useful backstop for oversights at earlier stages.

Since flowcharting, like COBOL, is problem-oriented, we have been able to present the problem and its solution techniques by using only three basic symbols, two programming symbols, and the flowlines and directional arrows. The following manner of use should be noted:

- The input/output parallelogram is used only for the four operations directly connected with input and output data at the beginning and end of the chart.
- The "decision" diamond is used to frame questions to which more than one answer path is available.
- The process rectangle is used to designate a specific operation or operations on a given path. In its modified form, which occurs twice, it indicates that the specified operations are charted elsewhere.
- The use of flowlines and connectors is perhaps clear except in the borderline cases where either could have been used to connect operations. The standard use of the connector is shown by those numbered 1 and 2. At the top of the page, 1 designates the starting point of the flowchart logic, and 2 designates a continuation point; these are entry functions. At the bottom of the page, 1 indicates the return point from an exit from the completion of the logic cycle; the same cycle is to be performed on the next pair of records. Connector 2 at the bottom of the page is introduced as a convenient reference to the continuation point at the top. Clearly, flowlines from bottom to top of page would have been awkward here. The use of connector 3 to designate exit from the FICA calculation and reentry to the main path could have been accomplished by use of a flowline; conversely,

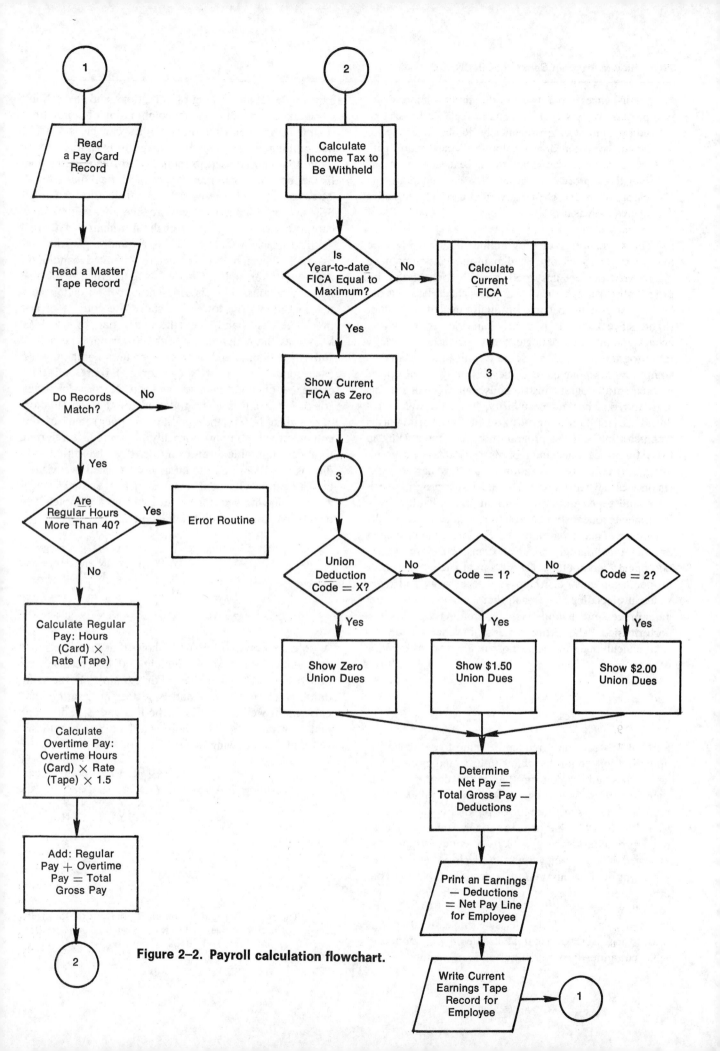

Figure 2–2. Payroll calculation flowchart.

the flowlines from two of the three "union dues" process symbols could have been replaced by a numbered connector. An identically numbered connector could have been drawn pointing to the "main" path from the third process box to the next (net-pay determination) process. In general, space limitations and clarity of reading should govern in cases of alternative choice of symbols.

The presentation of programmer flowcharting here may seem pedagogically peculiar in that questions have been raised but not answered, and no connection with program instructions has been established. The last deficiency, as should become gradually evident, is rather slight; since COBOL is a problem-oriented language, accurate statements of logic can be translated directly into program instructions. Some technicalities related to computer components and devices may have to be worked into program instructions, but we will do this as required. The first peculiarity, however, was introduced to emphasize the position of flowcharting as a technical link and the programmer as a human link in the data processing chain of user, systems, programming, and computer operations. The flowchart (or decision table, when required) is not just a programmer's technique to be dispensed with if the individual programmer erroneously believes that it does not expedite or improve his programming. Fallible human beings provide information, create systems, write programs, and operate computers. The person at each stage, using proper techniques, can help to detect errors and oversights at preceding stages, and thereby help create better data processing in both systems creation and systems performance. The programmer's flowchart is an essential technique for this purpose in the systems creation phase.

DECISION TABLES

Parts of programs are frequently found to be dependent upon multiple conditions that can be stated more clearly and concisely in table form than in flowchart form. For such a portion of a program, a decision table can be used as either a substitute for or preliminary supplement to a flowchart routine or subroutine. Almost any computer program, however, is likely to contain some processing that does not require a decision immediately preceding it. For this reason, a decision table or tables can seldom be used as complete replacement for a logic flowchart.

The principle of the decision table, it should be understood, is *not* a technique usable only in connection with computer programming; it is a method of or-

ganizing a detailed listing of conditions and the actions to be taken depending on the combination of conditions, so that a minimum number of rules can be stated for determining which action to take. It is a logic technique that can be used to reduce performance time and likelihood of error in many types of clerical and administrative operations based on manual decision-making.[3] For the programmer, it can reduce the volume and complexity of a program or of the flowchart for it.

The decision table format is a quadrangle, the upper half of which is concerned with stated conditions and the lower half of which is concerned with the possible actions to be chosen. The upper left side states the conditions; the lower left states the courses of action. The right-hand side (the upper part of which is known as the condition stub, the lower part the action stub) is columnarized, with each column containing for each condition a Y or N (yes or no) representing its existence or nonexistence, and an X for whichever course of action is to be followed for the combination of Y's and N's in the condition (upper) half of the column. Each column, normally numbered, is referred to in decision table terms as a *rule*. If we had three conditions (A, B, and C), and if any two existed, we wished to take action Q, but if fewer than two existed, action Z, the following decision table would be a complete list of possible combinations and actions:

		Rule:	1	2	3	4	5	6	7	8
Conditions:	A		Y	Y	Y	Y	N	N	N	N
	B		N	Y	N	Y	N	Y	N	Y
	C		N	N	Y	Y	N	N	Y	Y
Actions:	Q			X	X	X				X
	Z		X				X	X	X	

A close inspection of the table shows that there are some redundancies in it; some conditions that determine action occur more than once. For example, if the condition is Yes for both A and B, it does not matter what C is; and if we have a Yes for both B and C, it does not matter what A is. The table could be reduced to six rules, in the following form:

		Rule:	1	2	3	4	5	6
Conditions:	A		Y	N	_	_	Y	N
	B		Y	N	Y	N	N	Y
	C		_	_	Y	N	Y	N
Actions:	Q		X		X		X	
	Z			X		X		X

---

3. The reader is urged to consult a brief but thorough discussion of decision tables in Davis, Gordon B., *Computer Data Processing*, McGraw-Hill Book Company (second edition, 1973), pp. 234–243.

Frequently some specific qualification is made that can reduce the number of action choices. Suppose we said that to take action Q, B must be one of the two conditions in existence. This would reduce the decision table to one of only three possibilities:

		Rule:	1	2	3
Conditions:	A		Y	—	—
	B		Y	Y	N
	C		—	Y	—
Actions:	Q		X	X	
	Z				X

TECHNICAL-AID ASPECTS OF FLOWCHARTS AND DECISION TABLES

While we have emphasized so far that flowcharting and decision tables are general logic techniques which aid the entire system's construction and maintenance, they also have undeniable advantages specifically to the programmer. Because each basic step is related to others, the properly defined paths and subpaths in a flowchart, or the conditions and actions in a decision table will ordinarily indicate a pattern to the programmer which will enable him or her to choose the best instructions to use to give effect to the chart or table logic. This will become evident as the student becomes acquainted with the vocabulary and purposes of the various CO-BOL instructions. While some programmers tend to use programming language in flowcharts, it is safer for future reference (even for the programmer!) to employ *problem* logic at this stage of developing the program.

It is suggested that when the student has completed Chapter 12, he refer back to the flowchart and decision tables shown here and note where specific programming instructions are almost implicit in the program logic. In the flowchart, for example, some simpler decisions point to use of the "simple conditional" (IF statement), and certain subroutines suggest use of the PERFORM and others the GO TO branching instructions. In the decision tables, the first two should suggest using a counter to add a 1 for each positive condition's existence, and determining which action to take based on whether contents of the counter is a number less than 2 or greater than 1. The small decision table, of course, is the set of conditions to which the "nested conditional" statement is framed to apply. It is hoped that when the suggested review is made, the student will be impressed by the concept that if the flowchart or decision table is properly addressed to the *problem* (*not* to the program), the program itself will be properly addressed to the problem.

Two other major programming aids of flowcharting are (*1*) as a check on the completeness of the specifications given the programmer, and (*2*) as a checkpoint in debugging programming logic when compiling and testing a program. Both have been indicated in the description of a programmer's function in Chapter 1; the first was made evident in the payroll program flowchart, and the second will become evident as you check out compilations and test runs of your own programs.

REVIEW MATERIAL

Terms

Flowchart	Processing function	Path
Systems flowchart	Connector	Decision table
Logic flowchart	Flowlines	Condition
	Decision	

Questions

Why is flowcharting in the long run, a time- and labor-saving technique? Why do some managements try to short-circuit the flowcharting phase of a data processing project?

What functions are indicated by a systems flowchart? a logic flowchart?

What does the decision symbol indicate on a flowchart? How is it unique among flowcharting symbols?

What types of file manipulations can be shown on a flowchart?

Why should flowcharting precede programming? Why is it possible for one to draw a flowchart without knowing a programming language?

What kinds of mistakes or oversights are often detected during the flowcharting phase?

What types of programs lend themselves to analysis by decision table?

True-or-False Statements

It is good operating procedure to draw flowcharts at the completion of all systems and programming work for documentation purposes.

Flowlines, arrows, and connectors are used in flowcharts to depict the sequence of operations.

A decision symbol shows the choice of alternate paths depending on a condition or the answer to a question.

COBOL terminology should be used in flowcharting.

Decision tables are used in situations where multiple decisions call for a concise presentation.

PART C

COBOL as a Logical Tool in the Environment

3

THE STRUCTURE OF COBOL

COBOL'S OBJECTIVES

As pointed out earlier, one of the chief objectives which COBOL was intended to fulfill was making programming relatively independent of the computer being used. A second objective was to use English-language words for readability. A third objective was to employ terms that would describe the logic and operational steps in the problem or job being programmed rather than allow machine-language terms to represent the operations performed by the computer. Left to the computer manufacturer is the responsibility of producing a compiler program that will translate properly used COBOL instructions in a source program into machine-language instructions executable by that manufacturer's computer.

ADVANTAGES OF COBOL

Out of the CODASYL sessions which resulted in the first COBOL and the subsequent efforts to standardize COBOL more thoroughly, came a problem- or job-oriented language which had, by its very organization, certain advantages over assembly and machine languages:

1. Its required separation of a program into four sequential parts facilitated the location of specific program contents by anyone reading a source program listing to make changes in the program.

2. Its first part, the identification division, provides a convenient place to describe the purposes and limits of the program.

3. Its second part, the environment division (by specifying the computer and the devices on it being used in the program), indicates the basic places in the program that must be changed if a different computer is to be used for execution of the program.

4. Its third part, the data division, provides a specific place where input and output files must be described (in contrast to many other assembly languages which permit a somewhat disorganized approach to file definition by the programmer).

5. Its fourth and last part, the procedure division, provides instructions in English-language usage rather than in codes representing machine language.

6. The use of a language available on practically all commercially employed computers reduces reprogramming and retraining costs and time when a computer is replaced by another model or one made by another manufacturer.

CRITICISMS OF COBOL

In the dozen or more years of COBOL's history, much criticism, both favorable and unfavorable, has been directed at the language. Many of the unfavorable comments are partly true; all should be considered:

1. Programmers proficient in assembly language sometimes contend that:

a. Assembly-language programming takes less time because the instructions are abbreviations rather than full words, as in COBOL. Probably more than off-setting this, however, is the fact that many single COBOL instructions can be used in place of two or more typical assembly language instructions. This is particularly effective in COBOL instructions involving complex arithmetic and decisions.

b. Assembly language is really easier to understand and use because each instruction identifies a computer operation rather than masking it in a statement which includes other operations not specifically named. This is perhaps the most valid criticism, requiring an instructional approach to COBOL, which will be discussed shortly.

c. Assembly-language programming is more flexible and efficient than COBOL because every instruction can be used by itself and is not bound by the combinations of instructions represented by some COBOL verbs; consequently, assembly-language programming has a greater potential for programming difficult and complicated jobs. This objection, as well as the preceding one, usually comes from programmers who have learned and used an assembly language first before learning COBOL; a mental reservation is created that the assembly language is the mother tongue for programming. Although this criticism may be valid in some rather rare applications, there is not any specific or general range of business applications for which assembly language is feasible where COBOL is not.

2. Operations management may complain that:

a. COBOL programs require longer compilation time than assembly language programs. This is, in many instances, undeniable—if excessively sophisticated COBOL compilers are used. For smaller computers, some manufacturers (notably Honeywell) have made abridged COBOL compilers available.[1] These can also be used on larger computers; and the fact is that most commercial applications can be programmed using the abridged COBOL compilers, which compare favorably with assembly language in compilation time. In the early years of COBOL, some computer manufacturers supplied COBOL capability only with large computers, and then only to meet government bid specifications. Now a trend is setting in to supply abridged COBOL compilers on not only small (8K through 24K) computers but also for "minicomputers," and this objection should shortly be rendered obsolete.

b. COBOL programs, chiefly on large computers, use more execution time (for running actual computer jobs) than do assembly-language programs. This is—or was—a valid objection, having to do with the efficiency of the COBOL compiler. In recent years, however, as user preference for the advantageous features of COBOL has increased, computer manufacturers have worked to improve their COBOL compilers to produce more efficient object programs; notable improvements in execution time have been achieved.

It should also be pointed out that the efficiency of any program's execution time depends finally upon the programmer, whether assembly *or* compiler language is used. Unnecessarily used or repeated routines, failures to use available means to reference stored information quickly, and poor organization generally may cause a program to execute more slowly than necessary regardless of programming language.

3. Systems and general management may agree with the operations management objections to COBOL that are being at least partly overcome; but from a cost and systems viewpoint, acknowledge that conversion and training savings cannot be ignored as advantages of COBOL. Nor can the readability of COBOL source program listings and diagnostics be downgraded as a cost and time advantage when debugging or revising programs; COBOL does provide a wider area of communication both inside and outside the programming organization. Nonprogramming personnel familiar with application detail can aid a COBOL programmer in debugging to an extent not available with assembly-language programming.

In general, the simplicity, orderliness, ease in learning, and facility of communication in the use of COBOL are important cost-saving and time-saving factors in any EDP organization. While originating in the programming area, these factors are reflected in faster systems implementation and earlier operating results. Nevertheless, the two deficiencies sometimes occurring

---

1. The advent of minicomputers has added to the ranks; prior to this, Honeywell's COBOL B (for 8K and larger computers) was the smallest version. Now IBM's System 3 and Honeywell's Model 58 provide even smaller COBOL compilers.

in connection with COBOL usage may reduce the gains otherwise obtained:

1. Even with programming of optimum efficiency, some COBOL programs (primarily on large computers) may execute more slowly than assembly-language programs. Improved compilers have reduced this differential, but it continues to a reduced degree. However, since software and other nonoperating EDP costs tend to be higher than machine costs, the gains from COBOL tend to outweigh these losses.

2. The fact that COBOL is problem-oriented rather than machine-oriented, while focusing more effectively on the job to be done, can contribute to substantially greater hazard to efficient programming than does an assembly language. In this sense, a programmer's claim that assembly language is easier to understand *does* carry some weight. If a programmer is not aware of the number and kind of machine operations generated by a COBOL instruction, he has no way of knowing how many computer operational steps his program is performing or how much storage area he is using. If, for example, a COBOL programmer unfamiliar with machine language repeatedly uses a COBOL verb which must be translated into four instructions in an object program instead of using another COBOL verb which requires only two object instructions, he will be unknowingly producing an inefficient program. Mere statements in COBOL textbooks that specific practices are "inefficient" leave the programming student with conclusions supported by no detailed knowledge or logic. In many cases, the nature of basic computer operations permits an explanation as well as a conclusion; in some instances, an adequate answer may be dependent upon the specific computer manufacturer's compiler processing of the source program. A given COBOL statement will not necessarily result in the same number or pattern of machine language instructions in every compiler.

Some competent programmers are inclined to minimize the importance of either of these factors or the combination of them, pointing out that:

1. Even the fastest input-output devices (tape and disk units) have physical speeds so much slower than the internal processing speed of a computer that a relatively enormous number of internal operational program steps would be required to make total internal processing per item retard the physical speed of these devices. A program requiring so many internal steps that internal processing is slower than the fastest input or output device being used in its execution should be the exceptional case; normally, the speed of the program is bound by the speed of the slowest input or output device used in its execution. The reader-bound, punch-bound, tape- or disk-bound, or printer-bound program is the rule in commercial applications; the central-processor-bound program is the exception, and the chances are that when this is the case, assembly language would achieve only marginal gains in central-processor speed. In smaller computers, using input/output devices, there is even less likelihood of the occurrence of central-processor-bound programs.

2. The issue of efficient capacity utilization is raised primarily in two kinds of situations:

a. Small-computer operations, for which a single program, when written with maximum efficiency, may require close to the entire storage capacity of the computer. In such cases, both the compiler's efficiency and the programmer's understanding of what the *object* program's instructions must consist of may make the difference between writing the program in the requested form or recommending either that parts be eliminated or the needed processing be split up into two or more smaller programs.

b. Large-computer operations performed in a multiprogramming environment, in which different programs are being executed independently in separate areas of the computer. Here the combined effect of the compiler's efficiency and the programmer's knowledge of object language instructions will be somewhat similar. Either the ability to run multiple programs will be reduced, or the programs must be reviewed and improved program efficiency achieved to permit a wider range of concurrent use with other programs within the total capacity of the large computer.

Critics of COBOL contend that problems such as the above occur more frequently when COBOL is the programming language than when assembly languages are used. This criticism stems mainly from the two reasons cited. It is possible that the criticism is correct; yet it is also occasionally found that a COBOL source program will result in use of less computer storage than an assembly-language program of the same programmer-efficiency level. Here again, recent improvements in the efficiency of COBOL compilers have undoubtedly reduced both the margin and the frequency of deficiencies in object programs resulting from COBOL source programs.

Even the understanding of machine language and compiler contents does not in itself assure efficient programming. Ultimately, an efficient program depends on the programmer's keeping the number of instructions to a minimum. Doing this requires the ability to reduce a required series of instructions to the minimum necessary, and to avoid repeating any series of instructions unnecessarily. If this is done within the limits imposed by the structure of COBOL, the necessity of knowing the specific machine language is at a minimum; one basic objective of COBOL is thereby fulfilled.

COBOL VOCABULARY

Function of ANSI COBOL

The early versions of COBOL requirements formulated by the CODASYL conferences in the early 1960s set minimum contents for COBOL vocabulary and functions. Beginning about 1962, computer manufacturers, in competing for Federal government contracts for rental or purchase of computers in many areas, were required to have COBOL programming capability available on the computers they offered. Computer manufacturers placed varying emphases on needs beyond the minimum; in addition, differing internal construction of computers gave rise to different methods of implementing some COBOL instructions. The resulting variety of COBOL compilers, though not as disastrous as the effect of different programming languages, required significant effort to modify a COBOL source program written for manufacturer X's computer so that it could be compiled into an object program to be executed on manufacturer Y's computer of the same capabilities. Efforts at both national and international levels were made during the 1960s to standardize COBOL further, a major purpose in these efforts being to increase inter-computer COBOL compatibilities. By late 1968, a revised version of COBOL was agreed upon. This revised version is presently the base for current COBOL compilers. The then-United States of America Standards Institute (USASI) was assigned the responsibility for publication and maintenance of the standards for the new version of COBOL, which became known as USASI COBOL. When the Institute changed its name in 1969 to American National Standards Institute, the new reference—ANSI (or ANS) COBOL—became current.

ANSI COBOL is not a compiler. It is a set of specifications for COBOL compilers organized at three levels and in eight modules. A minimum COBOL compiler would contain only the lowest level of the three basic modules (nucleus, table handling, and sequential access); a so-called full COBOL compiler would contain not only the highest level of the three basic modules, but also the high level of the five optional modules (random access, library, segmentation, sort, and report-writer). Not all computers of 32K (32,768 positions) storage capacity or larger would require a full COBOL compiler; most of the five op-

tional modules are based on special hardware features or usages. Specifically, the *random-access* module is associated with disk systems; the *library* and *segmentation* modules assume external storage (tape or disk) of programs or parts of them for use when compiling or executing COBOL programs. The *sort* and *report-writer* modules are more dependent on the computer's capacity than on specific hardware features or usages.

For purposes of developing a working knowledge of programming in COBOL, the nucleus, table-handling, and sequential-access modules are necessary areas of detailed coverage. The sort and report-writer modules, though not parts of every COBOL compiler, are useful, readily understandable accessories that can save considerable operating and programming time; the basic techniques are given brief description in Chapter 15, as are those of the other three optional modules. These (particularly random access), however, require detailed treatment at their own levels to an extent not feasible in an introductory programming course; therefore, details of the programming techniques involved are left to areas of advanced instruction.

The COBOL "Character Set"

When writing a source program in COBOL, the programmer is confined to the use of fifty-one characters (the twenty-six letters of the alphabet, digits 0 through 9, and fifteen special characters, as indicated in Figure 3–1).[2] It will be noticed that such characters as %, ¢, &, ?, to name only a few, are not among the fifteen special characters in the COBOL character set. While they cannot be used as instruction symbols in a COBOL source program, they can appear in *data* that will be processed by the object program compiled from it, and will be printed, written on tape or disk, or punched as

---

2. Caution should be used in connection with the special characters. While some (particularly the slash, comma, and period) have the same card-punch and printout relationship on all computers, many do not. The punch configuration for parentheses, for example, may produce other characters on older keypunches. The comparing symbols ($= > <$) may be available on a keypunch used for a given computer, but the computer's printer may supply some other characters on printout. Finally, the punch configuration required by the particular computer to recognize a COBOL character for compilation purposes must be the governing guide, and source programs must be keypunched to conform to these requirements. For example, there has been some variation among computers as to the keypunch character recognized and the character generated by the computer line printer for the quotation mark. While the standard " is used in this text, the requirement in the particular compiler/computer relationship must govern program instructions and keypunching.

Figure 3–1. The COBOL character set.

Numeric digits:	0 through 9	
Alphabetic characters:	A through Z	
Special characters:	Printed as	Name or meaning

Printed as	Name or meaning
	space, blank
+	plus sign
—	minus sign, hyphen
*	asterisk
/	stroke, virgule, slash
=	equal sign, equals
$	currency sign, dollar sign
,	comma (sometimes decimal point)
;	semicolon
.	period, decimal point
"	quotation mark
(	left parenthesis
)	right parenthesis
>	"greater than" symbol
<	"less than" symbol

output card characters, if the computer used has "hardware" capability to recognize and process such characters.

COBOL "Reserved Words"

The COBOL vocabulary of "reserved words," numbering less than 250 in the full ANSI COBOL specifications, is a group of words available for programmer use in writing COBOL source programs. Most of them are words that, when translated by a COBOL compiler into machine language, result in one or more instructions in the object program either to perform internal operations or to control the operation of external computer components. Others describe characteristics of the data to be processed, the nature of the program, and the relationships of the various components of the computer in the program to be compiled. Not all of the reserved words used in a source program result in object-program functions. The ones that are necessary to producing an object-program operation are called *key words*. Those that have no object-program function but provide information about the source program itself or make source program instructions more readable are considered *optional words*.

While the ANSI COBOL reserved word list currently contains only 236 words, some COBOL compilers contain substantially more. Any COBOL compiler for a specific model computer is referred to as a "subset"; for example, the "IBM System/360 Disk Operating System Subset American National Standard COBOL." A COBOL subset for any specific computer

will include in its reserved word list special words to represent particular components (such as the reader, punch unit, printer, console) and their individual units (such as tape and disk units). In addition, it may contain "extensions" of ANSI COBOL specifications, in the nature of either special "hardware" characteristics or components, or internal operating techniques which require additional reserved words for identification of the hardware or generating operational instructions in the object program. As a result, a COBOL "full subset" may contain considerably more than 300 reserved words.

The 236 reserved words in the ANSI COBOL specifications are listed as Figure 3–2. Most of them are employed in all levels of the three basic ANSI COBOL modules; others are used in one or more of the five optional modules not available at the lowest level basic COBOL. To provide a perspective of vocabulary usage, a rearrangement of the reserved words, grouped by module with which they are typically used, is shown as Figure 3–3. In addition, the reserved words that are used in the nucleus module have been grouped by the source program division in which they are introduced or most typically used.

It should be pointed out that reserved words are not the only components of a COBOL source program. While a source program's procedure division instructions must always use reserved words to compile as object-program instructions, it is always necessary in the data division for the programmer to assign names to files, records, and parts (fields) of records for convenient reference to them in the related procedure division instructions. The names (data-names) assigned for this purpose *must not* be reserved words; the programmer can use other dictionary words or make up names for such use. The programmer will also have to assign names of his choice to paragraphs of his program containing groups of instructions; these are referred to as procedure-names and also must not be reserved words. In addition, as will be developed later, a programmer may need to create words of his own choosing, called *literals*, in a COBOL program procedure division or data division. And, third, for future reference to the source program, a programmer may desire to have brief explanatory notes incorporated in it.

The methods required for using literals and notes in a source program enable the programmer to use both reserved words and non-COBOL words in the literals and notes without interfering with compilation of the object program. The use of a reserved word as a *data-name* or *procedure-name*, however, will prevent the program's successful compilation. It should be understood, however, that the prohibitions concerning reserved word usage as names in source programs do

Figure 3–2. ANSI COBOL reserved word list.

ACCEPT	ENDING	MEMORY	RF
ACCESS	ENTER	MODE	RH
ACTUAL	ENVIRONMENT	MODULES	RIGHT
ADD	EQUAL	MOVE	ROUNDED
ADDRESS	ERROR	MULTIPLE	RUN
ADVANCING	EVERY	MULTIPLY	SAME
AFTER	EXAMINE	NEGATIVE	SD
ALL	EXIT	NEXT	SEARCH
ALPHABETIC	FD	NO	SECTION
ALTER	FILE	NOT	SECURITY
ALTERNATE	FILE-CONTROL	NOTE	SEEK
AND	FILE-LIMIT	NUMBER	SEGMENT-LIMIT
ARE	FILE-LIMITS	NUMERIC	SELECT
AREA	FILLER	OBJECT-COMPUTER	SENTENCE
AREAS	FINAL	OCCURS	SEQUENTIAL
ASCENDING	FIRST	OF	SET
ASSIGN	FOOTING	OFF	SIGN
AT	FOR	OMITTED	SIZE
AUTHOR	FROM	ON	SORT
BEFORE	GENERATE	OPEN	SOURCE
BEGINNING	GIVING	OPTIONAL	SOURCE-COMPUTER
BLANK	GO	OR	SPACE
BLOCK	GREATER	OUTPUT	SPACES
BY	GROUP	PAGE	SPECIAL-NAMES
CF	HEADING	PAGE-COUNTER	STANDARD
CH	HIGH-VALUE	PERFORM	STATUS
CHARACTERS	HIGH-VALUES	PF	STOP
CLOCK-UNITS	I-O	PH	SUBTRACT
CLOSE	I-O-CONTROL	PIC	SUM
COBOL	IDENTIFICATION	PICTURE	SYNC
CODE	IF	PLUS	SYNCHRONIZED
COLUMN	IN	POSITION	TALLY
COMMA	INDEX	POSITIVE	TALLYING
COMP	INDEXED	PROCEDURE	TAPE
COMPUTATIONAL	INDICATE	PROCEED	TERMINATE
COMPUTE	INITIATE	PROCESSING	THAN
CONFIGURATION	INPUT	PROGRAM-ID	THROUGH
CONTAINS	INPUT-OUTPUT	QUOTE	THRU
CONTROL	INSTALLATION	QUOTES	TIMES
CONTROLS	INTO	RANDOM	TO
COPY	INVALID	RD	TYPE
CORR	IS	READ	UNIT
CORRESPONDING	JUST	RECORD	UNTIL
CURRENCY	JUSTIFIED	RECORDS	UP
DATA	KEY	REDEFINES	UPON
DATE-COMPILED	KEYS	REEL	USAGE
DATE-WRITTEN	LABEL	RELEASE	USE
DE	LAST	REMARKS	USING
DECIMAL-POINT	LEADING	RENAMES	VALUE
DECLARATIVES	LEFT	REPLACING	VALUES
DEPENDING	LESS	REPORT	VARYING
DESCENDING	LIMIT	REPORTING	WHEN
DETAIL	LIMITS	REPORTS	WITH
DISPLAY	LINE	RERUN	WORDS
DIVIDE	LINE-COUNTER	RESERVE	WORKING-STORAGE
DIVISION	LINES	RESET	WRITE
DOWN	LOCK	RETURN	ZERO
ELSE	LOW-VALUE	REVERSED	ZEROES
END	LOW-VALUES	REWIND	ZEROS

Figure 3–3. Reserved word list analysis. To use these groupings as a study aid, the reader should refer to the comments below.

NUCLEUS MODULE:

Identification division:

AUTHOR	INSTALLATION
DATE-COMPILED	PROGRAM-ID
DATE-WRITTEN	REMARKS
DIVISION	SECURITY
IDENTIFICATION	

Environment division:

ASSIGN	MODULES
CHARACTERS	OBJECT-COMPUTER
COMMA	OFF
CONFIGURATION	ON
CURRENCY	SELECT
DECIMAL-POINT	SIGN
ENVIRONMENT	SOURCE-COMPUTER
FILE-CONTROL	SPECIAL-NAMES
INPUT-OUTPUT	STATUS
IS	WORDS
MEMORY	

Data division:

ARE	OMITTED
BLANK	⎰PIC
BLOCK	⎱PICTURE
⎰COMP	REDEFINES
⎱COMPUTATIONAL	RENAMES
CONTAINS	RIGHT
DATA	SECTION
FD	STANDARD
FILE	⎰SYNC
FILLER	⎱SYNCHRONIZED
IN	TIMES
⎰JUST	USAGE
⎱JUSTIFIED	VALUE
LABEL	VALUES
LEFT	WHEN
OCCURS	WORKING-STORAGE
OF	

Procedure division:

ACCEPT	DIVIDE
ADD	ELSE
ADVANCING	END
AFTER	ENTER
ALPHABETIC	EQUAL
ALTER	ERROR
AND	EXAMINE
AT	EXIT
BEFORE	FIRST
BY	FROM
CLOSE	GIVING
COBOL	GO
COMPUTE	GREATER
⎰CORR	IF
⎱CORRESPONDING	INPUT
DEPENDING	INTO
DISPLAY	LEADING

LESS	REPLACING
LINES	ROUNDED
MOVE	RUN
MULTIPLY	SENTENCE
NEGATIVE	SIZE
NEXT	STOP
NOT	SUBTRACT
NOTE	TALLY
NUMERIC	TALLYING
OPEN	THAN
OR	⎰THROUGH
OUTPUT	⎱THRU
PERFORM	TO
POSITIVE	UNTIL
PROCEDURE	UPON
PROCEED	VARYING
READ	WRITE

The following words, having a rather special use, are known as figurative constants:

ALL	⎰SPACE
⎰HIGH-VALUE	⎱SPACES
⎱HIGH-VALUES	⎰ZERO
⎰LOW-VALUE	⎱ZEROES
⎱LOW-VALUES	⎱ZEROS
⎰QUOTE	
⎱QUOTES	

TABLE-HANDLING MODULE:

ASCENDING	INDEXED
DESCENDING	SEARCH
DOWN	SET
INDEX	UP

SEQUENTIAL-ACCESS MODULE:

ACCESS	MULTIPLE
ALTERNATE	NO
AREA	OPTIONAL
AREAS	POSITION
BEGINNING	PROCESSING
CLOCK-UNITS	RECORD
DECLARATIVES	RECORDS
ENDING	REEL
EVERY	RERUN
FILE-LIMIT	RESERVE
FILE-LIMITS	REVERSED
FOR	REWIND
I-O	SAME
I-O-CONTROL	SEQUENTIAL
INVALID	TAPE
KEY	UNIT
KEYS	USE
LOCK	WITH
MODE	

RANDOM-ACCESS MODULE:

ACTUAL	SEEK
RANDOM	

SORT MODULE:

RELEASE   SORT
RETURN   USING

REPORT-WRITER MODULE:

CF	LINE
CH	LINE-COUNTER
CODE	NUMBER
COLUMN	PAGE
CONTROL	PAGE-COUNTER
CONTROLS	PF
DE	PH
DETAIL	PLUS
FINAL	REPORT
FOOTING	REPORTING
GENERATE	REPORTS
GROUP	RESET
HEADING	RF
INDICATE	RH
INITIATE	SOURCE
LAST	SUM
LIMIT	TERMINATE
LIMITS	TYPE

SEGMENTATION MODULE:

SEGMENT-LIMIT

LIBRARY MODULE:

COPY   SD
RD

COMMENTS:

1. It should be kept in mind that many of the words listed for a specific module or division are used in other modules or divisions; for example, most of the words introduced in the sequential module are also necessary when making use of the random access module. Similarly, within the COBOL nucleus, some words appearing in the environment and data divisions (e.g., IS, ON, IN, OF, TIMES) are also used in the procedure division.
2. No attempt has been made above to classify by division the words related to modules other than the nucleus. In general, the sequential and random-access words are used mostly in the environment and procedure divisions; the report-writer vocabulary consists solely of data division and procedure division words; the four sort module words listed above occur in the procedure division; the segmentation module word is used in the environment division; the library words all appear in the data division, though COPY may also appear in the environment and procedure divisions.
3. The eleven pairs of bracketed words represent optional usages for the same purpose. Spelling or abbreviation preferences of the COBOL user for time-saving or readability will govern the choice; either of the bracketed words produces the same object-program result.

---

not apply to *data being processed by the object program*. When a COBOL source program has been successfully compiled into an object program, the object program (which is in the machine language of the computer executing the program) controls the processing of data by the computer. The presence of COBOL reserved words in the *data being processed* cannot have any bearing on the object program's execution of the machine-language instructions.

COBOL INSTRUCTION FORMAT

COBOL source programs are prepared on standard coding forms set up so that each line of program instruction can be keypunched into a standard eighty-column card. Any COBOL compiler[3] will cause the

related computer to read the punched information according to this format (see Figure 3–4). Coding forms vary somewhat: each computer manufacturer supplies its own; but all must have the same columnar usage, as follows:

Columns 1–6: While it is not essential to punch a page number in columns 1–3 or a serial number in columns 4–6, it is a desirable safety precaution to do so. Most compilers check the ascending sequence of the source program cards as shown by the numeric digits punched in columns 1–6 and will print a warning message if a card is in descending sequence. If columns 1–6 are not punched, and there has been some mishandling of the cards, the compiler cannot detect a sequence error. When columns 1–6 are keypunched, page numbers lower than 100 should be punched with leading zeroes (e.g., 001, 035)in columns 1–3, and the card number within the page should be punched in columns 4–5, with a zero in column 4 if the card number is lower than 10. Column 6 should be left blank when punching an original program. It is reserved for inserting supplementary instruction cards when needed to amend an original source program. If, for example,

---

3. It is essential to keep in mind that the compiler is itself a program. Its function is to translate the keypunched source program readable by human beings into a machine-language program readable by the computer. The object program, whether stored on cards, tape, or disk, contains the instructions which the computer executes upon the input data to achieve the results intended by the source program.

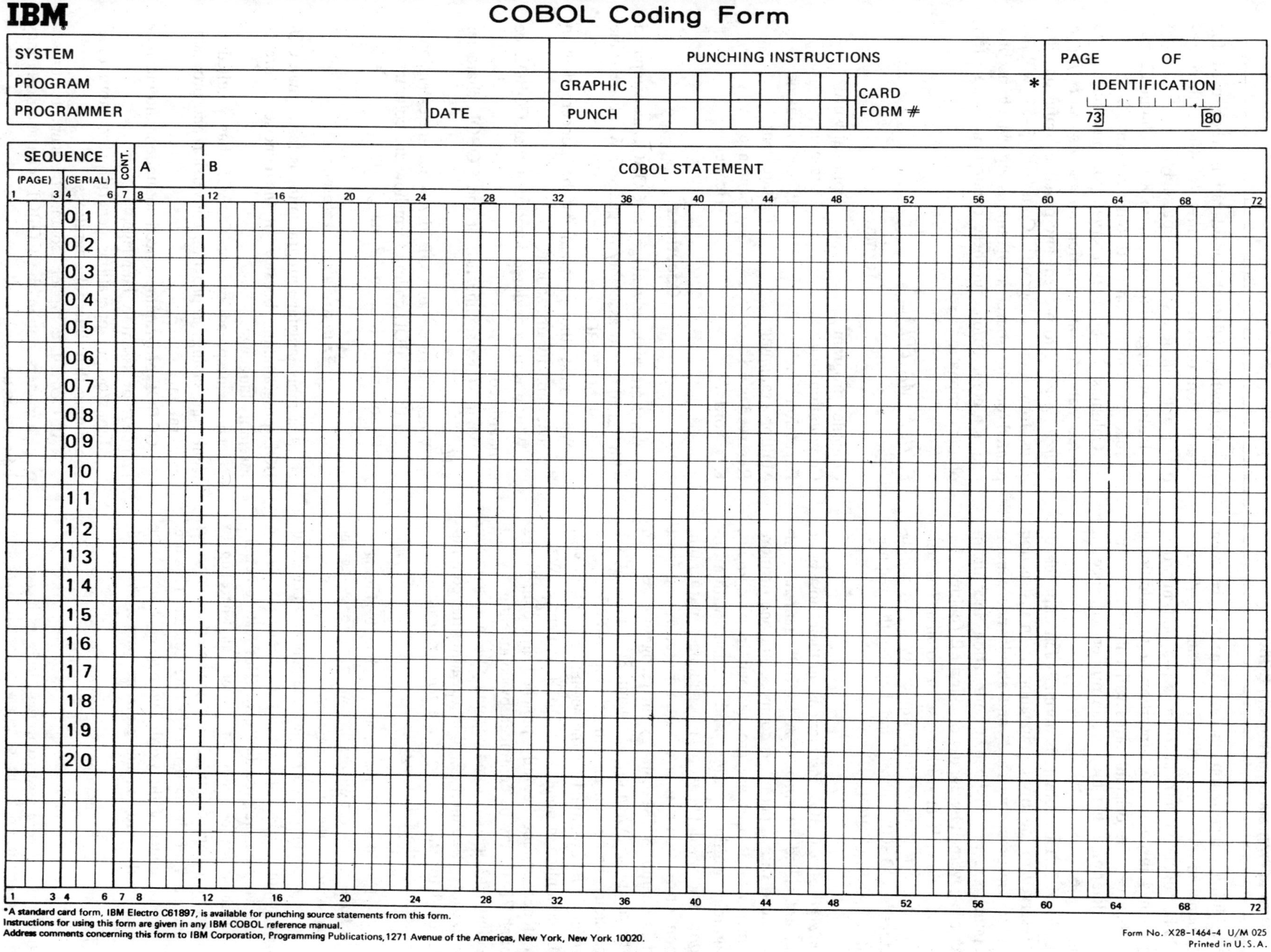

COBOL Coding Form

Figure 3–4. COBOL coding form.

four additional instruction cards are needed between cards punched 00603 and 00604 in columns 1–5, they should be punched 00603 in columns 1–5, and, in order, 1 through 4 in column 6.[4] Insertion of the additional cards between the original cards will enable the compiler to determine that they are in proper sequence on columns 1–6.

Column 7: This column is normally left unpunched; it is reserved to identify continuation of an instruction begun in the preceding card, and should not contain any punch except a hyphen. Continuation lines themselves are governed by the use of margin B (column 12) discussed below. If any other use of column 7 is permitted, it is a feature of the compiler for a given manufacturer's COBOL subset, and beyond the requirements of ANSI COBOL.

Margin A: COBOL instructions, in their most basic form, are called *statements.* A COBOL *sentence,* always ended with a period, is composed of one or more statements. Sentences are grouped within *paragraphs,* paragraphs within *sections,* and sections within *divisions.* The word (or words) beginning a paragraph, section, or division is referred to as a *header,* and must start in column 8 (Margin A) for recognition as such by the compiler. When use of column 8 is not required, there should be no punching in columns 9–11.[5]

Margin B: Column 12 is the beginning point, as well as the continuation point, for COBOL sentences. When a sentence cannot be fully punched in columns 12 through 72, it may be continued by completing a word on column 72 or sooner and beginning the next word on the next line at column 12. When reading the continuation card for an *ordinary statement or sentence,* the compiler does the following:

  • If column 7 is blank, the punching beginning on column 12 is considered a new word following the last word on the preceding card.

  • If column 7 is a hyphen, the punching beginning in column 12 is considered as the completion of the last word on the preceding card. This feature permits punching the beginning of a word anywhere up to and including column 72, and punching a hyphen in column 7 of the next card, where column 12 starts the remainder of the word. The hyphen is *not* to be used on the card containing the first part of the word.

The use of the column 7 hyphen requires special and somewhat different consideration when used for continuation of *nonnumeric literals,* where these requirements will be discussed separately.

Punching beginning in column 8 or column 12 will be read for compilation up through column 72.

Columns 73–80 are reserved for punching some unique name or abbreviation *in all the cards for a source program* to prevent any possible confusion with cards from other programs. Columns 73–80 will be printed on the source program listing which accompanies a compilation, but these columns have no effect on the compilation itself.

REVIEW MATERIAL

Terms

Compiler program	Optional word
Compilation time	Data-name
Execution time	Procedure-name
Multiprogramming	Statement
Reserved word	Sentence
Key word	Header

Questions

What are some advantages of COBOL as compared with machine and assembly languages? What are some criticisms of COBOL?

Why must the programmer be concerned with efficient capacity utilization?

Why was it considered important that COBOL be standardized?

What is the significance of the COBOL character set?

What is a subset of COBOL? What are extensions?

On the COBOL coding form how are columns 1–6 used? Column 7? Margin A? Margin B?

True-or-False Statements

Assembly-language programming is faster than COBOL programming because of the concise nature of assembly language.

The widespread use of COBOL has resulted in significant savings in program conversion and programmer training.

COBOL programmers need not understand machine language or assembly language.

Input/output operations generally are more time-consuming than internal operations.

All COBOL compilers contain the same features.

Characters not in the COBOL character set may be used as data.

Data-names cannot be reserved words.

A COBOL statement must be contained on one eighty-column punched card.

---

4. If the *computer* used recognizes blanks as higher than numeric digits, it would be necessary to punch a zero in column 6 of the original 00603 card.

5. An exception to this is permitted in indentations for data division definitions, but is seldom seen, probably because of carryover of force-of-habit coding of entries for other divisions.

4

THE DIVISIONS OF A COBOL PROGRAM

IDENTIFICATION DIVISION

The identification division entries provide reference information only. They supply data about the program itself, but nothing that is compiled into instructions in the object program. Since this division is the first in a COBOL source program, the source listing printout at compilation time begins with the identification division. Figure 4–1 is an example of a set of identification division statements. The following should be noted:

1. Only the first two lines, representing the division header and the PROGRAM-ID paragraph, are required. All other statements are optional, but, if used, must be in the order shown.

2. The division header consists of two reserved words followed by a period. (All division and section headers follow this rule.) Division and section headers must begin at margin A (column 8).

3. The remaining items are all considered paragraphs. The first word of a paragraph is called the paragraph header and is followed by a period. In the identification and environment divisions, a paragraph header must be a reserved word. (Verify this by checking against the reserved word list.)

4. A period following a word or the end of a sentence must be followed by at least one blank space.

5. The word following the PROGRAM-ID paragraph header is supplied by the programmer. It must *not* be a reserved word and must conform to the COBOL definition of a word as (*a*) containing no more than thirty characters which (*b*) can be only the letters *A* through *Z*, numeric digits 0 through 9 and (*c*) can include a hyphen (-) within the word but not at its beginning or end.

6. The sample identification division contains one continuation line (09). Note that it begins in *Area* B, but to the right of *Margin* B. It is permissible for continuation lines to begin at Margin B (column 12) or to the right of it.

Two significant items, not apparent from Figure 4–1, should also be noted:

7. Part of the program-name following PROGRAM-ID is incorporated by some COBOL compilers into the object program. Typically the part so processed is the first six or eight characters of the name. When this compiler feature is used, care should be taken to make the compiler-processed part of the program-name unique to avoid confusion with other object programs having names that begin with similar letter combinations.

8. A COBOL compiler feature present with some computers is utilized to supply the current date as the source program is compiled. When this feature is available, the date compiled, even if on the paragraph header card, will be replaced with the actual date of the compilation run.

It is important to recognize that even if little of the identification division becomes part of the object pro-

COBOL Coding Form

IBM

SYSTEM

PROGRAM

PROGRAMMER

PUNCHING INSTRUCTIONS

GRAPHIC   PUNCH

DATE

PAGE   OF

CARD FORM #

IDENTIFICATION 73 80

COBOL STATEMENT

SEQUENCE (PAGE) (SERIAL)	CONT	A	B	
01		IDENTIFICATION DIVISION.	
02		PROGRAM-ID. DAILY-VOUCHERS.	
03		AUTHOR. REX PENPUSHER.	
04		INSTALLATION. WESTERN CHEM. DIV.	
05		DATE-WRITTEN. FEB 2 1973.	
06		DATE-COMPILED.	
07		SECURITY. ACCOUNTING PERSONNEL ONLY.	
08		REMARKS. THIS PROGRAM LISTS NEW VOUCHERS DAILY, CHECKS MISSING	
09		NUMBERS, PRINTS ACCOUNT DISTRIBUTIONS.	
10			
11			
12			
13			
14			
15			
16			
17			
18			
19			
20			

*A standard card form, IBM Electro C61897, is available for punching source statements from this form.
Instructions for using this form are given in any IBM COBOL reference manual.
Address comments concerning this form to IBM Corporation, Programming Publications, 1271 Avenue of the Americas, New York, New York 10020.

Form No. X28-1464-4 U/M 025
Printed in U.S.A.

Figure 4-1. Identification division statements

gram, the source program listing that is printed during compilation time is an essential part of any program review for any kind of changes to the program, or for reference to determine what the program contains. The optional paragraphs that do not become a part of the object program often can contain information that must be noted in connection with these purposes. The SE-CURITY paragraph is not confined to military organizations; in a business, the information in it tells much about the purpose of the program. The SECURITY and REMARKS paragraphs, taken together, should provide perspective of the purposes, users, and content of the job done by the program. A programmer, assigned to make changes in a program written by a programmer no longer available for consultation, should be able to find such guideline information in the identification division before looking elsewhere to formulate the changes in program detail.

ENVIRONMENT DIVISION

The main function of the environment division is to set up the components of the computer to be used in the manner specified by the program. The required statements in this division become part of the object program. If an essential statement is missing, it may prevent the compilation of an object program; for example, if no statement has been included to select a tape unit on which to write a file of output records, the data division description of that file and its records and the procedure division statements on its handling cannot be used or performed.

The environment division, in referring to computer components, will be governed by the COBOL compiler for the specific computer. Names designated by the computer manufacturer will be assigned for use in this division of the source program to make proper reference to the reader, punch, printer, and tape or disk units. In addition, certain features of a computer may be given names that are included in the ANSI COBOL subset as reserved words for use in the SPECIAL-NAMES paragraph of the environment division. Both of these types of names are referred to in ANSI COBOL specifications as *implementor-names,* because they are created by the specific computer manufacturer (implementor) who provides the computer's components and special features to *implement* data division usages and procedure division operational instructions. Even if the implementor-names are reserved words, they are not part of the *ANSI reserved word list,* but are parts of only those *ANSI subsets* used by the specific "implementor's" computers.

There are two basic sections in the environment division: the configuration section and the input-output section. Because the division has to do with computer components and features of them, the requirements for the configuration section vary considerably from one implementor's subset to another. In some COBOL subsets, the compiler will process the source program even though the only entry in the configuration section is the section header itself. Even when this is the case, it is advisable to include both the SOURCE-COMPUTER and OBJECT-COMPUTER paragraphs in as complete a format as recognized by the compiler. The information given in these paragraphs, taken with the INPUT-OUTPUT SECTION, is a useful guide to the machine requirements of the program and the capabilities of the compiler needed to produce it.

Configuration Section

The SOURCE-COMPUTER paragraph must contain the header (SOURCE-COMPUTER) and the name of the computer to the extent specified by the implementor. Some computer manufacturers include enough data, such as a model number, to identify a particular combination of computer components.

The OBJECT-COMPUTER paragraph must contain the header and the computer-name entry. The object-computer may not necessarily be the same computer as the source-computer. Occasionally, a program written to be run on a small computer cannot be compiled on it because the amount of storage capacity required by the compiler plus the number and size of entries in the source program exceeds the computer's capacity though the object program, once compiled, does not. In such a case, the source-computer would be a larger one than the object-computer on which the object program would be used.

The format of the OBJECT-COMPUTER paragraph is a good example of the ANSI rules for COBOL entry formats. While somewhat awkward in appearance, these formats do show precisely and briefly what is necessary for compilation and what is optional for readability in any COBOL entry. Hereafter, the requirements for each new type of entry will be described in this format, whose characteristics should be kept in mind for ready understanding:

$$\underline{\text{OBJECT-COMPUTER}}\text{, computer-name}\left[\text{, }\underline{\text{MEMORY}}\text{ SIZE integer}\left\{\begin{array}{l}\underline{\text{WORDS}}\\\underline{\text{CHARACTERS}}\\\underline{\text{MODULES}}\end{array}\right\}\right]\text{.}$$

Words in capital letters are reserved words. If underlined, such a word must be used in the entry when that part of the entry is used; it is referred to as a *key word*. If not underlined, the reserved word need not be actually used in the entry; it is known as an *optional word* and is included only for readability of the source program listing. The compiler will develop the object program instruction properly from the entry even if the word is missing from it.

Words in small letters are programmer-supplied words which depend on the requirements of the program. They may be words which the programmer is using elsewhere in the program or words depending on the type of computer being used. As shown above, the computer-name is not only dependent on the type of computer, but is a reserved word in the implementor's subset of ANSI COBOL. For example:

```
ENVIRONMENT DIVISION.
CONFIGURATION SECTION
SOURCE-COMPUTER.   H-200.
OBJECT-COMPUTER.   H-200, MEMORY SIZE
                   32,768 CHARACTERS.
```

The computer-name used here refers to a Honeywell model. Other manufacturers would also include the computer model name and its subset's reserved word list; for example, IBM-360, B-3500 (Burroughs), UNIVAC-1108, XDS-SIGMA-7, CENTURY-200 (NCR).

The word "integer" means simply that the number representing the capacity of the object-computer must be indicated at this point in the entry. While dependent on the specific computer and its storage-capacity size, this number is not a reserved word. The memory capacity for most computers with COBOL availability is expressed in character positions, as shown here; for some, the term *words* or *modules* would be applicable.

When a portion of an entry is enclosed in brackets [ ], the enclosed portion may be included or omitted depending on the programmer's choice and the needs of the program. This does *not* mean that the bracketed portion is only for readability; as we will see in many instances later on, such items may be omitted only because the programmer has no need for their use in a specific program. When a bracketed entry portion is used, it must be in the order required by the format and very often (in a procedure division statement) it generates computer operations for which the programmer finds a need in the specific program. The bracketed area appears above as [, MEMORY SIZE 32,768 CHARACTERS]. Compare it with the ANSI format given a little earlier, and note that had it not appeared, a period would have been placed immediately following the computer-name.

The memory size clause of the OBJECT-COMPUTER paragraph happens to be primarily to supply information. A programmer assigned the task of enlarging a program to do more things would be forewarned of the computer's capacity limits by this statement and evaluate the feasibility of his task by the size of the existing program and the demands on capacity of adding the new features.

Two other items should be noted: In general, commas are not necessary for any purpose except readability. Here the comma could have been omitted and only a blank space left between the computer-name and the word MEMORY. Second, the word SIZE could have been omitted, though the words MEMORY and CHARACTERS could not. Had either of the latter two been omitted, the compiler would have caused some printout concerning incompleteness of the statement.

Braces { } are used in COBOL statement formats in somewhat the same manner as brackets; however, braces indicate that a selection must be made from two or more choices of words usable in the braced part of the statement, while bracketed items may be excluded altogether depending on program needs. In the data and procedure divisions, the choice within the braces usually depends on conditions in the program's purposes; in the environment division, as in this case, it depends on the kind of computer used.

The reserved word SPECIAL-NAMES is the name of a paragraph sometimes used in the configuration section. Its purpose is ordinarily to make use of special facilities in the object-computer. It will be employed only when the special facility is required in the program, and is usually in the format of:

implementor-name IS mnemonic-name.

ANSI COBOL specifications assumes IS will be a required word in all special-names entries; in some subsets, however, IS may be a key word in certain special-names entries and an optional one in others. The term "mnemonic-name" applies to most names created by the programmer; "mnemonic" is an adjective best defined as "memory-jogging." When a programmer makes use of a special computer component feature, he may refer to it in the procedure division by an abbreviated name he decides to use. The special-names entry will be needed to enable the compiler to associate the special feature, by its implementor-name, with the programmer's mnemonic-name. For example, suppose the programmer decides to use the abbreviation PCH for the punch unit for certain procedure division entries, and the punch unit's implementor-name is SYSPUNCH (as with IBM's 360). The required paragraph header and entry would be: SPECIAL-NAMES. SYSPUNCH IS PCH. Without the special-names paragraph and entry, the use of PCH in the program would fail to make the punch unit operative. In the source listing printout, a diagnostic would indicate that PCH had not been identified.

Input-Output Section

The basic function of this section is to allocate uses of specific computer components as required by the program. The basic computer components for input and output are the reader, the punch unit, the printer, and the file-storage units (usually tape or disk). It is customary to refer to any collection of data processed through any of these components as a *file*. An input file of cards is processed through the reader; each card is a record in the file. The card records may be copied on to tape or disk (in the same or different format) and become all or part of an output file. A file of tape or disk records may be read as input and part or all of it may be punched out as new card records in an output file from the punch unit. Any of the records of these files may be printed out; for programming purposes the printout is a file. The input-output section of the environment division, in a FILE-CONTROL paragraph, enables the programmer to select each data file to be used in the program and assign its handling to a specific computer component. The format of the simplest form of file-control statement is: SELECT file-name, ASSIGN TO implementor-name. The file-name is created by the programmer; the implementor-name is assigned by the computer manufacturer for each type of component, and must be spelled exactly as required, or the compiler will not be able to identify the component. The SELECT statements in a program to read input tape records and cards, write output disk records, and print a report during the processing might look like this for a Century 100 (NCR) computer:

```
INPUT-OUTPUT SECTION.
FILE-CONTROL.
    SELECT CARD-FILE ASSIGN TO
        NCR682-100.
    SELECT OLDTAPE ASSIGN TO
        NCR633-119.
    SELECT NEWDISK ASSIGN NCR655-101.
    SELECT PRINTFILE ASSIGN TO
        NCR640-102.
```

Note that the comma has been omitted from all, and the TO from one, of the entries. As indicated earlier, the comma's use is optional; and in this entry, TO is an optional word. (In certain other entries, TO is a key word.) Other relevant formatting details to be noted are:

1. Each statement is a sentence, ending with a period. Here all statements have been started at the same margin. The FILE-CONTROL paragraph header must start at Margin A, and end with a period. As long as a space follows each period, the SELECT statements can begin on the same *line* as the paragraph header and be continued at Margin B on new lines as required. The format shown above is used for easier reading.

2. Though the files are named in the environment division for the first time in a program, the FILE-CONTROL paragraph does not specify whether they are input or output. The tape and disk file names suggest which is the input and which the output file, but this determination is left for the procedure division.

The foregoing illustrations of environment division statements do not form a complete list. For segmented programs and library usages, special entries are applicable in the configuration section. Various functions of the SPECIAL-NAMES paragraph will be discussed later where relevant. Both the FILE-CONTROL and a special I-O-CONTROL paragraph can contain statements and clauses required for somewhat involved sequential and random-access operations and in library functions. At this point, however, only the contents of the environment division that are necessary for the basic handling of data division and procedure division functions are described. A complete basic environment division, including both configuration and input-output sections, is shown in Figure 4–2.

REVIEW MATERIAL

Terms

Paragraph header
Implementor-name
Source-computer
Object-computer
Special-names
    paragraph
Mnemonic-name

Questions

Which identification division entries are required? Which are optional?

Why might the object-computer not be the same as the source-computer?

In a COBOL entry format, what is an underlined word in capital letters? a word in capital letters but not underlined? a word in small letters?

COBOL Coding Form

SYSTEM			PUNCHING INSTRUCTIONS				PAGE	OF
PROGRAM			GRAPHIC			CARD	*	IDENTIFICATION
PROGRAMMER		DATE	PUNCH			FORM #		73 ☐ 80

SEQUENCE		CONT	A	B	COBOL STATEMENT
(PAGE)	(SERIAL)				
	0 1		ENVIRONMENT DIVISION.		
	0 2		CONFIGURATION SECTION.		
	0 3		SOURCE-COMPUTER. UNIVAC-1108.		
	0 4		OBJECT-COMPUTER. UNIVAC-1108.		
	0 5		INPUT-OUTPUT SECTION.		
	0 6		FILE-CONTROL.		
	0 7		SELECT CARDS-IN ASSIGN TO CARD-READER.		
	0 8		SELECT TAPE-IN ASSIGN TO UNISERVO TP1.		
	0 9		SELECT PRINTFILE ASSIGN TO PRINTER.		
	1 0		SELECT DISKMASTER ASSIGN TO MASS-STORAGE DSK1.		
	1 1				
	1 2				
	1 3				
	1 4				
	1 5				
	1 6				
	1 7				
	1 8				
	1 9				
	2 0				

* A standard card form, IBM Electro C61897, is available for punching source statements from this form.

Instructions for using this form are given in any IBM COBOL reference manual.

Address comments concerning this form to IBM Corporation, Programming Publications, 1271 Avenue of the Americas, New York, New York 10020.

Form No. X28-1464-4 U/M 025
Printed in U.S.A.

Figure 4-2. Basic environment division coding.

What is indicated by an entry enclosed in brackets? braces?

What is the function of the input-output section?

True-or-False Statements

The programmer chooses the paragraph headers in the identification and environment divisions.

The program is compiled on the object-computer.

Optional words are included for readability only and have no effect on the content of the object program.

A file is any collection of data processed through one of the input-output components of a computer.

A file is declared to be input or output in the environment division.

The SPECIAL-NAMES paragraph uses only programmer-chosen mnemonic-names.

5

THE DIVISIONS OF A COBOL PROGRAM
(continued)

DATA DIVISION

The data division always[1] contains a FILE SECTION, in which detailed description must be made of the files to be processed by the program, the types of records within each file, and the format of the contents of the records. The programmer has already assigned names to the files in the SELECT statements of the environment division's input-output section; now he must assign names to types of records within each file, as well as to the types of data fields within each type of record. In this way, the programmer can refer in his procedure division entries to the types of data fields by name and have specific computer operations performed on them. In addition, in ordinary programming it is normally necessary to have a WORKING-STORAGE SECTION where information to be created during the course of executing the object program will be stored or accumulated until needed in some other phase of execution. A simple example would be areas for accumulating group totals (such as sales by department) for printout as the processing of the data for each group is completed. These two basic sections and their contents will be discussed at some length now. A third part of the data division, the REPORT SECTION, is used only in connection with the report-writer module and will not be discussed in this text.

---

1. Theoretically, the FILE SECTION is also optional, depending on the need for it. It is unlikely, however, that a commercial program would be written with neither input nor output files.

File Section

The FILE SECTION header consists of the two named words followed by a period. On the next line, beginning at Margin A, the first description of a file begins, using the letters FD followed by two spaces and the name of a file exactly as spelled in the environment division SELECT statement. No period follows the file name; a number of entries may follow describing characteristics of the file and its records before the FD (file description) paragraph is terminated by a period. Only one of these entries is required by ANSI specifications; they may appear in any order within the FD paragraph. In their simplest form, the four most frequently used entries are:

1. RECORD CONTAINS integer CHARACTERS. If this refers to a card file, the record is a card; the entry would be RECORD CONTAINS 80 CHARACTERS, though RECORD 80 would suffice. A tape or disk record may contain a much smaller or larger number of characters, the number being determined by the need for retaining various kinds of data in a single record. Tape and disk records, however, are not "unit records" separable like cards; they are "written" on a continuous medium. The specification of size by this clause is usually checked by the compiler against the number of character positions specified in the descriptions of the data fields in the record. If records are written one-by-one on tape or disk, there is an unused space between any pair of records, referred to as an "inter-record gap." With tape, this may be a larger area than that occupied by

the record itself. For example, an eighty-position record written on magnetic tape at a density of 800 characters per inch would occupy about one-tenth of an inch. Let us assume that the computer generating the record would leave a standard gap of about one-half of an inch before writing the next record.[2] Writing records singly has the obvious disadvantages of leaving much unused space, and, just as serious, prolonging sorting time because the unused as well as the used areas occupy space that must be processed. The practice of writing records in blocks was developed to avoid this waste of time and media space.

2. BLOCK CONTAINS integer RECORDS. This clause, while not necessary if records are written singly, is a necessity when a file to be read or written contains blocked records. If twenty eighty-position records were written continuously (as if a 1600-position record), this clause would be BLOCK CONTAINS 20 RECORDS (or, BLOCK 20 RECORDS). Unblocked, twenty eighty-position records at 800/cpi density would occupy about eleven inches of tape. Blocked twenty, they would occupy about two inches. Nine of eleven inches would be saved by eliminating nineteen inter-record gaps. It should be noted, however, that processing blocked records necessitates reserving a considerable amount of storage capacity, which will not be available for executing program instructions.

3. LABEL $\begin{Bmatrix} \underline{\text{RECORD}} & \text{IS} \\ \underline{\text{RECORDS}} & \text{ARE} \end{Bmatrix} \begin{Bmatrix} \text{STANDARD} \\ \text{OMITTED} \end{Bmatrix}$ is the only required entry in the file description. When used in direct connection with card or print files, it will always be in the LABEL RECORDS ARE OMITTED (or the singular) form because the concept of label records is simply inapplicable to unit records and printouts.[3] The purpose of label records is to assure use of the correct mass-storage files in running jobs on a computer. Although it is good practice to place identifying stickers on reels of

magnetic tape or disk packs, stickers may be misplaced or identification incorrectly written. In creating mass-storage files, the practice of writing a "header label" record at the beginning of the file, containing a unique name, provides a means for any program using that file to check for the presence of the specified name as assurance that the required file is in use, and that some other file (containing a different name on the "header label," or no label record) has not been put to use in error. Each implementor has its own "standard" label specifications to be followed. The OPEN statement in the procedure division automatically initiates header label checking and/or writing.

When label records of a special nature are required, a programmer-created data-name or names may be substituted for STANDARD in the label record entry. The data-name for the label must not appear in the DATA RECORDS clause (see below), but must be the subject of a record description connected with the FD paragraph for the file.

4. DATA $\begin{Bmatrix} \underline{\text{RECORD}} & \text{IS} \\ \underline{\text{RECORDS}} & \text{ARE} \end{Bmatrix} \begin{Bmatrix} \text{data-} & [, \text{data-} \\ \text{name-1} & \text{name-2}] \end{Bmatrix}$ while an optional clause, is a convenient way of indicating how many types of records are contained in the file. The record descriptions which follow for the file normally contain the record names just as used in the DATA RECORDS clause. Any record description not named in the DATA RECORDS clause, or in a LABEL RECORD IS data-name entry connected with the same file, would result in a diagnostic printout at compilation time on some computers.

At this point, a simple but representative set of file and record description entries will serve to point out some of the basic COBOL requirements for describing data to be processed. Figure 5–1 is based on a file of eighty-column cards which are punched in the same content format and contain employee names and addresses. The content is arranged in each card as follows:

Columns

1–2	Department number
3–5	Employee number
6–25	Employee name
26–50	Employee street address
51–74	Employee city and state
75–79	Zip code
80	Card code (numeric)

The card-file is, we will assume, to be printed out. This requires definition of the print-file as well as of the card-file. We will further assume that SELECT state-

---

2. Although three-quarters of an inch may currently still be the most typical inter-record gap, improvements in magnetic tape devices have reduced the gap length considerably, and some computer tapes can now be written with inter-record gaps shorter than the hypothetical one-half of an inch.

3. This is true when a program is executed from beginning to end as one process. Some operating systems provide for "spooling" both input and output files so that input card reading or output file printing can be done separately from the program execution. In such cases, an input card file or the formatted contents of a printed report may be written on tape for later processing, and though the tape contents may represent card input or printed output, as tape data it could have header label records.

IBM

COBOL Coding Form

SYSTEM | PUNCHING INSTRUCTIONS | PAGE OF

PROGRAM | GRAPHIC | CARD FORM # | * | IDENTIFICATION 73–80

PROGRAMMER | DATE | PUNCH

SEQUENCE (PAGE) (SERIAL) | CONT. | A | B | COBOL STATEMENT

```
002010 DATA DIVISION.
   020 FILE SECTION.
   030 FD  CARD-FILE
   040     RECORD CONTAINS 80 CHARACTERS
   050     LABEL RECORDS OMITTED
   060     DATA RECORD IS EMP-NA.
   070 01  EMP-NA.
   080     02  DEPTNO              PIC 99.
   090     02  EMPNO               PIC 999.
   100     02  EMPNAME             PIC A(20).
   110     02  EMPADDR             PIC X(25).
   120     02  EMPCITY             PIC A(24).
   130     02  ZIP                 PIC 9(5).
   140     02  CARDNUM             PIC 9.
   150 FD  PRINT-FILE.
   160     RECORD 132 CHARACTERS
   170     LABEL RECORDS ARE OMITTED
   180     DATA RECORD IS PRINTOUT.
   190 01  PRINTOUT.
   200     02  FILLER              PIC X(14).
```

*A standard card form, IBM Electro C61897, is available for punching source statements from this form.
Instructions for using this form are given in any IBM COBOL reference manual.
Address comments concerning this form to IBM Corporation, Programming Publications, 1271 Avenue of the Americas, New York, New York 10020.

Form No. X28-1464-4 U/M 025
Printed in U.S.A.

Figure 5–1. Data division coding.

COBOL Coding Form

IBM

SYSTEM _____

PROGRAM _____

PROGRAMMER _____ DATE _____

PUNCHING INSTRUCTIONS

GRAPHIC		CARD FORM #	
PUNCH			

PAGE ____ OF ____

IDENTIFICATION [73] ____ [80]

```
SEQUENCE
(PAGE) (SERIAL)  CONT  A  B    COBOL STATEMENT
00030 1                02  P-DEPT        PIC 99.
      02               02  FILLER        PIC X(5).
      03               02  P-EMPNO       PIC 999.
      04               02  FILLER        PIC X(5).
      05               02  P-EMPNAME     PIC A(20).
      06               02  FILLER        PIC X(5).
      07               02  P-EMPADDR     PIC X(25).
      08               02  FILLER        PIC X(5).
      09               02  P-EMPCITY     PIC A(24).
      10               02  FILLER        PIC X(5).
      11               02  P-ZIP         PIC 9(5).
      12               02  FILLER        PIC X(5).
      13       WORKING-STORAGE SECTION.
      14       77  PREV-DEPT     PIC 99 VALUE ZEROES.
      15       01  CAPTIONS.
      16               02  FILLER        PIC X(13) VALUE SPACES.
      17               02  HEADINGS      PIC X(106) VALUE "DEPT   EMP NO   EMPLO
      18     -                 "YEE NAME        STREET ADDRESS      CITY AN
      19     -                 "D STATE   ZIP CODE".
      20
```

*A standard card form, IBM Electro C61897, is available for punching source statements from this form.
Instructions for using this form are given in any IBM COBOL reference manual.
Address comments concerning this form to IBM Corporation, Programming Publications, 1271 Avenue of the Americas, New York, New York 10020.

Form No. X28-1464-4 U.M 025
Printed in U.S.A.

ments in a preceding environment division have already referred to the two types of data as CARD-FILE and PRINT-FILE, as they are called in the FD paragraph. Note the following:

1. The only period in each FD paragraph is at the very end. The entire paragraph is regarded as a single sentence.

2. A separate line has been used for each of the FD statements only for readability. Since they are all parts of the same sentence, each could have been started on the FD line, allowing one space after the file-name, and continued on successive lines as needed in Area B.

3. The FD statements have been varied slightly to emphasize the flexibility permitted with optional words. In the DATA RECORD statement, IS was left in only for readability.

The record description paragraphs must begin at Margin A with an 01 identification, followed by the record-name (exactly as spelled in the DATA RECORD statement, if present) and a period. This line is a paragraph header. The number 01 is a *level number* which refers to an entire record. A record may be divided into a number of areas (fields) at an equal level with each other, as in this case. Since the areas are parts of a record, they must be given a *numerically* greater level number, regarded as a *lower* (subordinate) level. Since in this case they are regarded as equally significant parts, they are all given the same level-number, 02. Notice that these data descriptions must be in Area B, beginning no further to the left than column 12.

It is relevant to note in advance here that there is often a need to place data fields in groups, and to refer either to a group of fields or a single field within the group. When this is done, the single fields are referred to as elementary items, and are given a different level-number. For example, we might have needed to use the department and employee numbers both as separate fields and as a single field. In that case, the descriptions could have been:

```
02   EMP-IDENT.
03   DEPTNO      PIC 99.
03   EMPNO       PIC 999.
```

The 02-level item becomes a group item by doing this; the 03-level items in this case are elementary items. Note that only elementary items are accompanied by the cryptic PIC and other digits.

Note that each line of data description is regarded as a sentence, ending with a period. The level-numbers usable for describing data fields within file records are 02 through 49 in full COBOL compilers. Three other level-numbers (66, 77, and 88) have special uses, some of which will be discussed later. Names given to data fields depend on the programmer's ingenuity; they must conform to the COBOL definition of a word already stated and must not be reserved words.[4] Data-names must be unique; that is, the same data-name should not be used to refer to two or more data fields representing a different record or records.[5] Notice that here this could easily present a problem; the data record PRINTOUT is intended to present the information that is on each card record. The solution is simple: use the same data-name as a base, but add a prefix letter to identify the particular record containing the data. It is fairly obvious that the card field EMPNAME will have to be transferred to the print field P-EMPNAME, but the programmer will be able to refer to each field separately in the procedure division without confusion.

One last note with respect to data-names: a data-name must be only one word. The use of a blank space within a data-name makes it two words; the compiler then must attempt to identify the logical purpose of the second word, which is nonexistent in COBOL programming terms. For this reason, hyphens are used frequently to connect mnemonic abbreviations, otherwise difficult to read, into a single word.

Each data-name that is an *elementary* item must be followed by information which describes the number and type of characters that make up the data field; in short, a PICTURE of the data field must be given. Either of the reserved words PICTURE or PIC may be used following the data-name, followed in turn by one of three possible digits identifying the type of characters in the data. The digit 9 indicates that the information in the data field will always be numeric; an A indicates that it will always be alphabetic or spaces; the letter X indicates that it is alphanumeric—it can be either alphabetic or numeric and/or can contain special characters as well as numbers and letters. For example, a data field which contains only alphabetic data separated by occasional commas and periods should be identified as X, *not* A, since commas and periods are special characters rather than alphabetic. The identification of EMPNAME and EMPCITY by an A means that these data fields must contain neither

---

4. See page 47, item 5, in connection with the identification division.

5. A permissible, though awkward, technique to be discussed later uses the same data-name for two or more data fields that are in different file records, requiring "qualifiers" to be added in data-name references. This technique should be discouraged, except in special cases.

special nor numeric characters. EMPADDR has been identified as X because of the probability of house numbers and occasional special characters occurring in otherwise alphabetic data. The other fields are identified by a 9 as being exclusively numeric data.

The number of characters in a data field can be shown in either of two ways:

1. By repeating the character symbol, if the field is small. Note that the numeric fields DEPTNO, EMPNO, and CARDNUM are shown to be two-, three-, and one-position fields by the number of 9's shown following PIC.

2. For fields containing five or more character positions, by showing the applicable character symbol followed by parentheses surrounding the digit number representing the size of the field. Note that when this is done, no spaces precede or follow either parenthesis when the number of characters in the field completes its description.

When all fields in a record have been fully described, the number of characters shown in the elementary item pictures should be added up to make sure that they agree with the total indicated in the RECORD CONTAINS clause. The number of characters shown for the seven elementary items in the EMP–NA record is $2 + 3 + 20 + 25 + 24 + 5 + 1 = 80$, the number shown in the related clause. Both must agree with the size of the actual record described—in this case an eighty-column card record.

Describing a print record necessitates some advance work. Any computer program generating a printed report should have the printout requirements described on a printer spacing chart before work on the program is started. The printout format is prepared by either the systems analyst or the programmer, depending on the way functional responsibilities are assigned in the particular data-processing organization. In either case, the programmer should always have the charted format of print requirements as specifications to which his or her descriptions of the print file records must conform. Figure 5–2 shows the print requirements for each line of the data record described as PRINTOUT. The following items are relevant:

1. Computer line printers generate a printing line of ten characters to the horizontal inch (the same size as characters on an ordinary pica typewriter) and can be adjusted to print six or eight lines to the vertical inch. Most printer chart forms are arranged to reflect six lines to the vertical inch and ten spaces to the horizontal inch; the chart from which Figure 5–2 was reduced does this. Note that the horizontally numbered spaces total 144.[6] One or two types of printers can print a line of 144 character-spaces; a standard full-size printer can generate a 132-character line; and printers for smaller computers typically have capability for 100 or 120. The vertical broken lines toward the right edge of the chart form indicate these limits; the positioning of the printed data in Figure 5–2 is such as to center the printing on a 132-character-space line.

2. The printout required takes up far fewer than 132 characters. Fourteen character spaces are unused at each of the two sides of a line, and five spaces are

---

6. Based on the specific manufacturer's line printer maximums. Another manufacturer has a 160-character-space line available on one of its models; and it would be only a minor surprise if a printer would become available soon with an even longer line capacity.

Figure 5–2. Spacing chart for a printer report.

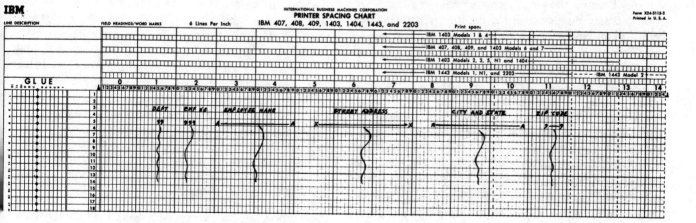

unused between each pair of items. Notice how this has been handled in the data division record description for PRINTOUT. Each data field to be printed has a picture the same as its comparable field in the card record described as EMP–NA; but the 14- and 5-space areas are all described as FILLER and given a picture of X. The term FILLER is a reserved word, and can be used as a data name any number of times in data division entries, each time as an indication that the area or field described is not being used.

Working-Storage Section

The working-storage section is used to hold information of various types for use as needed in the execution of the program. Such information may originate in records of a particular input file but be of a nature requiring use after the originating record has been processed. Or the information may be programmer-created, such as the headings on the report format (see Figure 5–2) to be printed at the top of each page of data printed. Sometimes data in the working-storage section is simply a single field; in other cases, it assumes the nature of a record. COBOL rules require that all single-field items be listed first, being defined as 77-level elementary items, followed by any record-type items defined at an 01 level.

The working-storage section of the data division shown in Figure 5–1 contains one 77-level field named PREV-DEPT and described as a two-digit numeric field. Presumably the cards that are input data are in employee-within-department sequence; the intention is probably to regard department number as a *control field* and provide for leaving an area on the report blank between departments or perhaps start a new report page for each department. To do this, the department number of any card read in must be held in storage until the next card is read, so that on each card reading a comparison can be made with the department number from the preceding card. If the numbers are the same, printing will continue as before. If different, procedure division instructions will cause blank lines to occur or move the continuous-form paper to the top of the next page and print headings before printing the card just read.

Notice that the PREV-DEPT picture has two words following it: VALUE ZEROES. For improved readability, the wording could be VALUE IS ZEROES; the use of IS is optional. The VALUE clause in a working-storage entry has an operational function (equivalent to the procedure division MOVE instruction, to be discussed later); it results in moving the information described by VALUE to the data area, where it will remain from the start of program execution until changed by the action of some procedure division instruction. The VALUE information may be either (as in this case) a figurative constant or (as in the next instance) a *literal*. The figurative constant ZEROES is numeric—VALUE ZEROES will result in placing the digits 00 in the storage area assigned to PREV-DEPT. Since it is expected that other numeric digits representing department numbers will later be placed in this area, the PICTURE had to be numeric, in turn restricting any information specified in the VALUE clause to numeric data. Placing blanks in the area could not be done in this case; to do that would require a VALUE IS SPACES clause, and SPACES, though also a figurative constant, is alphabetic, and cannot be moved into an area whose picture is numeric. Question: Why be concerned with having zeroes in a specific working-storage area at the beginning of program execution? The answer is that any data once read into a computer's internal storage will stay there until replaced. At the beginning of any job run (execution of an object program), data from the last previous job that was run is very likely to be left in many storage areas, including those which may be assigned for working storage in the current job. Causing zeroes or spaces to be placed in working-storage areas that are to be used in the program replaces unknown and unrelated data with data whose value we know and can deal with accordingly.

The data description for a record-level item is often used in working storage for making page-heading information available. The description begins with an 01-level entry beginning in Margin A, assigning the name CAPTIONS to the heading line. No picture is supplied for an 01-group item. The detail specifications for the heading data must be aligned to print above the card data as shown on the printer spacing chart. Since the first thirteen printing positions are not occupied by heading data, a FILLER description has been assigned with a picture of X(13). The entire line of heading data has been given the description HEADINGS, and, complete with the proper intervening number of spaces between heading words, has been enclosed in quotation marks.[7] The heading area has been given a picture of X(106) and a VALUE of the data described within the quotation marks. *Programmer-generated data* that is not strictly numeric must be enclosed in quotation marks. This type of data is known as a *nonnumeric literal* and must conform to the following rules:

---

7. HEADINGS is close to being a reserved word, but is not. It would not have been permissible to use the word HEADING, which is a COBOL reserved word.

1. A nonnumeric literal may contain any of the characters in the COBOL character set except quotation marks. (Since quotation marks indicate the beginning and the end of the nonnumeric literal, use of a quotation mark within a nonnumeric literal would be recognized as terminating it.) *A space counts as a character.*

2. A nonnumeric literal may be as long as 120 characters (*not* including the quotation marks). ANSI specifications impose this as a *minimum* requirement for COBOL compilers; it is permissible for a compiler to allow nonnumeric literals of greater length, but currently 120 is the typical limitation for the length of nonnumeric literals.

3. When coding-sheet limits require continuation of a nonnumeric literal on an additional line, the beginning line must be filled completely up through column 72, a hyphen (-) placed in column 7 of the continuation line, Area A (columns 8–11) left blank, and a quotation mark entered in Margin B (column 12) followed immediately (column 13 on) by the next letter or space that begins the continuation of the literal.

The following should be noted concerning the nonnumeric literal heading data coding: Within the beginning and ending quotation marks, there are exactly 106 characters. Spaces are counted as characters. The continuation-line quotation marks are not included in the character count; the COBOL compiler, after reading the column-7 hyphen, treats the column-12 quotation mark as a signal that more characters within the nonnumeric literal follow it. It is not regarded as part of the literal; it will not be stored or printed as part of the literal.

It is important to remember, when continuing a long nonnumeric literal, that it is essential to use all spaces exactly as you want them to appear when finally printing the data represented by the literal. Notice that the number of spaces allowed between words on the coding sheet is the same number as allowed between the corresponding words for the heading line on the printer spacing chart. For this same reason, the coding of the literal must be carried all the way to and including column 72 before it is continued on the following line. The words EMPLOYEE and AND are preserved as complete words in this way, aided by the column-7 hyphen and column-12 quotation mark. Had AND not been started on column 71, and spaces left in columns 71 and 72, with AND starting in column 13 of the continuation line, the compiler would be required to regard columns 70–72 as spaces within the literal. It would then find that the picture of 106 characters did not correctly define the literal (now 108 characters) and

would print at least a warning diagnostic, indicating the contradiction and probably the decision made by the compiler that the last two (seemingly excess) characters were being excluded from the literal.

Notice also that another choice was available to us rather than showing the first thirteen blank spaces separately as FILLER. Since these spaces plus the nonnumeric literal did not exceed 120 characters (the acceptable maximum), we could have given HEADINGS a longer picture [one of X(119)] and included in the VALUE the thirteen spaces between the beginning quotation mark and DEPT. This would have eliminated the need for the 02-level FILLER of thirteen positions.

A brief check of the data-division words listed in the Figure 3–3 analysis indicates that a number of them have not been discussed or even mentioned at this point; they involve uses not required in simple programs for which the data division illustrated here would be used. As the need for some of the yet-unused data-division reserved words develops, descriptions and explanations will be provided. At this point, after definition of one more term, we will turn to the necessary procedure-division knowledge and entries required to produce the simple printout implied by the data division set up in Figure 5–1.

The use of the term *nonnumeric literal* suggests that there must be such a thing as a *numeric literal*, as indeed there is. ANSI specifications require COBOL compilers to provide for accepting numeric literals of from one digit to at least eighteen digits in length. The numeric characters 0 through 9 and three others (the plus sign, minus sign, and decimal point) can be used in a numeric literal. The plus and minus signs may be used only as the leftmost character in the numeric literal; the decimal point may be used anywhere in the numeric literal except as the last (rightmost) character. If the numeric literal has no plus or minus sign, it is considered positive. It is treated as numeric in category; if it appears as a VALUE in a working-storage entry, its PICTURE would be 9's. A numeric literal should not be enclosed in quotation marks if it is to be considered numeric; but if it is desired to treat such a literal as nonnumeric, it can be made a nonnumeric literal by enclosing it in quotation marks (in which case a PICTURE for it would be X's).

REVIEW MATERIAL

Terms

Blocked records	Elementary item	Nonnumeric
Header labels	Field	literal
Level number	Data-name	Numeric literal
Group item	Literal	

Questions

What two sections normally appear in the data division?

Which clause must appear in the FD paragraph?

Which data descriptions do not contain a PIC clause?

Which of the following are proper data-names?

EMPNAME   EMP NAME
EMPNAME.   EMP-NAME-
EMP-NAME

What do the symbols A, 9, and X mean in a PIC clause?

When is FILLER used as a data-name?

What kind of data is described in the working-storage section?

What is the function of the VALUE clause?

Which of the following is a correctly stated numeric or nonnumeric literal? What is the error in each incorrectly stated item?

12–34	2.20	NUMERIC LITERAL
"12–34"	$2.20	"NONNUMERIC LITERAL"
1234–	220.	.0585
+1234	"$2.20"	

True-or-False Statements

All input records contain eighty characters.

Blocking of records on tape or disk saves space and time.

Blocking of records requires use of additional internal storage capacity.

All files must be labeled.

Level number 01 is used with a record-name.

Group items are made up of elementary items.

Records are defined in the file section but not in working-storage.

All literals are enclosed in quotation marks.

6

THE DIVISIONS OF A COBOL PROGRAM
(continued)

SOME IMPLICIT PROCESSING CONSIDERATIONS

As has been pointed out earlier (see page 39), the computer functions of reading input, processing data internally, and writing output all take place at different speeds; internal processing is the quickest function and the speed of the other two functions varies with the relative speed of the devices used. (For example, in reading card input and using the printer for output, the relative speed of reader and printer would determine which took less time per input or output item.) If each cycle of input–internal-processing–output had to be completed before the next cycle were begun, every complete cycle would take as long as the sum of the total time of each phase, as follows:

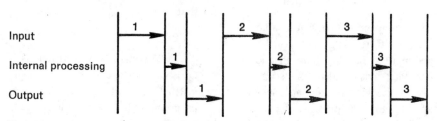

If, as in current computers, the next input phase could be performed while internal processing and output of the first were taking place, and the next internal processing could be done while waiting for preceding output to be completed, this overlapping of operations would reduce the time of the complete cycle to no more than required for the slowest of the three phases, as follows:

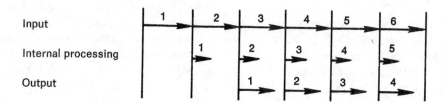

To accomplish this effect, it is necessary to have at least two sets of areas for each phase of the cycle, so that while input-1 is being processed internally, input-2 can be stored in another area to await the next internal processing. Similarly, at the output end, while output-1 is taking place, the results of internal-processing-2 can be placed in an alternate area. While the earlier phases of a new cycle are in process, output-2 can be done from the data in the alternate area. The alternate areas made available for holding information are referred to as "buffer areas," and the process of using them to make overlapping possible is known as "buffering." Buffering is done automatically by the hardware; the programmer is not required to specify alternate areas, although it is possible to do so. Occasional conditions arise when it may even be necessary or preferable to eliminate a buffer area by programming means even though such action slows down computer processing.

Ordinarily, however, one alternate area for each cycle phase will be provided without programming effort. The programmer, however, must be aware of the existence of buffer areas since output areas that are not completely filled with processed data must be properly cleared to prevent unwanted data from appearing in output. The MOVE SPACES instruction for such clearing purposes must be understood in terms of the necessity of clearing not one, but two areas.

PROCEDURE DIVISION

As evident from the discussion, the identification, environment, and data divisions have primarily descriptive functions—of the program, the computer and the components it uses, and the data files and records to be processed or created. The environment division also does some preparatory work in relating files to the computer components assigned to handle them in the course of the program. The data division also does some make-ready work (mostly in the working-storage section), identifying the capacity needed for storing program-generated data that will be needed to produce the results sought in the program. The procedure division provides the instructions that govern the action of the program in using input data to create output files in the form of card, tape, disk, or printed-report records.

Procedure division instructions are sometimes classified into four functional types: I/O (input-output), data movement, logic or sequence control statements, and arithmetic. There are a few instructions that do not fall into any of these specific categories; these will be discussed as necessity arises. Only the first three of the four functional types just mentioned will be needed to produce the listing of cards described in the Figure 5–1

data division; use of arithmetic statements will be developed in subsequent chapters.

Figure 6–1 is the procedure division for a simple printout program, using the information provided in the Figure 5–1 data division. The print format will follow the Figure 5–2 spacing chart, printing the heading line *only* on the *first* page of the listing, leaving one blank line following the heading, then printing one line for each card that is read. A blank line will occur after the last card is printed for each department. After one preliminary set of comments, let us examine how this listing will be accomplished by the program as written.

In the procedure division, paragraph headers must be single words (but not reserved words) and begin at margin A. The function of a paragraph header is to provide identification for a group of logically connected instructions, so that if the group of instructions to be followed is used out of its written sequence, it can be referred to readily in the source program. Partly for this reason, it is convenient (though not required) to connect a number as a prefix to the paragraph header. Notice that numeric prefixes 010, 020, and 030 have been assigned to paragraph headers in Figure 6–1. If we wished to add other groups of instructions to the program, we could use numbers in-between 020 and 030 as prefixes to the new paragraph headers, since these instructions would almost surely be introduced between these two existing paragraphs. An added convenience to using numeric prefixes to paragraph headers, since the prefixes become part of the single word for the header, is that it makes impossible the occasional absent-minded (and prohibited) use of a reserved word as a paragraph header.

Looking at the Figure 6–1 instructions in order, we find that:

1. The first two instructions in paragraph 010-OPEN are to open the card and print files. An OPEN instruction must be used for every file used by the program. OPEN instructions are referred to as I/O statements since they refer to input or output files. In effect, they are "ready" signals to the computer components (in this case, the card reader and printer), to which the files named are assigned, that processing is about to begin. Note that the OPEN statements name the files and identify them either as input or output. When the LABEL RECORDS ARE STANDARD statement is used in the data division, the OPEN statement for an input file causes checking of the header label on the file to make sure that it is the one specified; for output files (tape or disk) the OPEN instruction causes the specified header-label record to be written on the file before any data records are

COBOL Coding Form

IBM

SYSTEM			PUNCHING INSTRUCTIONS		PAGE	OF
PROGRAM			GRAPHIC			*	IDENTIFICATION
PROGRAMMER	DATE		PUNCH			CARD FORM #	

SEQUENCE		CONT.	A	B	COBOL STATEMENT
(PAGE) 3 4	(SERIAL)	6 7	8	12 16	
	01		010-OPEN.	
	02			OPEN INPUT CARD-FILE.
	03			OPEN OUTPUT PRINT-FILE.
	04			MOVE SPACES TO PRINTOUT.
	05			WRITE PRINTOUT FROM CAPTIONS.
	06		020-PROCESS.	
	07			READ CARD-FILE AT END GO TO 030-FINISH.
	08			MOVE SPACES TO PRINTOUT.
	09			IF DEPTNO > PREV-DEPT WRITE PRINTOUT.
	10			MOVE SPACES TO PRINTOUT.
	11			MOVE DEPTNO TO P-DEPT PREV-DEPT.
	12			MOVE EMPNO TO P-EMPNO.
	13			MOVE EMPNAME TO P-EMPNAME.
	14			MOVE EMPADDR TO P-EMPADDR.
	15			MOVE EMPCITY TO P-EMPCITY.
	16			MOVE ZIP TO P-ZIP.
	17			WRITE PRINTOUT.
	18			GO TO 020-PROCESS.
	19		030-FINISH.	
	20			CLOSE CARD-FILE.
	21			CLOSE PRINT-FILE.
	22			STOP RUN.

*A standard card form, IBM Electro C61897, is available for punching source statements from this form.
Instructions for using this form are given in any IBM COBOL reference manual.
Address comments concerning this form to IBM Corporation, Programming Publications, 1271 Avenue of the Americas, New York, New York 10020.

Form No. X28-1464-4 U/M 025
Printed in U.S.A.

Figure 6-1. Procedure division coding.

written on it. In this case, there are no label records to be checked or written.

2. To make sure that the first buffer area set aside for print-file records is clear of information possibly left from recent computer processing, spaces (blanks) are moved to the print record area. Notice that the 01-level name used—PRINTOUT—is the one that describes the print-file record in the data division. A MOVE instruction for alphabetic data is executed from left to right—spaces are moved into positions from 1 to 132 in that order, replacing whatever data had previously been there.

3. The next instruction is considered an I/O statement. WRITE is a COBOL verb that can be used to record data on tape, disk, or other external-storage components or to cause printing to take place—it creates output data. A simple WRITE statement may consist only of the verb and a record-name, as does the WRITE instruction in the 020-PROCESS paragraph. A full COBOL compiler enables information stored in another area to be moved to the print-storage area and printed by using the instruction format: WRITE record-name FROM identifier. Here the identifier is the 01-level record, CAPTIONS, in working-storage. The 02-level elementary items that make up CAPTIONS are, by the WRITE . . . FROM . . . instruction, moved to the first 120 positions of the print-storage area and printed as a line by the printer.

4. We have now not only opened the print file but printed the heading; however, at this point, no input data has been read, let alone printed. The 020-PROCESS paragraph contains the instructions for reading the cards that contain input data and printing each one. The first instruction of the paragraph is a READ statement, considered an I/O entry since it involves an input file. The file-name, as used in the SELECT clause of the environment division, must follow the verb READ. Every time the READ statement is executed, a card is read and its data is placed in the area reserved for it by the data-division record description entries. When the last input data card has been read and processed, and no more records can be read from the CARD-FILE file, we are AT END and instead of executing move and write instructions, the computer will bypass them and proceed to execute the instructions in the 030-FINISH paragraph. Every READ statement must contain an AT END clause.

5. Whether we have just printed the heading line, or data from a preceding card, the READ statement causes the information on an input card to enter the card-file record area described for it in the data division. Most of the instructions in the 020-PROCESS paragraph are to move data from the card-file record area, a field at a time, to the field areas in the print-

file record. It is not advisable to do this immediately after reading, because information from the last preceding print line may be retained in areas not used in the print record for card data. At this point, when data from the *first* card is to be moved to print areas, the buffer area available has not yet been used for printing in this program. It is the *second* area, the first having been used to print the heading line. To prevent any data left in this area from appearing in the FILLER areas in the print line, the instruction MOVE SPACES TO PRINTOUT (the print-file area) is inserted after the READ statement. This also assures that when any subsequent card is read, there will be a clean print-line area ready to receive the card data moved to it.

6. When we print any line of data, single-line spacing will take place automatically, so that the next printing will be on the line below it. We had decided to allow one blank line before printing employee data for each new department number. PREV-DEPT, at the time the first card is read, contains two zeroes. Undoubtedly, the lowest number that may be in the first data card's department-number field (DEPTNO) is 01. The next statement, IF DEPTNO > PREV-DEPT WRITE PRINTOUT, will cause "printing" of a blank line, because the condition specified is met and we have just moved spaces to PRINTOUT. We could have used the words GREATER THAN instead of the relational sign $>$. In either case, the data in DEPTNO will be compared to the data in PREV-DEPT and found to be a larger number; the instruction WRITE PRINTOUT will be executed, and a blank line will be left below the heading line (since we have just moved spaces to PRINTOUT). After this "printing," done from the second available area, the first buffer area will be available for the next print instruction. This area was used to receive heading-line data and has not been cleared. The second MOVE SPACES TO PRINTOUT now clears this buffer area for the next printout operation.

7. The next six instructions simply move card-record data fields to their related printing areas to assemble a line of print. Note, however, that the first of the six is slightly different; it appears to move DEPTNO to *two* areas—the print area P-DEPT and the working-storage area PREV-DEPT. A MOVE instruction may specify two receiving fields, as it does here, or more than two, for a single sending field.[1]

---

1. The reverse, however, is *not* true. An attempt to move the data from two different sending fields to one receiving field is obviously a contradiction in terms: the data from the second sending field would replace the data from the first if such a MOVE were possible.

We are moving DEPTNO to PREV-DEPT at this point so that when the next card is read, and the IF statement compares DEPTNO in that card with what we have just now moved to PREV-DEPT, the computer will print a blank line if DEPTNO is higher than PREV-DEPT or, if it is not, will simply execute the MOVE instructions which follow. Notice that each of the six MOVE instructions moves information from a card field, now stored in an area assigned in the data division, to its corresponding print-area storage location. No printing takes place, however, until the instruction, WRITE PRINTOUT, is reached.

8. The WRITE instruction, because it produces an output record, is regarded as a I/O statement. Unlike the other three I/O statements (OPEN, READ, and CLOSE), which are required to name *files*, the WRITE verb is always followed by a *record* name. Note in Figure 5-1 that PRINTOUT is the 01-level record name whose contents are described by the 02-level elementary items that form its pattern. WRITE does not always mean "print," as it does here. WRITE is also used in instructions to create tape, disk, or other forms of output storage records; even for punching out cards, WRITE is the verb normally used.

9. Note that after printing the data from a card, the statement is one that instructs the computer to go back to the paragraph just completed; it requires the reading of another card and execution of the same routines; spaces will be moved to the print-storage area, clearing it of the data last printed from that buffer area; then the comparison will be made between the second card's DEPTNO and PREV-DEPT, which now contains the digits 01 moved there from the first card. If the second card contains 01 as a DEPT-NO, there is no condition to cause the WRITE statement to be executed; the remaining MOVE instructions will be carried out, a print line will be written for the second card, and the GO TO 020-PROCESS will cause reading of a third card. This "loop" will be repeated until finally there are no more cards to be read; this is the END, at which the GO TO 030-FINISH clause of the READ instruction will transfer program control to the 030-FINISH paragraph.

10. The final paragraph of the program contains end-of-job instructions. There is a variety of operations for which instructions may be present in this paragraph; these will be indicated later as specific conditions occur. Two types of statements, however, are always present in the end-of-job paragraph—a CLOSE statement or statements, and the imperative statement, STOP RUN. A CLOSE statement must be followed by one or more file-names, stated precisely as occurring in the environment division SELECT statement and in the FD entry in the data division. Note that the CLOSE statement does *not* indicate whether the file being closed is input or output; it merely names the file.

The STOP RUN statement terminates program execution. Since no instructions in the program can be executed once the STOP RUN statement is reached, it is necessarily the last instruction in the program to be executed.[2] When the computer is being used for processing of separate jobs, each governed by a different program and run independently, the computer stoppage requires the operator to manually select the next object program and feed it into the computer while readying components for program execution. When the computer is being used in an "operating system" pattern, and tape- or disk-stored programs are "called in" in some predetermined order, the STOP RUN stoppage may be only a momentary pause as control is switched to another object program and processing is begun of input files set up while the just-completed program was running, on storage-unit devices not required by that program.

At this point, let us review what we have learned so far. We have found how to write a program to print a listing of input-card data, providing a heading on the first page of the listing, and supplying blank lines to separate heading from detail data and groups of detail data from each other. Necessarily, we have found that all four input/output instructions (OPEN, READ, WRITE, and CLOSE) and the STOP RUN instruction are basic to any program. The only additional instructions we have used are the MOVE and GO TO statements, though we have found that the WRITE . . . FROM . . . statement is, in reality, two instructions—a MOVE of data in one record area (and 01-level group item) to another record area, followed by a WRITE. We have also found that placing a VALUE clause in a data division elementary item area has the same effect as a procedure division MOVE statement at the beginning of program execution—the moving to the data area of the "literal," which is the VALUE specified. We have also used a simple conditional clause— an IF statement. Now we will learn some rules that cover additional basic uses of the MOVE, GO TO, and IF statements.

---

2. In the program illustrated, the end-of-job paragraph happens to be the last in physical sequence in the source program. It is not unusual, however, to find source programs in which many other paragraphs *physically* follow the end-of-job paragraph. The source program *logic*, nevertheless, must be such that when the object program is executed, the end-of-job routines are the last performed.

SOME MOVE INSTRUCTION RULES AND CHARACTERISTICS

We have already seen basic MOVE statements that transferred elementary items of data from one storage area to another of the same size. In each case the "sending" field of data had the same PICTURE as the "receiving" field, both as to type of data and number of characters. As is suggested by the WRITE . . . FROM . . . statement, it is also possible to move data from a whole record area to another record area.[3] If, for example, we wanted to create an eighty-position tape record from each card, we could MOVE the 01-level card record contents to the 01-level tape record area instead of moving each elementary item of card data to each corresponding field of tape data. To move data at a record level assumes that it is desired to have the receiving record area in exactly the same layout as the sending one. Where this is not the case, each data field often must be moved separately. This had to be done in moving card fields to the print area because each print field was to be separated from the next by five blank spaces. Had the instruction been MOVE EMP-NA TO PRINTOUT, the eighty positions of EMP-NA would have been moved to the first eighty positions of PRINTOUT, and the WRITE PRINTOUT instruction would have caused printing to take place considerably to the left of the heading areas with no spaces separating fields from each other.

In general, it is permissible to MOVE:

• Numeric data to either alphanumeric or numeric fields, but *not* to alphabetic fields.
• Alphabetic data to either alphabetic or alphanumeric fields, but *not* to numeric fields.
• Alphanumeric data to alphanumeric fields. Although a MOVE of alphanumeric data to numeric or alphabetic fields is possible, results are rather unpredictable, since special characters in the sending field may not be fully transferred in either case, nor will alphabetic characters going to a numeric field.

When data is moved from one area to another, the data moved in replaces any data that was in the receiving area before the move. In one important respect, alphabetic and alphanumeric moves differ from numeric, as governed by the *receiving* area's type of data. Data representing whole numbers (integers)[4] is moved into a numeric field from right to left; into alphanumeric and alphabetic fields from left to right. Where the sending and receiving fields contain the same number of characters, this creates no problem. When the receiving field has the greater number of characters, spaces will be moved into the receiving field at the right to fill the unused portion of an alphabetic or alphanumeric field, and zeroes will be moved in at the left for a numeric integer field. When the sending field is longer, the excess characters at the right are truncated (cut off) in an alphabetic or alphanumeric field; for a numeric field the excess integer characters at the left and the excess decimal characters at the right are truncated. Atop facing page are illustrations of equal-length and short and long fields in moves. Note that in all cases where the receiving field is at least as long as the sending field, no problem is caused by a smaller number of significant characters in the sending field. On any MOVE, all characters in the receiving field before the MOVE are replaced as a result of the MOVE instruction. Notice also that where the sending field is larger than the receiving field, the truncation occurs at the right side for alphabetic and at the left for numeric integer information.

Further rules concerning MOVE statements will be developed as we encounter the necessity of using numeric fields containing decimal amounts and for "editing" alphanumeric and numeric data for report printing.

THE GO TO INSTRUCTION

The basic format for this instruction is GO TO procedure-name. The procedure-name must always be the name of a paragraph or section header in the procedure division. In terms of internal computer operations, it is, by itself, an unconditional branch—it diverts the path of the program to the first statement in the paragraph called for in the GO TO. If GO TO 020-PROCESS were not in the Figure 6–1 procedure division, observe that the various MOVE and WRITE statements would be executed for the first card read in, the 030-FINISH paragraph instructions would be followed, and the program would be executed after processing only one card. The GO TO 020-PROCESS causes a branch back to reading another card as long as there are cards in the reader feed. This is undoubtedly one of the most-used functions of the GO TO instruction—branching back, after processing a record, to read another input record. Another necessary use is the function of a GO TO statement following the READ . . . AT END instruction. Here, when there are no more input records to

---

3. It is also possible to move a group item within a record to a group item in another record area within the rules governing MOVE in other respects.

4. Numeric values lower than whole numbers, i.e., decimals, are moved from left to right, as will be shown in the discussion of arithmetic statements.

SENDING FIELD		RECEIVING FIELD		
Picture	Contents	Picture	Contents before move	Contents after move
X(15)	JOHN JONES	X(15)	ALBERT SMITHERS	JOHN JONES
9(5)	00012	9(5)	62897	00012
9(3)	734	9(6)	928375	000734
A(8)	LINCOLN	A(10)	WASHINGTON	LINCOLN
9(6)	123456	9(4)	8923	3456
X(15)	SEARS, ROEBUCK	X(10)	BAMBERGERS	SEARS, ROE

be read, and therefore none to process, the GO TO branches forward to bypass all the processing instructions between it and the 030-FINISH paragraph, causing that paragraph's instructions to assume control of program execution. The GO TO statement can be used in many other branching operations besides those of assuring continuation of reading input data or initiating end-of-job routines. Quite often, a GO TO instruction will be an unconditional one, as is the GO TO 020-PROCESS here; perhaps just as often, it will be conditional, introduced by an IF.

THE IF STATEMENT

In its simplest form, this statement contains a possible condition and an instruction to perform an operation if the condition exists. When the condition does not exist, execution of the program continues with the instruction contained in the program's next sentence. A check of the one IF statement in Figure 6–1 shows it to be of this type: IF condition; statement. It is permissible, *though usually unnecessary*, to add the words ELSE NEXT SENTENCE; for example, IF A = B MOVE C TO D ELSE NEXT SENTENCE. Occasionally these three words may be necessary for clarity to anyone reading the source program, but they add nothing; without them, program execution would continue with the next sentence's instruction when the IF condition does not exist anyway. Sometimes it is convenient to use an IF statement and NEXT SENTENCE in the opposite way: IF G = H NEXT SENTENCE ELSE MOVE X TO Y. The same effect could be had by rewording this instruction as: IF G IS NOT EQUAL TO H MOVE X TO Y. In either case, when G and H are equal, the MOVE instruction will be bypassed and the execution of the program's next sentence will take place.

Another fairly simple variation of the IF statement is to state either of two possible choices; for example,

IF E = F MOVE S TO T ELSE MOVE J TO K. Implicitly, one of these conditions will be met; one of the two moves will be performed, and program execution will continue with the operation called for in the program's next sentence.

The variations of the simple IF statement can be listed as follows:

IF condition; statement-1; ELSE statement-2
IF condition; statement-1　　　　(ELSE NEXT SENTENCE implied)
IF condition; statement-1; ELSE NEXT SENTENCE
IF condition; NEXT SENTENCE; ELSE statement-2

Two or more IF statements may be used in the same sentence, creating a form known as a "nested conditional." This is a more complex version of the IF statement, which we will consider somewhat later.

It should also be noted that the terms "statement-1" and "statement-2" do not limit the programmer to use of single imperatives following IF and ELSE. The instruction, IF A = B MOVE G TO H MOVE J TO K MOVE R TO S ELSE MOVE W TO X MOVE Y TO Z is an acceptable simple IF statement in the first of the four formats listed above.

REVIEW MATERIAL

Terms

Overlapping	Sending field	Truncation
Buffer area	Receiving field	Branch
Paragraph	Loop	Condition

Questions

What is the function of the paragraph header in the procedure division?

What instruction determines whether a given file is to be used as input or output?

Why is it necessary to MOVE SPACES TO PRINTOUT?

What is the function of the AT END clause of the READ instruction?

What unit of data is output by the execution of a WRITE statement?

What I/O statements require the use of file-name? record-name?

What combinations of sending and receiving fields are allowed in a MOVE statement?

When a MOVE is executed, what happens to the data that was in the receiving field prior to the move?

When moving a numeric field to a smaller numeric field, which characters will be truncated? Which characters would be truncated if the fields were alphanumeric?

If the instruction IF A = B WRITE PRINTOUT ELSE GO TO 030-FINISH is executed, what will happen if the condition is true? false?

True-or-False Statements

Paragraph headers in the procedure division are reserved words.

The OPEN statement reads the first data record of the file.

The WRITE statement creates output data, writing records on tape, disk, the printer, or other output devices.

A MOVE statement can specify more than one receiving field.

All input/output statements require a file-name.

Each file used in a program should be CLOSED before the STOP RUN statement is encountered.

Nonnumeric data should not be MOVED to a numeric field.

When an alphanumeric field is MOVEd to a larger alphanumeric field, spaces are moved into the receiving field at the left.

The statements following ELSE in an IF statement are executed if the condition is false.

Programming

6–1: Write a program to print the following from cards which are in the following format:

Column:			Field is:	
1	Card number			numeric
2–3	Department number			numeric
4–7	Employee number			numeric
8–32	Employee name			alphabetic
33–57	Street address			alphanumeric
58–75	City and state			alphabetic
76–80	Zip code			numeric

Required: Print all fields, providing for two blank spaces between each pair of fields.

6–2: Add instructions to the above program to obtain double spacing of print lines.

6–3: Add to the program the necessary statements in the environment, data, and procedure divisions to write a tape record for each input card. Assume a 200-position record, blocked 10. Do not write the card number on the tape record; place the fields in card columns 2–80 in positions 1–79 of each tape record.

7

**BASIC STORED-FILE CREATION: SOME
BASIC PRINTING AIDS**

FILE CREATION

The program just described is perhaps of the simplest type possible—a printout listing the contents of an already-created file. The file already in existence was not even created by the computer—it was created by keypunching cards and sorting them into a desired sequence. No validation of data was made by the computer program: it was assumed that the cards were properly punched and in sequence by employee number within department. Two slight reading conveniences were performed by the program: a set of first-page headings was provided to identify the data fields and a blank line was "printed" between the last employee line in a department and the first employee line in the next department. Sorted card files are older than computers; computer devices are not needed to store them. External storage devices of computers provide more compact data-file storage than do cards, as well as far quicker access to large volumes of data. While punched cards are still frequently used as original data input to computers to *create* or update files, they are now seldom used as continuing permanent files. Magnetic tape and, to an increasing proportion, magnetic disk records are used as the media for data file storage now almost to the exclusion of cards.

Basically, creation of a stored tape or disk file from cards involves only one more file description in the data division and one more set of MOVE and WRITE instructions in the procedure division than a program for

printout from a card file. Actually, printout is not even necessary in a program for creation of a tape or disk stored file; but a printout is normally provided for easier reading than the alternative of creating the file by a printless program and then using an implementor-provided "dump" program, which prints a listing of the file directly from the tape or disk storage on which it was "written." Although a "dump" printout is proof that the file was created to the precise extent shown in the printout, the typical "dump" is difficult to use for visual reference because each entire data record is printed continuously, just as it occurs in storage, with no spaces between data fields. A third approach is to create the file without printout during the file creation and to supply later a printout from the stored file in a form similar to that of the one just described for printout from a card file. In fact, such a print program would differ from the one described only in that the data division would contain a tape or disk file description instead of one for a card file.

Of the three approaches to stored-file creation, we will use the one of concurrent printout while creating the file from card input. We will assume that the card input contains the same kind and format of data as just described in the card-to-print program. For the time being, we will add just enough to the program to create a stored file and do only a minimum of checking (validation) of the card input data for correctness. In this process, we will make a change or two in the print arrangement, but only as required for input-data validation. We will assume that the card input is intended to be in ascending sequence by employee number within department, but we will check to make sure that only those cards that are in proper sequence (not duplicates or low numbers) are written on the stored file which we are creating. To guide the user of the printed report, we must print a line for each card, whether written on the stored file or not. We will print an "error message"—REJECTED—to the right of each print line for a card containing a duplicate or low-sequence identification number.

We must make a few data division changes to accomplish our purposes. For sequence-checking, we must now regard the *combination* of DEPTNO and EMPNO in the card file as a single area; but we must also continue to use them as separate fields for printout, and continue to use DEPTNO separately as a means of checking for a change in department numbers. Reference back to page 58 tells us that this can be done by identifying the two fields together as an 02-level group item, with no picture but a different name, and considering the two fields separately as elementary items with pictures. We will consider the change made as shown; the 02-level group item is now EMP-IDENT. EMP-IDENT must be compared on a card-just-read to previous-card-read basis in the same way as DEPTNO and PREV-DEPT were; this requires us to set up a 77-level field in working storage for comparison. The entry: 77 PREV-IDENT PIC 9(5) VALUE ZERO. should suffice. Also needed is provision for an area in the print record where the error-message can appear. Figure 6–1 shows a 14-position FILLER area available following the zip-code field. The message REJECTED contains eight characters. Let us change the 14-position FILLER picture to one of X(6) and add an entry: 02 ERRORMESSAGE PIC A(8).

One more data division addition must be made—the file description of the tape or disk records to be created. The file-name itself must, of course, be the same as that in a SELECT statement to be provided in the environment division, naming the file and typically assigning it to the implementor-name for the tape or disk device being used. For creation of simple sequential files, the name of the device in the SELECT statement might be the only indication in the source program as to whether the file were being written on tape or disk; for more complex programs and larger files, other environment and data division entries could be required, which would differ depending upon the type of storage device used.

Let us assume here that we will need to add more data (such as social security number, job title, pay rate, etc.) to each employee master record later on and assume a 200-position record will be required. Assuming that the data-name MASTERFILE has been used in the SELECT statement, we will define the file as follows:

```
FD   MASTERFILE
     RECORD CONTAINS 200 CHARACTERS
     BLOCK CONTAINS 20 RECORDS
     LABEL RECORDS ARE STANDARD
     DATA RECORD IS MASTER-REC.
01   MASTER-REC.
     02   M-EMP-IDENT.
          03   M-DEPT          PIC 99.
          03   M-EMPNO         PIC 999.
     02   M-EMPNAME            PIC A(20).
     02   M-EMPADDR            PIC X(25).
     02   M-EMPCITY            PIC A(24).
     02   M-ZIP                PIC 9(5).
     02   OTHERDATA            PIC X(121).
```

Note that we are not including the card number as part of the master record; this leaves 121 unused positions, into which we will MOVE SPACES so that we will, where necessary in subsequent programs, be able to determine whether or not data has been supplied in this area.

Since we are going to print all card input, but write a master record only for those cards in good sequence, we must test each card before processing it. Depending on the test outcome, card data will either (a) be written as a master output record *and* printed without an error message or (b) be printed with an error message and *not* written as a master record. This requires splitting our original 020-PROCESS routine into two separate paragraphs. Consider the following:

```
020-PROCESS.
    READ CARD-FILE AT END GO TO 030-FINISH.
    MOVE SPACES TO PRINTOUT.
    IF DEPTNO > PREV-DEPT WRITE PRINTOUT MOVE
        SPACES TO PRINTOUT.
    IF EMP-IDENT IS NOT GREATER THAN PREV-IDENT
        MOVE "REJECTED" TO ERRORMESSAGE GO TO
        025-PRINT.
    MOVE EMP-IDENT TO PREV-IDENT.
    MOVE DEPTNO TO M-DEPT PREV-DEPT.
    MOVE EMPNO TO M-EMPNO.
    MOVE EMPNAME TO M-EMPNAME.
    MOVE EMPADDR TO M-EMPADDR.
    MOVE EMPCITY TO M-EMPCITY.
    MOVE ZIP TO M-ZIP.
    MOVE SPACES TO OTHERDATA.
    WRITE MASTER-REC.
025-PRINT.
    MOVE DEPTNO TO P-DEPT.
    MOVE EMPNO TO P-EMPNO.
    MOVE EMPNAME TO P-EMPNAME.
    MOVE EMPADDR TO P-EMPADDR.
    MOVE EMPCITY TO P-EMPCITY.
    MOVE ZIP TO P-ZIP.
    WRITE PRINTOUT.
    MOVE SPACES TO PRINTOUT.
    GO TO 020-PROCESS.
```

Notice that very little has been added. The new (additional) IF statement will cause "REJECTED" to be added to the print line if the card just read has the same or lower employee identification number than the number left in PREV-IDENT; in that case, all the statements relating to writing a master record will be bypassed, the 025-PRINT routine will take place, and the next card will be read. If the card EMP-IDENT is a higher number than PREV-IDENT, card data will be moved to the master-record area, and the master record will be written. After this the printing of the card data will take place through operation of the 025-PRINT routine. Notice that the contents of PREV-DEPT and PREV-IDENT are not changed until a card is read containing an EMP-IDENT higher than the last card written as a master record. Suppose, for example, that the first five cards had numbers of 01503, 01505, 01301, 01367, 01602. The first two numbers would each be greater than PREV-IDENT and would be moved to PREV-IDENT; the card-record data would be moved to the master-record area and both master records and print lines would be written. The third and fourth cards would be read and *printed*, with the error-message REJECTED, but the IF statement would cause all the sentences following it in the 020-PROCESS routine to be bypassed. When the EMP-IDENT in card 01602 is compared to PREV-IDENT, the latter's contents are still 01505, and 01602 would be moved in to replace it.

Note that the instruction, WRITE MASTER-REC, follows each set of MOVE instructions. The questions might logically be raised: Why is this WRITE occurring each time card-record data is moved to the MASTER-REC area? Aren't we writing twenty records at a time? Though the answer to the second question is Yes, the action of the WRITE instruction for blocked output records is somewhat different than it is for unblocked. An unblocked output record is "written" on output tape or disk immediately after the detail data for it is moved to the single internal storage area reserved for it by the FD statements. The BLOCK CONTAINS clause, however, sets up as many consecutive areas in internal storage as the number of records specified in the block. The WRITE instruction for an output record causes the data to be moved for the single record to the first "unused" consecutive area. When all of the areas are filled, the actual data transfer to the output device storage area takes place for the entire block of records. In effect, the blocking operation is an implementor-supplied technique, which requires no special WRITE instructions. Typically, if the data file ends before the last block of records is complete, the unused portion is "padded" with spaces, again a technique requiring no special programming instruction.

REPORT PRINTING AIDS

The program as amended to produce an externally-stored output file record, after making sure that the input record was in proper sequence, also produces a listing of all input data, with some limited reading aids. The column headings for the printed data will appear only once—on the first page of the report. Printing of data will continue line after line, single-spaced vertically, except when a change of department number causes a blank line to be "printed." When the continuous-form paper is "burst" at the horizontal perforated lines to permit its assembling in separate pages, printing on each page will begin at the very top line and end at the very bottom—a standard eleven-inch page will contain sixty-six lines of printing. This may get maximum use of printing area per page, but at the loss of other advantages. Four desirable aids to convenient usage suggest themselves:

1. Headings to appear at the top of *each* page, not merely the first.

2. Top and bottom margins on each page, to permit notations and avoid possible splitting of top and bottom printing lines should slight misalignment occur.

3. Starting a new page with each new distinct group of data (such as department number). This is especially desirable in a departmentalized report, of which specific sections may be distributed to specific departments or personnel in a business.

4. Page numbering, either from beginning to end of the entire report or from beginning to end of each section of it. This is normally the most efficient check against missing or out-of-sequence pages in a report.

A COBOL compiler that includes the report-writer module enables the programmer to provide for these basic aids by setting up report format descriptions in the data division and writing a minimum of procedure division instructions. However, many COBOL compilers, even for relatively large computers, are obtained at the user's choice without the report-writer option. This absence may require more procedure division entries to obtain the same results, but it does not create a serious problem. All computer manufacturers provide some "hardware" feature to implement printer control of line spacing for positioning to the first printing line on a page. Usually this is done by means of a carriage-control tape, which is a paper and/or plastic tape supplied by the computer manufacturer. The computer-user cuts the tape into lengths corresponding to one or more report pages by punching a hole at a designated distance from the tape margin at repeated intervals corresponding to a page length. The ends of the tape are then glued so that it becomes a belt; and it is fitted over the rotating carriage device which controls the upward spacing of the platen over which the continuous-form paper is fed into the line printer. The computer manufacturer's COBOL compiler contains a reserved word that relates to the marginal tape position on which the punched hole is located. A wire brush is in contact with the tape as it is moved over the metal carriage device; when the brush contacts the metal through the hole in the tape, an electrical impulse is available to either start or stop carriage motion to position the paper. To make use of this type of page-control device a SPECIAL-NAMES entry in the environment division is needed in the format: SPECIAL-NAMES. implementor-name IS mnemonic-name. The implementor-name is the reserved word assigned in the computer's compiler for control use of the contact impulse; the mnemonic-name is a programmer-assigned word (not a reserved word) that is used in the procedure division to cause paper movement to the top of the next page before printing takes place. Assuming that the programmer has selected PAGETOP as the mnemonic-name, the SPECIAL-NAMES sentence on IBM's 360 or 370 would be: C01 IS PAGE-TOP; on a Burroughs 5500 it would be: CHANNEL 1 IS PAGETOP. Other implementor-names vary from specific single words to combinations with numbers. The latter is used for printer carriage-control tapes with a number of columns or channels (typically twelve). This permits the selection of a number of points on a page where printing may be positioned after causing paper movement and stoppage at the point of electrical contact of the wire brush with the metal surface (through the punched hole in the tape). Normally, the last channel is punched at the point where the last printing line on a page is to occur; contact through this punched hole can be used to *start* paper movement to the next page top by means of a procedure division IF statement that tests before or after each print-line writing for the sensing of the contact. Even when this feature is available, however, most programmers prefer to use the line-count technique to determine when the end of a page has been reached and a new page is to be started. Except for dependence on the electromechanical stoppage of paper movement, the line-count technique places control over the number of printed lines per page strictly within the program.

The line-count technique requires an area to be set up in working-storage to be used as a counter. An initial value of 0 is given the area; a digit 1 is added for each single-spaced print line as the instruction to print occurs; before data is moved to the print-record area for printing each line, an IF statement tests the counter area to determine whether the number it contains is greater than (or equal to) the number selected as the maximum number of lines per page. If it is not, normal line-printing takes place; if it is, control is passed to instructions which space the paper to the programmer-named position (in example above, PAGE-TOP) designated as the first printing line of the next page. We will describe the line-counter area as: 77 LINE-NUM PIC 99 VALUE ZERO. Since we want to number each page, an area to receive a page-count must also be set up: 77 PAGE-NUM PIC 999 VALUE 1. The value of 1 (it will be moved in as if 001) is assigned because the page number will be printed on the first page before any processing of data takes place; the number 1 must be available at that time. The 77-level entry provides a counter area, but no printing space. It is convenient to print page numbers on the heading line; there is ample space remaining in the CAPTIONS area, where we left thirteen printing positions unused. We can make use of them as follows:

```
02  FILLER       PIC X(5) VALUE SPACES.
02  PAGENAME      PIC X(4) VALUE "PAGE".
02  PAGE-NO       PIC ZZZ9.
```

The picture of ZZZ9 appears as something new. This is one of numerous ways of "editing" printed output, which we will discuss more comprehensively a little later. The "suppression" character Z is used to prevent leading zeroes from printing in numeric fields. If, say, PAGE-NUM contained a value of 020 and were moved into PAGE-NO, it would print as 20; no "leading" zero (any to the *left* of the 2) would print, though the zero to the right of the 2 would.

We have supplied the necessary supplements to the data division entries. Now we must carefully revise our procedure division entries so that paper movement to a new page will occur and so that page headings, properly page-numbered, will print under three conditions: at the beginning of the processing, when an input card has a higher department number than the card preceding it, and when a specified number of lines (let us specify fifty-five) have already been printed on a page. Let us analyze the following revised procedure division:

```
010-OPEN.
    OPEN INPUT CARD-FILE.
    OPEN OUTPUT MASTERFILE PRINT-FILE.
020-READ-TEST.
    READ CARD-FILE AT END GO TO 030-FINISH.
    IF PREV-DEPT > ZERO AND DEPTNO > PREV-DEPT
        MOVE 001 TO PAGE-NUM.
    IF DEPTO > PREV-DEPT GO TO 028-HEADLINES.
    IF LINE-NUM > 54 GO TO 028-HEADLINES.
021-CREATEMASTER.
```

```
       MOVE SPACES TO PRINTOUT.
       IF EMP-IDENT IS NOT GREATER THAN PREV-IDENT MOVE
            "REJECTED" TO ERRORMESSAGE GO TO 025-PRINT.
       MOVE EMP-IDENT TO PREV-IDENT.
       MOVE DEPTNO TO M-DEPT PREV-DEPT.
       MOVE EMPNO TO M-EMPNO.
       MOVE EMPNAME TO M-EMPNAME.
       MOVE EMPADDR TO M-EMPADDR.
       MOVE EMPCITY TO M-EMPCITY.
       MOVE ZIP TO M-ZIP.
       WRITE MASTER-REC.
   025-PRINT.
       MOVE DEPTNO TO P-DEPT.
       MOVE EMPNO TO P-EMPNO.
       MOVE EMPNAME TO P-EMPNAME.
       MOVE EMPADDR TO P-EMPADDR.
       MOVE EMPCITY TO P-EMPCITY.
       MOVE ZIP TO P-ZIP.
       WRITE PRINTOUT AFTER ADVANCING 1 LINES.
       ADD 1 TO LINE NUM.
       GO TO 020-READ-TEST.
   028-HEADLINES.
       MOVE SPACES TO PRINTOUT.
       MOVE PAGE-NUM TO PAGE-NO.
       WRITE PRINTOUT FROM CAPTIONS AFTER ADVANCING
            PAGETOP.
       MOVE SPACES TO PRINTOUT.
       WRITE PRINTOUT AFTER ADVANCING 1 LINES.
       ADD 1 TO PAGE-NUM.
       MOVE 2 TO LINE-NUM.
       GO TO 021-CREATEMASTER.
   030-FINISH.
       CLOSE CARD-FILE.
       CLOSE MASTERFILE.
       CLOSE PRINT-FILE.
       STOP RUN.
```

Two new types of instructions have been added to the program, which now has two more paragraphs than before. Let us analyze the changes, beginning with the more general ones first.

The decision to advance the paper to a new page is based on three possible conditions already stated. Each of these conditions requires reading of a card before deciding whether to process the card further or to advance the paper and print a heading line on the new page. At the beginning of the processing, the counter area PAGE-NUM already contains a value of 001, and PREV-DEPT has a value of zero. The first IF condition is not met; but since DEPTNO in the first card read is greater than PREV-DEPT, the second IF statement will cause the 028-HEADLINES paragraph to take control. During the processing of cards, if one is read containing a higher department number than in PREV-DEPT (the number moved there from the last previous error-free card), *both* conditions in the first IF statement are met; 001 is moved to PAGE-NUM to assure that the page number 1 will appear on the first page for the new department; and the second IF state-

ment transfers control to the 028-HEADLINES paragraph to head up a new page. Finally, if enough lines have been printed to cause LINE-NUM to accumulate to fifty-five, and a card is read which contains the same DEPTNO as the last good card preceding it, the first two IF statement conditions are not satisfied, but the third IF statement will cause control transfer to 028-HEADLINES to start a new page with a heading. Note that this statement does not move the value of 1 to PAGE-NUM; whatever number is already there should be moved to PAGE-NO for printing on the new page.

The 028-HEADLINES paragraph has been set up so that regardless of which of the three conditions above transfers control to it, the processing operations will be the same. Spaces are moved to the PRINTOUT record area to clear it of any data that might have been on the last card print-line in areas not used by CAPTIONS, or, for the first page heading, data left in storage from prior processing.[1] The contents of PAGE-NUM, whether 001 or a larger number, are moved to PAGE-NO, where the picture of ZZZ9 will replace leading zeroes with spaces; and the WRITE PRINT-OUT . . . will cause printing of the heading and page number to take place after moving the paper up to PAGETOP through the interaction of the implementor's COBOL compiler with implementor printer controls. The AFTER ADVANCING clause which aids in doing this, as well as in controlling spacing between print lines, will be discussed in more detail shortly. For the moment, we will consider the remaining requirements to resume detail-line printing and keep accurate count of page- and line-numbers. After printing the heading line, spaces are moved to the print-file record area PRINTOUT, and a line of spaces is written to provide a blank open line between the heading and first detail lines on the page.[2] At this point, we add 1 to PAGE-NUM so that the proper consecutive number will be available for the next page if detail from the

---

1. In this particular case, we are being unnecessarily careful, since all unused positions of CAPTIONS have been assigned a value of SPACES. In principle, however, it is good practice to clear a print area just prior to moving data to the print area for writing a print line, unless information from the preceding line is to be repeated.

2. If we assume that print buffer 1 received the print-line for CAPTIONS, the MOVE SPACES after printing CAPTIONS cleared print buffer 2, permitting the next WRITE PRINTOUT to print a blank line. Following this, the next printing will be from print buffer 1 again, where the CAPTIONS data is still stored. Before any further printing is required by the program, however, 021-CREATEMASTER will be executed, which will, for the first card on the first page, clear print buffer 1 and for subsequent card printing, alternately clear buffers 2 and 1.

same department is continued on it. At this point also, we have used up two print lines (heading and blank line) on the new page. We must record the line count; since LINE-NUM may contain a high number (the number of lines printed on the preceding page), we MOVE (*not* add) 2 to LINE-NUM to *replace* contents left from the preceding page; and now, since a card has been read but not processed, we transfer control back to 021-CREATEMASTER, which tests each card for proper sequence, after it is read, and, depending on test outcome, prints card information or writes a stored-file record before printing. Notice that 021-CREATEMASTER contains all but the first three instructions of the former 020-PROCESS paragraph it replaces. The first of the three instructions is now in 020-READ-TEST verbatim, the second is in 028-HEADLINES, and the third, changed to fit one of three conditions for headings, is in 020-READ-TEST.

The ADD 1 TO LINE-NUM is an essential count of each line printed. Since it takes place *after* printing, LINE-NUM will contain a count of fifty-five only *after* the fifty-fifth printing line is written. When the next card is read, LINE-NUM will for the first time contain a count greater than *54* per page, a condition which will transfer control to the heading routine. We might have used the relational expression IF LINE-NUM = 55 instead of IF LINE-NUM > 54; in this program it would have been adequate. In many cases, however, conditions and routines may be introduced that will require more than one line to be printed as the end of the page is approached; it is a safer general principle to test for greater than the full-page line-count minus 1 than to test for equality to the full-page line-count itself.

The AFTER ADVANCING Option

It is possible, as done in our first procedure division, to WRITE print-lines with no mention of the number of lines for the paper to be moved up. When no mention is made, printing will take place with an automatic spacing up of one printing line; what we ordinarily call single-spaced printing results. To achieve any other (say double- or triple-) line-spacing, or to cause "skips" of the paper to the top of a new page, one of the ADVANCING options shown in the format below may be used:

WRITE record-name [FROM identifier-1] $\left[\begin{array}{l} \underline{BEFORE} \\ \underline{AFTER} \end{array}\right]$

ADVANCING $\left\{\begin{array}{l} \text{identifier-2 LINES} \\ \text{integer LINES} \\ \text{mnemonic-name} \end{array}\right\}$

Note that the first WRITE statement in 028-HEADLINES is in the format of: WRITE record-name FROM identifier-1 AFTER ADVANCING mnemonic-name. Note also that the word ADVANCING could have been omitted; we could have said: . . . AFTER PAGETOP.

The other two WRITE statements involving print lines are in the format of: WRITE record-name AFTER ADVANCING integer LINES. We could have coded these as WRITE PRINTOUT AFTER 1. The word LINES is also optional. Why did we use the ungrammatical "1 LINES"? The ANSI COBOL reserved word list includes LINE; but this is reserved for specific data division usage in the report-writer module which (*a*) is not part of every COBOL compiler, and (*b*) does not permit the use of LINE for this WRITE statement format.

It should be kept in mind, however, that the use of the ADVANCING option supersedes the automatic single-line printer spacing, so that once the ADVANCING option is used in a program, the automatic spacing is canceled; therefore, if there are three WRITE instructions referring to the same file, two containing the ADVANCING option and one not, overprinting will occur when the WRITE instruction *not* containing the ADVANCING option is executed.

When the BEFORE ADVANCING option is available in a COBOL compiler, some programmers occasionally find it more useful than AFTER ADVANCING; but many compilers do not contain this variation. The AFTER option is just about universally available.

The reference to "identifier-2 LINES" covers instances where the number of lines to be advanced is governed by the numeric contents of a data field in an input or output record area or in working-storage. If, let us say, the linespacing were to be governed by a single-column input-data record field to which we gave the data-name LINECODE, and each input record might contain any number from 1 to 9 in this field, we might formulate an instruction to WRITE PRINT-LINE AFTER ADVANCING LINECODE LINES.

In using the ADVANCING option of the WRITE statement for printing, the programmer should check the COBOL compiler being used for (*a*) availability of the BEFORE option already mentioned, (*b*) the limit of the number of lines it is permissible to specify, and (*c*) the effect of the option on specification for print-record areas. Some older compilers have a limit of three lines per instruction which, by use of various programming techniques, can be enlarged considerably.

By far the most necessary of the three items above is checking the compiler's handling of printer control for its effect on the data division specifications. Some electromechanical control must be obtained over the movement of the printer platen and the related parts which cause paper movement. When the control is exercised by means such as a carriage-control tape, a practice appearing in IBM's 360 and 370 compilers may result. In these compilers (because of the type of printer control), an additional character position must be reserved in the description of the print record. Effectively, this is for storage of a carriage-control character for the integer representing the number of lines to be advanced. This requires, for the standard 132-character print record, that we specify RECORD CONTAINS 133 CHARACTERS, although only 132 will ever print on any line. In addition, a one-position FILLER (picture X) must be specified at the beginning of the definition of print-record data fields. If the first print-record field would have been FILLER anyway, one additional position can be added to it; but if a data field is to begin in printing position 1, the seemingly fictional 02-FILLER PIC X must precede the data-field entry. Including this extra position, the number of characters specified for the various fields in the print-record area must total 133, agreeing with the RECORD CONTAINS clause. Omission of the non-printing FILLER position when it is intended that a data field begin in print position 1 will result in non-printing of the first data-field character.

Theoretically, it is not absolutely necessary to use the ADVANCING option to govern line spacing; *in practice,* it is almost always necessary (or at least much more convenient) because of the need to allow top and bottom margins for pages, to number pages, and to provide page headings for improving readability of reports. Once the ADVANCING option is used in COBOL programming, compiler and printer control requirements may call for modification of data division entries in the manner just described for IBM's 360 and 370 ANSI COBOL programs.

ARITHMETIC: SIMPLE ADDITION

We have used two ADD instructions of the same type in the foregoing program, one to keep count of page numbers, the other to count lines printed on each page. ANSI COBOL specifications describe the function of the ADD statement as causing two or more numeric operands to be summed and the result to be stored. The term "operand" is used in ANSI COBOL to mean any "lower-case" word used in a COBOL program statement. As has been demonstrated so far, "lower-case" words are either implementor-names (which are reserved words in the implementor's ANSI COBOL subset) or programmer-supplied words, such as file-names, record-names, data-names, numeric or non-

numeric literals, and procedure division paragraph headers. Either of our entries adding the numeric literal 1 to a data field in working-storage would be described in the following format: ADD literal TO identifier. In the above format, neither operand may exceed eighteen decimal digits in length. The identifier area added to must be a data-name field in a storage area. We cannot add a literal to a literal or a data-name area to a literal, since a literal generated in the procedure division is not stored in a location that can receive data. We may add (the contents of) a data-name identifier to another data-name identifier that is located in a data division storage area; we may also, in a single instruction, add two or more literals or data-name area contents to the contents of another numeric data area.

The operands to which we added page and line counts in our program were numeric fields with pictures of 9s. The pictures did not indicate whether the fields were positive or negative; the fields are referred to as *unsigned* and are regarded as if they were positive. When subtraction needs to be done in a numeric data area in which a negative result may occur, the 9's in the picture must be preceded by an S, which occupies no character space in the storage area but provides for the possibility of the area containing a negative result. The only times when it is safe to define an arithmetical-result field without a sign are, as here, when there is no possibility of negative results. Even in simple addition, however, two rules must be observed:

1. Make sure that the result-field area is large enough to meet the maximum requirements. Here two positions were enough for LINE-NUM, since 55 was the maximum number it would contain; and three positions for PAGE-NUM seemed adequate as long as the maximum number of pages for a department would be less than a thousand.

2. Adding or other forms of arithmetic must not be done in a field with a picture edited for printing. Note that PAGE-NO with a picture of ZZZ9 is such a field. We did our addition in PAGE-NUM (picture 999) and later MOVED the result to PAGE-NO, which avoided any violation of the rule.

At this point, it is both convenient and relevant to describe a simple option of the ADD (and other arithmetic) statements, which also avoids violation of the rule. It is sometimes useful, when adding two or more operands, to have another field available to which the result will be transferred. Suppose we want to add FIELDA, FIELDB, and the literal 50, but because we need to use one or both of the data fields unchanged at a later point in the same program, we do not want the result to be entered in either of the fields. Let us assume that FIELDC is edited for printing, and that it is otherwise feasible in the program to transfer the results of the addition to it. The following is permitted: ADD FIELDA FIELDB 50 GIVING FIELDC. With the GIVING option, the operands to the left of GIVING are summed in an accumulator area (not defined as a data division item in the program) and the sum stored (in effect, moved to) the operand area to the right of GIVING. While the GIVING option makes it possible to work around the dangers of using an edited field for arithmetic, it can be used also where the result is to be stored in an unedited field. The GIVING option is discussed in further detail in Chapter 9.

REVIEW MATERIAL

Terms

Sequence (of a file)	Suppression (of leading
Page and column headings	zeroes)
Carriage-control tape	Operand
Counter	Signed and unsigned fields
	Result field

Questions

Why are tape and disk, rather than cards, normally used as file-storage media?

What does a "dump" program do?

What happens when a record is written to a blocked file?

Why is the VALUE clause used in the data description of a field that is used as a counter?

What does the symbol Z mean in a PIC clause?

In the file creation program described in this chapter, what is the function of the field PREV-DEPT?

In what situations is it desirable to advance the printer paper to a new page?

What does the AFTER ADVANCING option provide for?

What is the restriction on the use of an edited field in an arithmetic statement?

What is the function of the GIVING option in an arithmetic statement?

True-or-False Statements

Sequence-checking of card files is necessary to screen out duplicate or out-of-sequence cards.

Blocking of records on tape requires only that the BLOCK CONTAINS clause be included properly.

The carriage-control tape allows the printer to print upper- or lower-case characters.

Programmers use the line-count technique to signal the operator that more paper must be fed into the printer.

A field with VALUE ZERO may not be changed during the execution of the program.

The first character in a print record is reserved for the carriage-control character when the ADVANCING option is used.

Arithmetic operands cannot exceed eighteen decimal digits in length.

The ADD verb is limited to two operands.

Programming

7–1: Write a program to create from card data a tape file of customer names and addresses. The tape records are to be 120 positions long, and are blocked 20. Write the print and tape records as shown below:

Card Columns and Contents		PICTURE	Print Positions	Tape Record Positions
1	Sales region	9	4	1
2–3	Salesman number	99	8–9	2–3
4–7	Customer number	9999	13–16	4–7
8–30	Customer name	X(23)	20–42	8–30
31–55	Street address	X(25)	46–70	31–55
56–74	City and state	X(19)	74–92	56–74
75–79	Zip code	9(5)	96–100	75–79
80	Card code	9	Not used	Not used

The cards are in ascending sequence on columns 1–7. The printout is to be single-spaced, with a blank line following the last customer for a salesman. Begin a new page for each sales region. Each page is to contain a maximum of 54 lines. All cards are to be printed, but no tape record is to be written if either of the following conditions exists:

1. A card is out of sequence; that is, columns 1–7 contain a lower number than that of the last preceding card that was in sequence. Print BAD SEQUENCE in print positions 119–130.

2. A card has no punching in any one of the three alphanumeric fields. Print DATA MISSING in print positions 119–130.

7–2: Add headings and page-numbering to the program in Problem 7–1. Each region is to start with page 1. The headings and their print positioning are:

REGN	2–5
SLSMN	7–11
CUSTOMER NUMBER AND NAME	13–36
STREET ADDRESS	50–63
CITY AND STATE	75–88
ZIPCODE	94–100
PAGE	122–125

Allow for three page-number positions in 127–129

7–3: Incorporate the following in your program as amended by item 2: Assume that there is a second card for each customer, containing the same data in columns 1–7, and a 2 in column 80. This card follows the first, which is punched 1 in column 80.

A second line is to be printed for each customer, and additional information written on the tape record, based on the 80/2 card contents, as follows:

Card Columns and Contents		PICTURE	Print Positions	Tape Record Positions
8–30	Bill-to department	X(23)	20–42	80–102
31–32	Credit rating code	XX	104–105	103–104
33	Credit limit code	X	108	105
34	Billing terms code	X	111	106
35–36	Customer class code	99	115–116	107–108

Add the following to heading-line data:

RTG	LMT	TMS	CLS

in printing positions:

103–105	107–109	111–113	115–117

8

UPDATING A STORED FILE: DATA
AND PROCESSING CONTROLS

DATA VALIDATION

In the preceding section, the creation of a stored file was described. It was assumed that the records would be written in low-to-high sequence based on the five-digit employee identification code field. Only one type of input data validation was done: before processing an input data record, we tested to make sure that the code field in it was greater (a higher number) than the preceding record and if it was not, we wrote no output file record for it. We indicated this action by printing the error message REJECTED on the printing line for the out-of-sequence input record.

To update even the simplest stored file, additional validation of input data is essential. Moreover, since there will be two *input* files to be processed (the stored file and the updating data), the *relative* sequence of records in each of the two files will have to be given some consideration in planning the pattern of procedure division instructions. For example, in the simplest updating, there are normally at least two kinds of update data—additions and changes. An addition should have an identification code field that does *not* match any stored-file record; a change should have one that *must* match a stored-file record. These two different types of update data will have different effects on the stored file: one will add a complete new record; the other will only alter part of an existing record. This requires a different set of instructions for each; moreover, it suggests that some means in addition to the code-number field be used to identify each update data record. Suppose, for example, that an update record

intended to be an addition to the stored file was given a code number of a record already on the file, or an item intended as a change was miscoded with a number not on the stored file. These possibilities of human error are typically checked against by requiring the updating data-preparers to use a single-digit code (such as A for an addition, C for a change, D for a deletion), which is then keypunched as an update data record field. While this does not detect all miscoding errors, it supplies a *consistency check* which will prevent confusion between the intent of the update data and its actual content.

Updating of a stored file may be done either by "writing" the entire file in its updated form as a new output file while leaving the original input file intact (as is done with sequential tape and disk records), or by recording changes and additions on the input file itself, which then becomes an output file as well (as is done with random-access files on disk). For present purposes, we will assume separate input and output files (as on tape).[1]

---

1. In this type of updating, an internal processing rule known as the grandfather principle is followed in orderly computer centers. The "father" input file, as well as the update data, is retained until the output file ("son") has been used on one subsequent updating (as a "father" input file) and the output of that updating been accepted as correct. When a "father" file has thus become a "grandfather", neither it nor the update data used with it is needed for further verification of existing file data. Manual mishandling of tape files which causes one master file to be rendered useless is reduced from disaster to nuisance by use of this principle.

SEQUENTIAL FILE RECORD COMPARISON

Updating a file requires brief but careful consideration of the principles of comparing data in two files in ascending sequence, in order to prepare an adequate flowchart and write the proper IF statements in a program based on that flowchart. The relatively simple illustration which follows should, it is hoped, convince the beginner that flowcharting ought to precede, and be the base for, writing even a simple updating program. Assume that the card input is to be used to update a tape file; that unmatched tape records will be copied onto an output tape; that matched tape records will be written, as changed by matching card data, on the output tape; and that unmatched card data will be written as additions to the file on the output tape. Assume also that at the beginning of each input file, the identification code numbers of data occur as follows:

    Update data cards: 103, 107, 111, 112
    Input tape file: 101, 102, 103, 104, 106, 108, 113

Having read the first record from 'each file, a comparison of the code numbers indicates a rule of action: if the master record code number is lower than the update record code number, copy the input master record to the output master file and read the next master record. This course will be taken on the first two master records (101 and 102). When the third master record (103) is read, we get a different condition: master record code number equals update record code number. This requires creating an output master record partly from the input master (the unchanged portions) and partly from the update record (new data replacing parts of the input master); following this (changing of record 103), we must read *both* the next input master *and* the next update record. Since the next two input master records (104 and 106) are lower than the update record (107), they will be copied to the output master file, bringing master record 108 to be compared with update record 107. Now we have the third possibility: the master record code number is higher than the update record code number, indicating that the *update* record is an *addition* to the master file. The action needed is to write the update record out as an output master record, and read the next update record.

END-OF-FILE CONSIDERATIONS

A second necessary consideration in updating a file sequentially is providing alternative end-of-file routines based on three possible conditions:

1. Update records may end while there are still input master records to be read and processed.

2. Master input records may end while there are still update records to be read and processed.

3. The last update record may match the last input master record.

While there are numerous ways in which these alternative conditions can be set up in a program, perhaps the simplest is to take advantage of either of two figurative constants provided as reserved words in COBOL. HIGH-VALUE (or HIGH-VALUES) represents the character that is the very last (highest) in the collating sequence recognized in the computer being used. In computers with a collating sequence based on EBCDIC, ^F_F is the high-value character; others recognize different characters (for example, in Honeywell's 200 family, a character keypunched as zero-7-8 is the last in the collating sequence). Regardless of what the high-value character is in the particular computer, an instruction to move HIGH-VALUES to an area for comparison with an input record code area will always result in the record code area being found low.

In creating a stored file, only one end-of-job routine was necessary because only one input file was being used to create the stored file. In an updating program with two input files being used, an end-of-file routine must be set up for *each* input file (to cover its termination and continue processing the other input file), and an end-of-job routine must be provided when all records from *both* input files have been processed. To illustrate: Assume two input files (update and master data), and a field for each defined in working-storage to be used for holding each record code number for comparing master and update code numbers. We will call these fields UPDATEHOLD and MASTERHOLD. We will also provide end-of-file routines called EOFC and EOFM and designate the end-of-job routine as EOJ. The first READ routines in the program will be:

    READ-UPDATE.
        READ UPDATEFILE AT END GO TO EOFC.
        MOVE UPDATECODE TO UPDATEHOLD.
    READ-MASTER.
        READ MASTERFILE AT END GO TO EOFM.
        MOVE MASTERCODE TO MASTERHOLD.

This will be followed by a paragraph headed COMPARE, in which the decisions for output-record writing will be made based on the comparative codes in master and update files. The paragraph will conclude with an attempt to read either the next master or the next update record. What should EOFC and EOFM do? They will be precisely alike, except for reference to the UPDATEHOLD and MASTERHOLD areas:

```
EOFC.
    MOVE HIGH-VALUES TO UPDATEHOLD.
    IF MASTERHOLD = HIGH-VALUES GO TO EOJ.
    GO TO COMPARE.
EOFM.
    MOVE HIGH-VALUES TO MASTERHOLD.
    IF UPDATEHOLD = HIGH-VALUES GO TO EOJ.
    GO TO COMPARE.
```

EOJ will contain any cleanup operations and conclude with file-closing and STOP RUN statements. Let us test EOFC and EOFM statements with the three end-of-file conditions just stated:

1. If the last update record has been processed through the COMPARE and subsequent routines, a READ UPDATEFILE will be necessary, and the AT END condition will occur. The program will branch to EOFC, and HIGH-VALUES will be moved into UPDATEHOLD, replacing the code number of the last update record. If there is still a master-record code number in MASTERHOLD, there is still at least one master record to be processed, and COMPARE routines will follow. The compare routines will always now result in the master-record code being low (since it will be compared to HIGH-VALUES), the master record being processed and written as an output record, and another attempt to read a master record. For example: Say the last update record is 918, and the last master records are 922, 924, and 925. Update number 918 will be processed and, whether or not there is a master record 918, the program will attempt to read the next update record, find none, and go to EOFC, where it will move HIGH-VALUES to UP-DATEHOLD, and go to COMPARE. Master 922 will be found low as compared to HIGH-VALUES, and be written as output data. Since the master record was low, the next master must be read and the cycle repeated. When the last master record is processed, the next attempt to read will cause a branch to EOFM.

2. The program will also branch to EOFM when the last master record has been read and processed and there are still update records to be read. Since the first step in EOFM is to move HIGH-VALUES to MASTERHOLD, any comparisons of update and master code numbers will show the *update* record to be low, cause it to be processed, and result in an attempt to read another update record. This is the same cycle as in *1*. above, with the comparative code-number situation reversed as between the two files. The processing of the last update record will cause a branch to EOFC on the next attempt to read an update record.

3. In cases *1*. and *2*. above, the ultimate branch to the "opposite" end-of-file routine when the second

file (the one with higher ending code numbers) runs out will encounter the IF condition as a fact: HIGH-VALUES will be in the HOLD area for the other file and the GO TO EOJ will take place. In the event that the last update record is a change to be made in the last master record (each will then have the same code number), the EOJ condition will materialize as follows: Since both input file records must be processed to write an output record, the subsequent operation will require an attempt to read both update and master files; and, in order to go to EOJ from the end-of-file routine for the *first* file read, will have to find HIGH-VALUES in the hold area for the second file. The end-of-file routines do not create this condition; if either routine contained a MOVE HIGH-VALUES to the *other* file's hold area, EOJ would be reached prematurely (while there were still records to be processed in the other file). One possible way to assure the presence of HIGH-VALUES in the hold areas in both files following a last-records-equal situation is to provide for it in the last instructions in the paragraph governing processing of matched records.

Checking back to the READ and comparing routines just described shows that after making the file changes required by an UPDATEHOLD = MASTER-HOLD condition, we would need to read both the next update record and the next master record and compare them. If we were not concerned with the possibility of simultaneous last records in the two files, the last statement in the file change routine could be simply GO TO READ-UPDATE, which would be followed by READ-MASTER and comparing routines. This will cover cases where there are records available to be read in both files or only one file. If both files are at an end, however, this normal processing sequence will produce only one end-of-file routine (for the update file) and one HIGH-VALUES (in UPDATE-HOLD). We need HIGH-VALUES in both hold areas to get to EOJ. Could we somehow write (instead of GO TO READ-UPDATE) a series of instructions that would read a master record—and if at end (no master record) would move HIGH-VALUES to MASTER-HOLD, then do the READ-UPDATE paragraph (which at end moves HIGH-VALUES to UPDATEHOLD), and then go to the COMPARE routines? The answer is Yes; we can do it using only types of instructions already illustrated or by using in addition a COBOL verb not yet illustrated—the PERFORM statement, which provides saving of considerable COBOL coding though in itself producing more *machine* instructions than a GO TO.

The PERFORM Statement

A PERFORM statement in its simplest form is: PER-FORM procedure-name. The procedure-name must be a paragraph or section[2] in the procedure division. PERFORM (properly used) causes the paragraph or section named to be executed and permits the program to be resumed with the instruction following the PER-FORM. It is different from a GO TO principally in the following respect: Assume a series of four paragraphs (PARA1, PARA2, PARA3, PARA4), with the first paragraph containing seven instructions. If the fifth statement in PARA1 contained a GO TO PARA4, PARA4 would be executed; the last two statements in PARA1 and all of PARA2 and PARA3 would be by-passed. Other GO TO statements elsewhere in the program could cause PARA2 and PARA3 to be executed, but GO TO instructions could not return directly to the sixth and seventh instructions in PARA1.

If the fifth statement in PARA1 was PERFORM PARA4, PARA4 would be executed, followed by the sixth and seventh instructions in PARA1 and PARA2, PARA3, *and* PARA4 in their normal sequence, as long as PARA4 (the procedure named by the PERFORM statement) did not contain a GO TO or an AT END. Occurrence of the condition governing the GO TO or specified by the AT END that would transfer program control outside of the paragraph to be PERFORMed would also prevent the return of control to the instruction following the PERFORM statement.

A PERFORM statement, then, permits an interruption of program sequence to execute the instruction to be PERFORMed, followed by resumption of program sequence immediately following the point of interruption. On this basis, we could follow our file-change instructions based on UPDATEHOLD = MASTER-HOLD conditions with this series of statements:

```
READ MASTERFILE AT END MOVE HIGH-VALUES TO
    MASTERHOLD.
IF MASTERHOLD LESS THAN HIGH-VALUES MOVE
    MASTERCODE TO MASTERHOLD.
PERFORM READ-UPDATE.
GO TO COMPARE.
```

If there is at least one more record available to be read in each file, the AT END condition will not be met when the master record is read, but the next statement, which is the same as the remaining statement contained

2. A procedure division section is a paragraph or a group of paragraphs in a segmented program. See page 157 for further detail.

in the READ-MASTER paragraph, will be executed. This will be followed by the READ-UPDATE para-graph and a return to the process of comparing the newly-read master and update records, assuring normal required processing.

If there are no more records available in either file, HIGH-VALUES will be moved to MASTER-HOLD, execution of the READ-UPDATE will find the AT END condition, and EOFC will be executed. MASTERHOLD will be found to contain HIGH-VALUES and EOJ will be executed.

If there is no record remaining in the master file, but one or more available in the update file, HIGH-VALUES will be in MASTERHOLD when the update record is read, and since UPDATEHOLD will be lower than MASTERHOLD, the update record will be proc-essed as a new output record and the program will return to its first reading routine (READ-UPDATE), repeating the cycle of update record reading and proc-essing until the end of the update file forces EOJ.

If there is no record remaining in the update file but the master file still has records to be read, the next master record will be read, its code number moved to MASTERHOLD, and the PERFORMance of READ-UPDATE will uncover the AT END condition, trans-ferring program control to EOFC. The process de-scribed under *1.* on page 82 will then take place.

It may appear that we have examined end-of-file and end-of-job conditions in excessive detail. The detail may be considerable, but it is necessary. All conditions must be checked out; the object program must be tested with data representing high, low, and equal conditions for the ending of each input file, and "dumps" taken of the latter part of the output file. The dumps must show the effects of the last records from each input file upon the output file under each of the three basic conditions. It is extremely easy to leave one type of possibility unaccounted for in end-of-file routines and, particularly when some master-file records near the end of the file have little activity, have the omission go un-discovered for months, until some chance transaction reveals that a master record is no longer on the file. This can happen only when an updating program is not thoroughly tested; and when it does happen, it requires not only testing to discover the original program error but, based on the type of error, a determination of the extent of the damage to the completeness and accuracy of the file since the program has been in use. Controls, established by the user of the computer-produced file-updating reports, and incorporated in the program itself, may supplement the program testing and help to assure the user that the program is working properly each time it is used.

RECORD COUNTS

One aid in checking update program performance is a controlled record count. If the user department furnishes the computer area with the number of records on the last updated master file, the number of each type of update data record furnished, and the number of records that the new master file should contain as a result of the updating, these counts can be verified during execution of the program while serving as a check on the functioning of the program itself.[3] The control counts may be stated in this form:

Input master count	5,381
+ Additions	46
− Deletions	21
Output master count	5,406
Changes	219

Notice that (*a*) the total of output records is the input master count plus or minus the difference in number of additions and deletions, and (*b*) changes do not affect the output master count. Care must be taken in the program to count each type of input and output data at the proper point in processing; for example:

- Input master records should be counted at file-reading time.
- Additions, deletions, and changes should be counted after validation tests have taken place and miscoded update input has been rejected.
- Output master records should be counted at output-writing time.
- If counts are taken of input data errors that are rejected by the tests made in the program, these counts should be taken during the error-flagging routines initiated by the error conditions.

Since validation tests may result in *processing* counts that differ from the user's *control* counts, counts of rejected data should also be made during program execution and printed out in "recap" form at the end of processing so that they can be reconciled to the user's control counts. The printout might show:

INPUT MASTER COUNT	5,381		
+ ADDITIONS MADE	43	ALREADY ON FILE	3
− DELETIONS MADE	20	UNMATCHED	1
OUTPUT MASTER COUNT	5,404		
CHANGES MADE	212	UNMATCHED	7

---

3. The master file input and output total counts are usable as controls only in sequential updating. In random-access updating, these counts are not obtained because by this method it is not likely that all master records will be accessed and read.

Note that the combinations of processed and rejected item counts for each type of update data should equal the control count for that type. A difference between the record count recap and the control count may indicate error in either (*a*) the control count itself, (*b*) the user data preparation, (*c*) the computer-area data preparation (such as in keypunching), or (*d*) a computer processing error, of either an operational or programming nature. Errors caused by programming should not occur if a program has been adequately tested. Incorporating record counts into an update program will aid not only in establishing processing proofs of control counts, but in locating errors in the program's handling of the update data and of the instructions that take the counts. Once testing has assured that each count has been taken at the applicable point in the program, the counts become useful in testing end-of-file and end-of-job routines to locate programming errors that may result in output file records being omitted or duplicated.

SPECIFICATIONS FOR AN UPDATING PROGRAM

With the essentials for validation, multiple-file sequence-checking, end-of-file, and data-control techniques in mind, let us write specifications for updating the file created by our last program. This file will be the input master file to our update program; it will have the same data division record description as the output file in the program creating it. The other input file will consist of cards in the same format as the cards in the file-creation program, with one exception—column 80 will be alphabetic and contain one of the following letters:

A   if the card represents an addition to the file.
C   if the card represents changes of data in a record already on the file.
D   if the record identified by the card is to be deleted from the file.

The output master file will be the same size and format of record as the input master, and will be created as follows:

1. Each unmatched input master record will be copied as output.

2. Each unmatched "80/A" card will be formatted and written as an output record.

3. Each input master matched by an "80/C" card will be copied as output, except that any fields with name or address data in the 80/C card will replace the input master data on the output record.

4. Any input master record matched by an "80/D" card will *not* be copied as an output master.

These four requirements imply that the program should test matched and unmatched update cards for consistency with the column-80 code letter. To provide for (*a*) reasonable validation of update data, (*b*) a report of valid changes made as between input and output master files, (*c*) an indication on the report of each update item rejected as invalid, and (*d*) a recap of valid and rejected record counts, we will have the program do the following:

1. Print a line for each update record in the same format as the printout for our file-creation program. We will enlarge the error-message area so that the disposition of each valid or invalid update card can be printed:[4]

If a valid addition (80/A)	ADDED
If a file-matching 80/A	MATCHED ADD
If a valid change (80/C)	CHANGED
If an unmatched 80/C	UNMATCHED CHANGE
If a valid deletion (80/D)	DELETED
If an unmatched 80/D	UNMATCHED DELETE

2. Accumulate counts of records processed and rejected, for verification by the user to control counts.

3. As with the file-creation program, provide page headings, page-numbering, and starting of a new page at the beginning of a new department. This last provision will involve checking of department number in records of *two* input files rather than one but is merely an extension of an already described technique. The record count recap is to be printed on a separate page after detail printing of the update data has been completed.

4. We are assuming here that the user is satisfied that the pre-computer sort of update data on the employee and department number codes will preclude any out-of-sequence condition occurring during program execution; however, attention will be called to points in the program where use of the previous-number principle can be employed, in conjunction with techniques to be discussed in Chapter 12, to minimize wasting computer time when there are serious sequence errors in input data.

---

4. The possibility of codes other than A, C, or D being punched can be readily checked and detected by sorting on column 80 immediately before the cards are sorted on the employee identification number field, as they must be before sequential processing takes place.

THE FLOWCHART

Note that the flowchart shown in Figure 8–1 is in several segments—one main section containing the basic processing sequence and questions to be decided, and a number of subsections, each representing a path taken following a positive response to a question. The main section poses only the basic questions in the program: tests for end-of-file, tests for comparative high, low, and equal conditions of the two input files, and tests for conditions (end-of-page or new department) requiring starting of a new printed page. The subsections say more specifically what operations need to be done as a result of making additional tests. Notice that (*a*) in all cases except end-of-job, a connector indicates the point of return to the main processing, and (*b*) with one exception, the terms used relate to the kind of data handling to be done rather than to programming instructions. The exception is the use of the word PERFORM since this word, used in the programming sense, enables us to avoid additional flowchart steps and to indicate where programming instructions may be minimized.

While the primary purposes of flowcharting prior to programming have been discussed already, it is worthwhile to point out specific advantages for this particular program. Each of the three types of update data cards is to be printed; each has a possible type of error. This makes six variations of the printed line, which would otherwise be the same. Preparation of a flowchart requires the programmer to coordinate the six possibilities so that the six differences will be handled separately while the operation common to all can be planned to be coded only once. Here the very preparation of the flowchart points out to the programmer preparing it the points where the six different messages and record counts must be provided. The flowchart also shows that only one print routine need be used.

Quite often it is preferable to set up the file section of the data division before flowcharting. This helps the programmer to check the adequacy of the specifications provided by making sure that the file and record descriptions contain the necessary data to reach the specified results. Usually, most of the working-storage section can be detailed at this point also; occasionally, some of the needs for working-storage will come to light only as the flowcharting develops the program plan.

The procedure division coding should begin only after the completion of the flowchart and should follow the flowchart outline, as has been done in Figure 8–2, which contains the data and procedure divisions required.

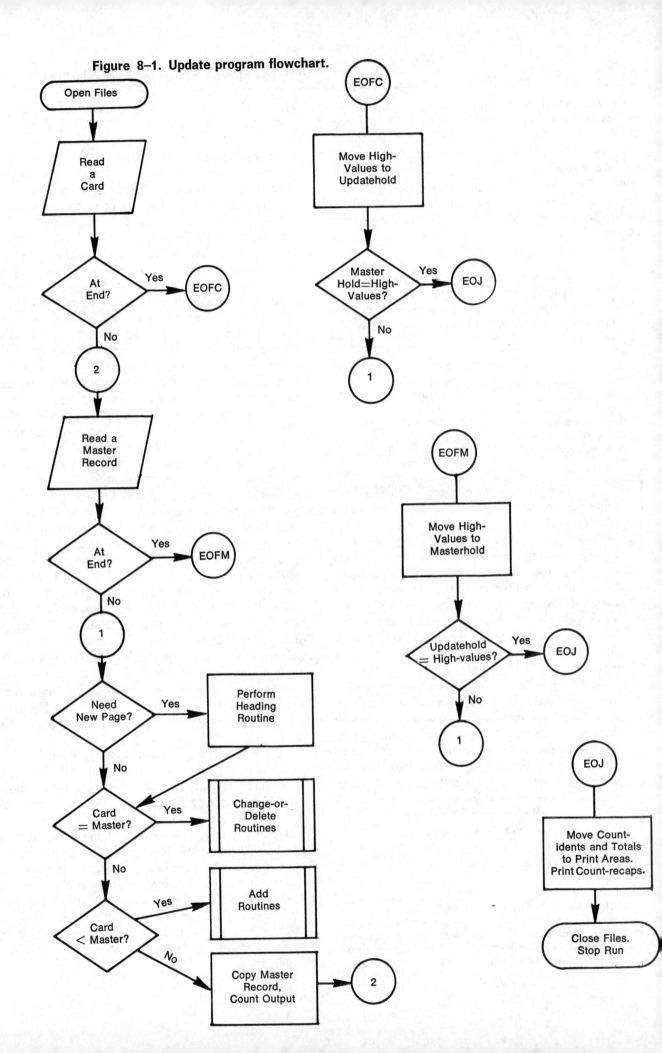

Figure 8-1. Update program flowchart.

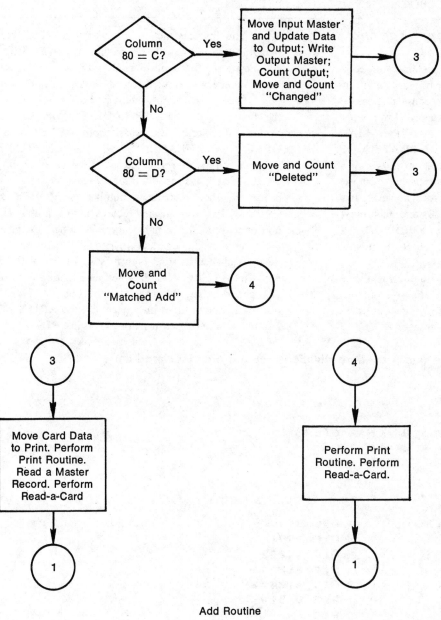

Change-or-
Delete Routines

Column 80 = C? — Yes → Move Input Master and Update Data to Output; Write Output Master; Count Output; Move and Count "Changed" → 3

No ↓

Column 80 = D? — Yes → Move and Count "Deleted" → 3

No ↓

Move and Count "Matched Add" → 4

3 → Move Card Data to Print. Perform Print Routine. Read a Master Record. Perform Read-a-Card → 1

4 → Perform Print Routine. Perform Read-a-Card. → 1

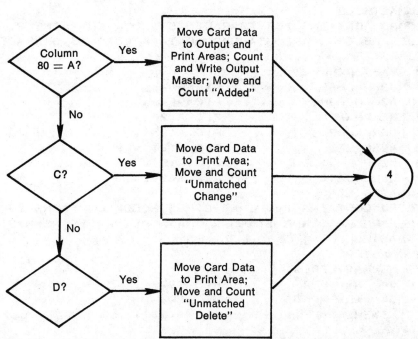

Add Routine

Column 80 = A? — Yes → Move Card Data to Output and Print Areas; Count and Write Output Master; Move and Count "Added" → 4

No ↓

C? — Yes → Move Card Data to Print Area; Move and Count "Unmatched Change" → 4

No ↓

D? — Yes → Move Card Data to Print Area; Move and Count "Unmatched Delete" → 4

NOTES ON CODING OF FILE-UPDATE PROGRAM

1. The 010-OPEN paragraph requires no comment. The 020-READ-UPDATE paragraph is essentially as described under end-of-file considerations. If any test is to be made for out-of-sequence (low) cards, it should be made immediately after the READ CARDFILE statement by comparing UPDATECODE to PREV-IDENT, which we have set up in working-storage but not made use of for comparing purposes for reasons indicated on page 85. Note, however, that instructions in paragraphs 035, 043, and 054 move either master or update data codes into PREV-IDENT just prior to moves for writing output records to permit such comparisons.

2. The 025-READ-MASTER paragraph is also as described under end-of-file considerations. Note that as soon as a master record is read, it is counted in the MASTERSIN area in working-storage.

3. The first instruction in the 030-MATCHING paragraph will initiate page headings both (a) before comparing the first records read and (b) when subsequent update and master records just read both contain a new department number. Before comparing the first records read, PREV-DEPT's contents are zeroes, necessarily less than both MDEPT and DEPTNO; 075-HEADLINES will be PERFORMed before any records are processed, assuring a heading on the first page of the report. Once records are processed, the department number is MOVEd to PREV-DEPT from master records in paragraph 035 and update records in paragraph 066. When a department number higher than PREV-DEPT appears in newly-read records from both files, 075-HEADLINES will also be PERFORMed. If neither situation (a) nor (b) above exists, but execution of 066-PRINT has occurred enough times on a page and the ADD 1 TO LINE-NUM (last instruction in 066-PRINT) has

Figure 8–2. Data and procedure divisions for a file update program.

```
001160 DATA DIVISION.
001170 FILE SECTION.
002030 FD  CARDFILE
002040     RECORD CONTAINS 80 CHARACTERS
002050     LABEL RECORDS ARE OMITTED
002060     DATA RECORD IS CARDREC.
002070 01  CARDREC.
002075     02  UPDATEDATA.
002080     03  UPDATECODE.
002090         04  DEPTNO          PIC 99.
002100         04  EMPNO           PIC 999.
002110     03  EMPNAME             PIC A(20).
002120     03  EMPADDR             PIC X(25).
002130     03  EMPCITY             PIC A(24).
002140     03  EMPZIP              PIC 9(5).
002150     02  CCODE               PIC A.
002160 FD  OLDMASTFILE
002170     RECORD CONTAINS 200 CHARACTERS BLOCK CONTAINS 20 RECORDS
002180     LABEL RECORDS ARE STANDARD DATA RECORD IS OLDMASTREC.
002190 01  OLDMASTREC.
002200     02  MASTERCODE.
002210         03  MDEPT           PIC 99.
002220         03  MEMPNO          PIC 999.
002230     02  MEMPNAME            PIC A(20).
002240     02  MEMPADDR            PIC X(25).
003010     02  MEMPCITY            PIC A(24).
003020     02  MZIP                PIC 9(5).
003030     02  OTHERDATA           PIC X(121).
003040 FD  NEWMASTFILE
003050     RECORD CONTAINS 200 CHARACTERS BLOCK CONTAINS 20 RECORDS
003060     LABEL RECORDS ARE STANDARD DATA RECORD IS NEWMASTREC.
003070 01  NEWMASTREC.
003075     02  MASTERDATA.
003080     03  NEWMASTCODE.
003090         04  NEWDEPT         PIC 99.
003100         04  NEWEMPNO        PIC 999.
003110     03  NEWEMPNAME          PIC A(20).
```

```
003120          03   NEWEMPADDR              PIC  X(25).
003130          03   NEWEMPCITY              PIC  A(24).
003140          03   NEWZIP                  PIC  9(5).
003150          02   NEWDATA                 PIC  X(121).
003160 FD   PRINTFILE
003170          LABEL RECORDS ARE OMITTED DATA RECORDS ARE PRINTOUT COUNTS.
003180 01   PRINTOUT.
003190          02   FILLER                  PIC  X(5).
003200          02   P-DEPT                  PIC  99.
003210          02   FILLER                  PIC  X(5).
003220          02   P-EMPNO                 PIC  999.
003230          02   FILLER                  PIC  X(5).
003240          02   P-EMPNAME               PIC  A(20).
004010          02   FILLER                  PIC  X(5).
004020          02   P-EMPADDR               PIC  X(25).
004030          02   FILLER                  PIC  X(5).
004040          02   P-EMPCITY               PIC  A(24).
004050          02   FILLER                  PIC  X(5).
004060          02   P-ZIP                   PIC  9(5).
004070          02   FILLER                  PIC  X(5).
004080          02   ERRMESSAGE              PIC  X(18).
004081 01   COUNTS.
004082          02   FILLER                  PIC  X(38).
004083          02   GOODCOUNTS              PIC  X(25).
004084          02   GOODTOTALS              PIC  ZZZZ9.
004085          02   FILLER                  PIC  X(5).
004086          02   BADCOUNTS               PIC  X(18).
004087          02   BADTOTALS               PIC  ZZ9.
004088          02   FILLER                  PIC  X(38).
004090 WORKING-STORAGE SECTION.
004100 77   UPDATEHOLD               PIC  X(5) VALUE ZERO.
004110 77   MASTERHOLD               PIC  X(5) VALUE ZERO.
004120 77   PREV-DEPT                PIC  99 VALUE ZERO.
004130 77   PREV-IDENT               PIC  9(5) VALUE ZERO.
004140 77   MASTERSIN                PIC  9(5) VALUE ZERO.
004150 77   OUTPUTCOUNT              PIC  9(4) VALUE ZERO.
004160 77   BADADD                   PIC  9(3) VALUE ZERO.
004170 77   CHANGES                  PIC  9(4) VALUE ZERO.
004180 77   DELETES                  PIC  9(4) VALUE ZERO.
004190 77   BADCHANGE                PIC  9(3) VALUE ZERO.
004200 77   BADDELETE                PIC  9(3) VALUE ZERO.
004210 77   GOODADD                  PIC  9(4) VALUE ZERO.
004220 77   LINE-NUM                 PIC  9(2) VALUE ZERO.
004230 77   PAGENUM                  PIC  9(3) VALUE 1.
005010 01   CAPTIONS.
005020          02   FILLER                  PIC  X(4) VALUE SPACES.
005030          02   HEADINGS                PIC  X(118) VALUE "DEPT     EMP NO   EMP
005040-     "LOYEE NAME           STREET ADDRESS                  CITY AND
005050-     " STATE           ZIP CODE      STATUS  ".
005060          02   PG                      PIC  X(5) VALUE "PAGE ".
005070          02   PAGENO                  PIC  ZZ9.
005080          02   FILLER                  PIC  XX VALUE SPACES.
006010 PROCEDURE DIVISION.
006020 010-OPEN.
006030          OPEN INPUT CARDFILE OLDMASTFILE.
```

```
006040          OPEN OUTPUT NEWMASTFILE PRINTFILE.
006060    020-READ-UPDATE.
006070          READ CARDFILE AT END GO TO 080-EOFC.
006075          IF UPDATECODE NOT > PREV-IDENT MOVE "OUT OF SEQUENCE" TO
006076          ERRMESSAGE PERFORM 066-PRINT GO TO 090-EOJ.
006080          MOVE UPDATECODE TO UPDATEHOLD.
006090    025-READ-MASTER.
006100          READ OLDMASTFILE AT END GO TO 085-EOFM.
006110          MOVE MASTERCODE TO MASTERHOLD. ADD 1 TO MASTERSIN.
006120    030-MATCHING.
006121          IF PREV-DEPT < MDEPT AND < DEPTNO MOVE 001 TO PAGENUM PERFORM
006122          075-HEADLINES. IF LINE-NUM > 54 PERFORM 075-HEADLINES.
006130          IF UPDATEHOLD = MASTERHOLD GO TO 040-CHANGE-OR-DELETE.
006140          IF UPDATEHOLD < MASTERHOLD GO TO 050-ADDCHECK.
006150    035-MASTERLOW.
006160          MOVE OLDMASTREC TO NEWMASTREC. MOVE MASTERHOLD TO PREV-IDENT.
006170          WRITE NEWMASTREC. MOVE MDEPT TO PREV-DEPT.
006180          ADD 1 TO OUTPUTCOUNT. GO TO 025-READ-MASTER.
006190    040-CHANGE-OR-DELETE.
006200          IF CCODE = "C" GO TO 043-CHANGE.
006210          IF CCODE = "D" GO TO 046-DELETE.
006220          MOVE "MATCHED ADD" TO ERRMESSAGE ADD 1 TO BADADD.
006230          GO TO 063-ADDPRINT.
007010    043-CHANGE.
007020          MOVE OLDMASTREC TO NEWMASTREC. MOVE MASTERHOLD TO PREV-IDENT.
007030          IF EMPNAME NOT EQUAL TO SPACES MOVE EMPNAME TO NEWEMPNAME.
007040          IF EMPADDR NOT EQUAL TO SPACES MOVE EMPADDR TO NEWEMPNAME.
007050          IF EMPCITY NOT EQUAL TO SPACES MOVE EMPCITY TO NEWEMPNAME.
007060          IF EMPZIP IS NUMERIC MOVE EMPZIP TO NEWZIP.
007070          MOVE "CHANGED" TO ERRMESSAGE. ADD 1 TO CHANGES.
007080          WRITE NEWMASTREC. ADD 1 TO OUTPUTCOUNT.
007090          GO TO 060-MATCHPRINT.
007100    046-DELETE.
007110          MOVE "DELETED" TO ERRMESSAGE. ADD 1 TO DELETES.
007120          GO TO 060-MATCHPRINT.
007130    050-ADDCHECK.
007140          IF CCODE = "A" GO TO 054-ADD.
007150          IF CCODE = "C" MOVE "UNMATCHED CHANGE" TO ERRMESSAGE ADD 1 TO
007160          BADCHANGE GO TO 063-ADDPRINT.
007170          IF CCODE = "D" MOVE "UNMATCHED DELETE" TO ERRMESSAGE ADD 1 TO
007180          BADDELETE GO TO 063-ADDPRINT.
007190    054-ADD.
007200          MOVE UPDATEDATA TO MASTERDATA. MOVE UPDATEHOLD TO PREV-IDENT.
007205          MOVE SPACES TO NEWDATA.
007210          MOVE "ADDED" TO ERRMESSAGE. ADD 1 TO GOODADD.
007220          WRITE NEWMASTREC. ADD 1 TO OUTPUTCOUNT. GO TO 063-ADDPRINT.
008010    060-MATCHPRINT.
008020          PERFORM 066-PRINT.
008030          READ OLDMASTFILE AT END MOVE HIGH-VALUES TO MASTERHOLD.
008040          IF MASTERHOLD < HIGH-VALUES MOVE MASTERCODE TO MASTERHOLD
008045          ADD 1 TO MASTERSIN.
008050          PERFORM 020-READ-UPDATE.
008060          GO TO 030-MATCHING.
008070    063-ADDPRINT.
008080          PERFORM 066-PRINT
```

```
008090        PERFORM 020-READ-UPDATE.
008100        GO TO 030-MATCHING.
008110  066-PRINT.
008120        MOVE DEPTNO TO P-DEPT PREV-DEPT.
008130        MOVE EMPNO TO P-EMPNO.
008140        MOVE EMPNAME TO P-EMPNAME.
008150        MOVE EMPADDR TO P-EMPADDR.
008160        MOVE EMPCITY TO P-EMPCITY.
008170        IF EMPZIP NUMERIC MOVE EMPZIP TO P-ZIP.
008180        WRITE PRINTOUT AFTER ADVANCING 1 LINES.
008190        MOVE SPACES TO PRINTOUT.
008200        ADD 1 TO LINE-NUM.
008210  070-HEADINGTEST.
008220        IF PREV-DEPT < MDEPT AND < DEPTNO MOVE 001 TO PAGENUM PERFORM
008230        075-HEADLINES.
008240        IF LINE-NUM > 54 PERFORM 075-HEADLINES.
009010  075-HEADLINES.
009020        MOVE SPACES TO PRINTOUT.
009030        MOVE PAGENUM TO PAGENO.
009040        WRITE PRINTOUT FROM CAPTIONS AFTER ADVANCING PAGETOP.
009045        MOVE SPACES TO PRINTOUT.
009050        WRITE PRINTOUT AFTER ADVANCING 1 LINES.
009070        MOVE SPACES TO PRINTOUT.
009080        ADD 1 TO PAGENUM.
009090        MOVE 2 TO LINE-NUM.
009100  080-EOFC.
009110        MOVE HIGH-VALUES TO UPDATEHOLD.
009120        IF MASTERHOLD = HIGH-VALUES GO TO 090-EOJ.
009130        GO TO 030-MATCHING.
009140  085-EOFM.
009150        MOVE HIGH-VALUES TO MASTERHOLD.
009160        IF UPDATEHOLD = HIGH-VALUES GO TO 090-EOJ.
009170        GO TO 030-MATCHING.
009180  090-EOJ.
009190        MOVE SPACES TO COUNTS.
009200        MOVE "INPUT MASTER RECORDS" TO GOODCOUNTS.
009210        MOVE MASTERSIN TO GOODTOTALS.
009220        WRITE COUNTS AFTER ADVANCING PAGETOP.
009230        MOVE SPACES TO   COUNTS.
009240        MOVE "+ ADDITIONS MADE" TO GOODCOUNTS.
010010        MOVE GOODADD TO GOODTOTALS.
010020        MOVE "ALREADY ON FILE" TO BADCOUNTS.
010030        MOVE BADADD TO BADTOTALS.
010040        WRITE COUNTS AFTER ADVANCING 2 LINES.
010050        MOVE SPACES TO   COUNTS
010060        MOVE "-DELETIONS MADE " TO GOODCOUNTS.
010070        MOVE DELETES TO GOODTOTALS.
010080        MOVE "UNMATCHED" TO BADCOUNTS.
010090        MOVE BADDELETE   TO BADTOTALS.
010100        WRITE COUNTS AFTER ADVANCING 2 LINES.
010110        MOVE SPACES TO   COUNTS.
010120        MOVE "OUTPUT MASTER RECORDS" TO GOODCOUNTS.
010130        MOVE OUTPUTCOUNT TO GOODTOTALS.
010140        WRITE COUNTS AFTER ADVANCING 2 LINES.
010150        MOVE SPACES TO COUNTS.
```

```
010160          MOVE "CHANGES MADE" TO GOODCOUNTS.
010170          MOVE CHANGES TO GOODTOTALS.
010180          MOVE "UNMATCHED" TO BADCOUNTS.
010190          MOVE BADCHANGE TO BADTOTALS.
010200          WRITE                  COUNTS AFTER ADVANCING 2 LINES.
010210          CLOSE CARDFILE OLDMASTFILE NEWMASTFILE PRINTFILE.
010220          STOP RUN.
```

brought LINE-NUM's contents to more than 54, the second statement in paragraph 030 will cause HEAD-LINES to be PERFORMed. Notice that HEAD-LINES is essentially the same routine used in the file-creation program, but that there is no longer any need for a GO TO instruction as its last sentence; when the MOVE 2 TO LINE-NUM has been executed, program control will be returned to the sentence following the PERFORM instruction which caused HEADLINES to be executed, and execution of the next instruction in 030-MATCHING will take place.[5]

4. The first test for type of update data looks for an equal condition between update and master record codes. If equality exists, a further test is made by a GO TO 040 to identify the card as a change or a deletion. A change results in GOing TO 043-CHANGE, where the first instruction may appear a bit confusing. The MOVE of OLDMASTREC to NEWMASTREC is a group move, which is perfectly safe since the data fields and picture characters have corresponding field lengths and types of characters. The MOVE does not write the new master record on the output storage device; it merely transfers the input master data to the internal-storage area from which it will be written on the output external-storage device. Meanwhile, there is ample time for the four IF statements to determine whether there is significant data in each of the update card fields that is to replace input master data in the new master record. If an alphabetic or alphanumeric card field is equal to SPACES (blanks), no data will be replaced; if not blank, each card field will be moved to its corresponding new master record area, replacing the old data. Note that we could not use the test against SPACES for the EMPZIP field, which is de-

fined as numeric.[6] Instead, we tested positively for a numeric condition, which would occur only if the numeric zip code were actually punched in the update card.

Continuing the CHANGE routine, an identifying literal is moved to the message area on the print-file record, 1 is added to output master and change counts, the new master record is written, and control is transferred by a GO TO to paragraph 060-MATCH-PRINT (whose first instruction causes a PERFORM of the 066-PRINT paragraph, which moves card data to the print record and prints it). Note that immediately thereafter, control returns to the second instruction in 060-MATCHPRINT. This is the series of instructions that must include the possibility of both files ending with a matched-record condition (see pages 82–83). If *both* files do not end, control will be returned to 030-MATCHING.

5. Note that the second test in 040 (which results if the matched card is not a C) results in GOing TO the very brief 046-DELETE routine (which consists of moving the literal "DELETED" to the print message area, counting the deleted record, and GOing TO 060-MATCHPRINT, the purpose of which was just described).

6. A matched card that is neither a C nor a D must be an A if we assume proper sorting of cards has preceded processing (see page 85n). An error-message move, an error-count, and printing by way of paragraph 063 will result, followed by reading of the next card and a return to the MATCHING routine.

7. If the next card record has a lower number than the next master record (second 030-MATCHING instruction), control goes to 050-ADDCHECK. If the first test there shows that the card is properly coded as an addition, control passes to 054-ADD. There we find that group levels in the data definitions of the card and new master records have been arranged to

---

5. Note that the AFTER ADVANCING option in the HEADLINES and other paragraphs involving printing assume that record descriptions for print files meet the specific computer requirements. The total number of characters in the records in our data division is 132; an additional filler position at the beginning of each *could* be required. Also, a SPECIAL-NAMES environment division statement is assumed to identify PAGETOP.

---

6. See Chapter 14 for the basic ANSI test limitations. Some compilers enable this test to be made for a numeric field; it is not, however, a requirement for compilers meeting the ANSI specifications.

permit a single group MOVE of the first 79 columns of card data to the first 79 positions of the new master record area. Only one other MOVE is needed—of SPACES to the remaining 121 positions of the new master area. After taking the necessary counts, moving an ADDED message to the print area, and writing the new master record, we transfer control to 063-ADDPRINT. This must differ from 060-MATCH-PRINT after requiring a PERFORM of the 066-PRINT routine; since only a card record has been processed and an input master record is waiting to be compared to another card, only 020-READ-UPDATE needs to be PERFORMed before proceeding to 030-MATCHING.

Had the card been a C or D, the second or third IF statements in paragraph 050 would have resulted in a related error message, addition to error count, and printing by way of paragraphs 063 and 066 as above.

8. Note that paragraph 035 will be executed when neither of the two conditions in the 030 IF statements is present. The third condition, when the master record has a lower number than the update card, will cause 035-MASTERLOW to be executed—moving and counting the record in the process of writing it as output. Control is then returned to 025-READ-MASTER.

9. The foregoing notes trace the program through all routines except 090-EOJ. Note that this routine has more than a file-closing and STOP RUN function; it causes printing of the five lines of record counts before closing the files. The following items should be considered:

a. The 01-level COUNTS record has been located in the file section of the data division. It has no VALUE clauses which would force its placement in the working-storage section, as does CAPTIONS. Moreover, we can simply WRITE COUNTS if it is a print-file record, saving five *object*-program MOVEs which are implicit in the alternative of WRITE PRINTOUT FROM COUNTS had we placed COUNTS in working-storage.

b. The first record-count line will be printed on a new page as a result of the AFTER ADVANCING PAGETOP; the remaining lines will be double-spaced. Before printing each line, the count or counts and the literals describing them are moved to the corresponding print areas.

c. SPACES are moved to COUNTS after printing each line except the last to make sure that the error counts and names, which are not used on every line, are not retained and printed on a subsequent line where no data has been moved in for printing.

REVIEW MATERIAL

Terms

Updating	End-of-job	Record count
Identification	routine	Validation tests
code field	High value	Matched card
End-of-file	Procedure-name	
routine		

Questions

What are the three major kinds of update data?

Contrast the updating of a sequential file with that of a random-access file.

What are the three possible end-of-file conditions?

What is the function of the PERFORM statement? How does it differ from the GO TO?

How is HIGH-VALUES used in the update procedure described in this chapter?

What types of errors may be detected by the appropriate use of record count recaps and control counts?

Why is a matched addition an error? an unmatched change or deletion?

Why is it recommended that the procedure division be written after the completion of the flowchart?

What kind of statement is used in comparing the update and master record codes?

How do we determine if an alphanumeric field is to be updated? a numeric field?

True-or-False Statements

In updating of sequential files it is essential that update and master files be in the same sequence.

At the time a record is being added to a master file its code number should be higher than the master record code number.

HIGH-VALUES may have a different value on one computer than on another.

If the master input file ends while there are still update records to be read and processed, the remaining update records should all be additions.

The PERFORM statement allows us to execute some statements in a paragraph and not others.

Each update card should match a master record.

The procedure division should follow the sequence and decisions depicted in the flowchart.

Programming

8–1: Write a program to update the 120-position record file you created in the preceding chapter's program. The updating cards will be in the same format as the original ones, except that instead of having a 1 in column 80, the first card will contain an A, C, or D, representing either an addition, change, or deletion. Print all cards in the format of your file-creating program, and follow the rules described in this chapter for validating the update data. In addition, observe the following conditions:

For additions: An 80/A card must be followed by an 80/2 card with the same digits in columns 1–7. If it is not, do not write a tape record; print CARD MISSING in positions 119–130. If an 80/A matches a record on file, print MATCHED ADD in positions 119–130 and do not write a tape record.

For changes: An 80/C card may be, but need not be, followed by a matching 80/2 card. If there is no matching tape record (on columns 1–7), print NOT ON FILE for the update data. For valid changes, move only those fields which are punched in the update data cards to the output tape record. A blank field in change data cards means that the tape-file record data is to be copied onto the output tape record.

For deletions: There will be only an 80/D card, with punching in columns 1–7 and 80. If there is no matching tape record, print NOT ON FILE for the update data.

Page length, page numbering, and headings and skips to new pages should follow the same rules as in your file-creating program. You may find that you can avoid considerable coding by duplicating many of the data division and procedure division cards from your file-creating program.

9

REPORT PRINTING INVOLVING ARITHMETIC, GROUP TOTALS, AND PRINT EDITING

NATURE OF REPORTS

One of the oldest and most frequent uses of computers is the printing of reports from sorted file records showing accumulations of quantity or money figures and presenting one or more levels of group totals within the file as well as totals for the entire file. For example, a company-wide payroll report based on a file sorted by employee within department within plant might list each employee's earnings, showing departmental earnings totals at the end of each departmental listing of employees, and plant totals following the last departmental total within plant. The following small-scale illustration may help to visualize the group total concept:

PLANT	DEPT	EMPLOYEE	GROSS PAY
01	01	A ALBERTSON	205.88
01	01	B CURTIS	157.26
		DEPT TOTAL	363.14*
01	02	D EDWARDS	198.46
01	02	F GORDON	217.50
		DEPT TOTAL	415.96*
		PLANT TOTAL	879.10**
02	01	E ALLEN	153.06
02	01	C CALHOUN	147.85
		DEPT TOTAL	300.91*
02	07	B BAKER	222.44
02	07	J JINKS	200.00
		DEPT TOTAL	422.44*
		PLANT TOTAL	723.35**
		COMPANY TOTAL	1,602.45***

The least inclusive level of totals (in this case, department) is referred to as *minor*. When there are three levels of inclusiveness, an *intermediate* total includes all totals of all minor groups within it, and a *major* total includes intermediate totals within it. Note that the plant-01 total is the sum of the two departments within plant 01; likewise, the plant-02 total is the sum of the two plant-02 department totals. If there were numerous companies in the above report, plant totals would be regarded as intermediate, and company totals as major since each company total would include all plant totals within the company. In the above illustration, however, since only a single company is represented in the file, the company total is a *final* total. In the illustration used here, totals are identified by words indicating the group level represented by the total, and by one or more asterisks to the right of the total figure (the number of asterisks depends on the inclusiveness of the total). Often only one of these two ways is used, the choice being dependent on the space available within the report format as limited by the length of the computer printing line.

A report may consist *only* of total lines. If we have a file of sales data sorted by salesman within sales region within product, and any salesman may have numerous sales of a product, a report in product sequence would consist of a salesman (minor) total line; salesman totals would be accumulated to a regional (intermediate) total line, and all regional sales for each product would be accumulated in the product (major) total line.

To provide a programming exercise in the use of arithmetic, handling of more than one level of totals, and the editing of numeric data in report-printing, let us describe a sorted file to be used in preparing a sales analysis, specify the report details we want to get from it, and then, before writing the program, determine what additional COBOL rules we must know to be able to write the program.

SPECIFICATIONS FOR A REPORT

Assume a file of 100-character records containing sales data in sequence by salesman number within sales region number. From it we wish to obtain a report in the following columnar format: (Note that in Figure 9–1 this is set in a single line across the page)

REGION NUMBER	SALESMAN NUMBER	TOTAL SALES AMOUNT	–	TOTAL RETURNS AMOUNT	=	NET SALES AMOUNT	COMMISSIONS EARNED

The file record layout shows that region number occupies positions 1 and 2, that salesman number occupies positions 3–5, that both gross sales and returns are in the same area (41–47), expressed in dollars and cents, and that, though there is no dollar-and-cent figure for commissions, positions 67–69 in each record contain three digits indicating a commission rate (for example, 050 for 5%, 075 for 7½%). If we wish to have the report in tabulated form (no detail printing of each record), showing one line of data for each salesman within a region, a total line for each region, and a set of final totals, the following questions arise:

- How do we recognize the positive or negative condition of the sales amount?
- How are decimal points in the dollar-and-cent and commission rate fields handled in the arithmetic instructions?
- What instructions are necessary for addition, subtraction, and multiplication? (We must multiply sales by commission rate to get commissions earned.)
- How do we "edit" our printed report figures to show possible negative amounts, commas for thousands, decimal points preceding cents, and such identifying characters as $ and *?
- And, equally important, how do we coordinate the program routines to accumulate the three levels of totals and print them at the proper intervals within the report?

If we give attention to the arithmetic handling (including editing), we may then be able to flowchart our programming steps.

ARITHMETIC: DATA DIVISION REQUIREMENTS

Signed and Unsigned Fields; Decimal Place Recognition

Numeric fields used for arithmetic may be unsigned (have no indication whether they are positive or negative). In this case, if a whole number, the field is described in the same way as any other numeric field that is a whole number, and is treated as if positive. When it is a decimal, or contains a decimal, the field must be described in the data division in a way that locates the decimal point if it is to be used properly in arithmetic processing. This is done in the PICTURE clause by using a V at the decimal point location. The stored data field contains no character position with either a V or a decimal point; the V is not counted as a character in determining field length. The V merely marks the position of the decimal point for proper execution of arithmetic by the object program; since it takes up no storage space, the V is normally referred to as the *implied* decimal point.

Two of the numeric fields in our sales file record involve decimals. If neither required a sign, we would describe them as:

```
02   SALES        PIC 9(5)V99.
02   COMMRATE     PIC V999.
```

Notice that SALES is a seven-position field, the V marking the dividing line between dollars and cents. Notice also that COMMRATE is defined as *entirely* a decimal, since a rate of 7½% or 10% would be keypunched or recorded as 075 or 100 and would be a decimal value of .075 or .100. The handling of decimal values in MOVE statements should be recalled at this time. While whole numbers are MOVEd from right to left, decimals are MOVEd (like alphabetic and alphanumeric data) from left to right, and the receiving field is truncated or zero-filled accordingly. Check this principle in the following examples of possible MOVEs of these two fields:

Sending Field, Picture, and Contents			Receiving Field, Picture, and Contents		
SALES	9(5)V99	1234567	FIELDA	9(6)V999	012345670
SALES	9(5)V99	1234567	FIELDB	9(6)	012345
COMMRATE	V999	105	FIELDC	9V9999	01050
COMMRATE	V999	105	FIELDD	9V99	010
COMMRATE	V999	105	FIELDE	999	000
SALES	9(5)V99	1234567	FIELDF	9999V99	234567

The position of the decimal point in the field contents has been noted by the symbol   ; like the V, there is no character position existing in the field contents for it. The V in the data definition locates the decimal point. This is so that procedure division arithmetic instructions in the source program will cause the object program to allocate the proper number of character positions for the number of integer and decimal positions required in computing the result field. Notice in the above examples that the integer and decimal portions of a field are moved independently and in opposite directions: integer areas are either zero-filled or truncated at the left; decimal areas are zero-filled or truncated at the right. Note also that an attempt to move a complete decimal field to a complete integer field results in complete truncation of the decimal data and generates zeroes in the integer area. The results would be exactly the opposite if an attempt were made to move a complete integer field to a complete decimal field; the integer would be completely truncated and the decimal area generated as zeroes.

When one field in a card or stored-file record can hold either positive or negative numeric data, and there is no code elsewhere in the record to indicate which condition exists, the low-order (rightmost) digit in the field will carry some bit identity which indicates the condition of the field. When original data is keypunched, a positive field is usually punched with *no* additional punch in the rightmost column, but a negative amount is punched with an eleven-zone punch above the rightmost digit in the field. If properly defined in a program data division, the card field will be read as positive or negative and (also if properly defined) any internally or externally stored field receiving the data will carry some bit identity of the rightmost digit—the computer's *equivalent* of a twelve-zone punch for a positive field or an eleven-zone punch for a negative field.

To identify a data field as having the capacity of being either positive or negative, we must *sign* the field's picture at its origin in the data division; and if we transfer the data, whether by MOVEs or arithmetic, to some other field, the receiving field must also be signed if we wish to be able to recognize the negative values as such. In any data division record fields except those for print-file records, this is done by placing an S to the left of the PICTURE contents; for example: 02 SALES PIC S9(5)V99. Like the V, the S occupies no character position in storage; it serves as a source program signal for the object program's arithmetic execution to check the rightmost position of the field for bit recognition to determine whether to treat the field as positive or negative.

To add or move a quantity field to another quantity field, we must be sure that we have signed (or left unsigned) the data division PICTURE of each field, since signed fields are treated "algebraically" in arithmetic operations, while unsigned fields are treated as if always positive. For example, if we say ADD FIELDA FIELDB TO FIELDC, and all fields are signed, if FIELDA contents are +350 and FIELDB contents are −200, a net of +150 will be added to FIELDC, since adding a negative number is, algebraically, subtraction. If, even though these fields contained positive and negative bit identification, their PICTUREs did not contain the S sign, the same instruction would result in adding 550 to FIELDC, since the sign bit would be ignored and all fields would be treated as if positive.

Omission of the S in any arithmetic field PICTURE can alter the condition of the result. Assume that FIELDX can be either positive or negative, and that it is being added to a field called TOTALS. Consider the following three conditions:

FIELDX PICTURE	TOTALS PICTURE	Results in TOTALS
Has S	Has S	Positive or negative, depending on data.
No S	Has S	Always positive if only input is FIELDX.
Has S	No S	May be negative but cannot be identified as such on printout.

Except for the edit character P, which has a fairly special use, the characters S and V are the only ones used for editing data pictures in preparation for internal computer processing.[1] Most of the remaining edit characters are intended for editing numeric printing.

EDITING NUMERIC PRINTING

Unlike the S and V, any edit character for numeric printing *does* occupy a character position, in both storage area and printed data. The edit characters are included in the PICTURE of the edited data field that will eventually be printed. If they are *insertion* characters, they occupy a print character space for each insertion, adding to the length of the stored-field data as it appears in the field when printed. *Replacement* characters simply take the place of leading zeroes when printing the stored field that has been moved to the edited print area.

ANSI COBOL specifications classify editing by insertion into four methods:

---

1. The use of P for zero insertion in numeric fields, as well as the use of blanks in alphanumeric editing, is discussed in chapter 11.

1. Simple insertion, in which the editing character is positioned in the PICTURE between any two characters, and will be printed as positioned. Characters used for simple insertion are the comma (,), the letter B to represent a blank space, and zero (0).

2. Special insertion. This usage refers only to the period (.). Its normal use is as a decimal point, to be inserted as an additional character position where the implied decimal point (V) is indicated in the field being moved to the print area. The decimal point may be used only once in any PICTURE and may *not* be used as the last character in the PICTURE character-string.

3. Fixed insertion. This refers to the use of the edit character at a fixed position, either to the left or to the right of the edited field when it is printed. The characters used in this way are the currency sign ($), the positive sign (+), the negative sign (−), and either of two two-position symbols, DB and CR, also used as negative signs. Only one of the four positive–negative symbols may be used in a PICTURE; the reason for this will be evident from illustrations to follow.

4. Floating insertion. This is a repeated use of either the $, +, or − sign in the PICTURE, beginning one position to the left of the leftmost data character and continuing in all positions which might be leading zeroes. This usage results in having the floating sign print only once, immediately to the left of the first significant character in the numeric character-string.

The ANSI specifications also distinguish between two types of zero suppression:

1. Replacement with spaces, in which the letter Z is inserted in place of the leftmost character in the PICTURE and repeated as far as it is desired to replace leading zeroes with spaces. A simple version of this has been shown in connection with page numbering and record counts.

2. Replacement with asterisks, in which the * is used in the same way as just described for the Z. The result is to replace each leading zero with an asterisk (*). This is sometimes referred to as the check-protecting asterisk, though there is now a tendency to use the floating $ sign for this purpose. The replacement asterisk is the only usage of * in editing. When an asterisk is used to flag printed totals, as will be seen a little later, it is a nonnumeric literal, not an edit character.

Since zero suppression replacing with spaces is the most basic form of numeric PICTURE editing, and may be combined with simple, special, or fixed insertion (and often with all three!), it seems logical to begin a numeric editing description with a discussion of zero suppression of this type. Zero suppression is a *replacement* function; it does not itself change the length of the edited print-field PICTURE as compared to the length of the field whose data was moved to the print field. Consider a stored field, PICTURE 9(6), whose data is being moved to a six-position print area. Using the letter b to indicate a blank space, we can obtain these various results depending on the contents of the sending field and the absence or kind of zero suppression used in the print-field PICTURE:

Sending Field Contents	Print-Field PICTURE	Printed Results
004276	9(6)	004276
004276	Z(6)	bb4276
000000	Z(6)	bbbbbb
000000	ZZZZ99	bbbb00
010307	ZZZZ99	b10307
000005	ZZZZ99	bbbb05

Sometimes a smaller field is moved to a larger one for printing. Assuming a sending field with a PICTURE of 9(4), we might have the following:

1234	9(6)	001234
0012	Z(6)	bbbb12
0000	Z(6)	bbbbbb
0000	ZZZZ99	bbbb00

Zero suppression with replacement by asterisks is essentially the same as with replacement by spaces, except for one condition involving a fixed-insertion decimal point, as will be indicated. In the examples above, the use of asterisks instead of Zs in each print-field PICTURE would result in the printing of an asterisk instead of a space in each print position indicated by a b. In any one PICTURE, the Z and the asterisk are mutually exclusive as zero-suppression characters; either one or the other may be used, but not both.

Simple insertion characters (space, comma, and zero) may be placed anywhere within the print PICTURE character-string. The space (B) is ordinarily used to separate a data field into readable segments, as in the case of the date and social security number fields below. The zero is seldom used as an actual in-

tabular presentations of mathematical or financial data. The comma's ordinary use is to set off thousands, millions, etc. When zero suppression is combined with simple insertion characters, the comma will be replaced by the replacement character used. Consider the following:

DATA FIELD		PRINT FORMAT	
PICTURE	*Contents*	*PICTURE*	*Results*
9(9)	053260905	999B99B9999	053 26 0905
9(6)	070473	99B99B99	07 04 73
9(7)	0123456	9,999,999	0,123,456
9(7)	0123456	Z,ZZZ,ZZZ	123,456
9(7)	0000123	Z,ZZZ,ZZZ	123
9(7)	0000000	Z,ZZZ,ZZZ	
9(5)	04321	00099999	00004321
9(5)	04321	ZZZ99000	4321000

The "special" insertion character (.) in the edited PICTURE must be aligned with the V in the numeric data field moved to the edited PICTURE. When the data field has no V, the decimal point is implied as being to the right of the rightmost digit. When zero suppression is combined with decimal-point insertion, complete replacement with *spaces* will blank out the decimal point, but complete replacement with asterisks will not. The following are examples of special insertion and typical combinations of simple insertion and zero suppression with it:

DATA FIELD		PRINT FORMAT	
PICTURE	*Contents*	*PICTURE*	*Results*
9999	1234	9999.99	1234.00
9V99	123	999.99	001.23
9V99	123	ZZZ.99	1.23
9V99	001	ZZZ.99	.01
999V99	00000	ZZZ.ZZ	
999V99	00123	ZZZ.ZZ	1.23
999V99	00123	***.***	**1.23
999V99	00001	***.99	***.01
999V99	00000	***.**	***.**
999V99	00000	***.99	***.00
999V99	00000	ZZZ.99	.00
99999V99	0003456	**,***.99	****34.56
99999V99	0003456	ZZ,ZZZ.99	34.56
999V99	00001	ZZZ.ZZ	.01

Note that although the asterisk will replace a comma, it does not replace a decimal point when all zeroes are the data contents, as does a space when Z is the suppression character. Note also that the Z replaces leading zeroes with spaces until the decimal point or the first significant digit is reached, whichever occurs first, if the data contains any significant digits.

If the $, +, —, CR, or DB symbol is used for

fixed insertion, each symbol can be used only once in the character string. The $ can be used in the same string as any one of the other four; but with or without the $, only one of the other four symbols is permitted in a PICTURE. The use of one excludes the use of the other three. The $ and + can be used whether or not the field being moved to the print area is signed (though there is very seldom any purpose in printing the + beside items that are known to be always positive). The symbols DB, CR, and — will print only (*a*) when used in connection with a signed field that is being moved to the print area, and (*b*) when the contents of that signed field are negative. The + as an editing symbol has a double effect when used in connection with a signed sending field: when the contents are positive or zero, the + will print; when the contents are negative, the — will print.

When used as fixed-insertion characters, these five symbols must be positioned in the print PICTURE character-string as follows:

- The $ must be the leftmost character, except when a leftmost + or — is used.
- The + or the — may be used as either the first (leftmost) or last (rightmost) character.
- The DB or CR may be used only as the last (rightmost) two characters in the string.

Examples of these five edit symbols used in accord with the above rules and in combination with simple and special insertion and zero suppression follow:

DATA FIELD		PRINT FORMAT	
PICTURE	*Contents*	*PICTURE*	*Results*
9999V99	123456	$Z,ZZZ.99	$1.234.56
9999V99	000123	$Z,ZZZ.99	$ 1.23
999V99	01234	+$ZZZ.99	+$ 12.34
S999V99	01234	+$ZZZ.99	—$ 12.34
S999V99	01234	—$ZZZ.99	$ 12.34
S999V99	01234	—$ZZZ.99	—$ 12.34
999V99	01234	—$ZZZ.99	$ 12.34
9999	1234	+ZZZ9	+1234
S9999	0123	+ZZZ9	+123
S9999	0123	+ZZZ9	—123
S9999	0123	—ZZZ9	123
S9999	0123	—ZZZ9	—123
9999	0000	$ZZZ9	+0
999V99	01234	$ZZZ.99+	$12.34+
S999V99	01234	$ZZZ.99+	$12.34—
S999V99	01234	$ZZZ.99—	$12.34

Note: All of the foregoing illustrations of leftmost + and — can be changed to rightmost + and — editing with the results suggested by the preceding three samples. The + and — will appear at the right under the same conditions as they appeared at the left.

PICTURE	Contents	PICTURE	Results
999V99	12345	ZZZ.99DB	123.45
S999V99	12345	ZZZ.99DB	123.45
S999V99	12345	ZZZ.99DB	123.45DB
999V99	12345	ZZZ.99CR	123.45
S999V99	12345	ZZZ.99CR	123.45
S999V99	12345	ZZZ.99CR	123.45CR
S999V99	00000	ZZZ.99CR	.00
S999V99	00000	----.--	bbbbbbb
S999V99	00001	----.--	bbb-.01
S999V99	00001	----.99	bbb-.01

Since the fixed $, +, or − sign used at the leftmost position of a field which may contain a few or many digits can sometimes be difficult to read, or may permit (as in instances of altering checks) insertion of digits at the left to increase small figures, the *floating insertion* of the $, +, or − is provided for in ANSI COBOL. The edit PICTURE must contain the first floating character as an extra position at the left of the string and, except for the simple and special insertion characters (such as , or .), be repeated as far to the right as it is desired to have the single character print. Only one of the three ($, +, or −) signs may be used as a floating character in an edited PICTURE. In effect, the floating insertion character does the same job as zero suppression, except that it supplies an edit symbol one position to the left of the first significant character in the string. If a floating character is entered in the PICTURE all the way across, and if a decimal point is included and there are significant digits to its right in the field contents, the floating character will print to the left of the decimal point; but when the field contents are zero, with or without a decimal point, the entire printed field will be spaces—the floating character itself will not be printed. When the + or − is used as a floating edit symbol, it will print only if the sending data field PICTURE is signed and the condition represented by the sign occurs in the field. In the examples of floating edit symbols below, a space is represented by a b in order to show the actual number of printing positions to be provided.

DATA FIELD		PRINT FORMAT	
PICTURE	**Contents**	**PICTURE**	**Results**
999V99	56789	$$$$.99	$567.89
999V99	00123	$$$$.99	bb$1.23
999V99	00001	$$$$.99	bbb$.01
999V99	56789	++++.++	+567.89
999V99	56789	----.--	b567.89
S999V99	00012	++++.++	bbb+.12
S999V99	00001	++++.99	bbb+.01
S999V99	00001	++++.++	bbb+.01
S999V99	00000	++++.++	bbbbbbb
S999V99	01234	----.--	bb12.34
999V99	01234	----.--	bb12.34
S999V99	01234	----.--	b−12.34
S999V99	01234	++++.++	b−12.34

ARITHMETIC: PROCEDURE DIVISION REQUIREMENTS

Unsigned and Signed Fields; Basic Terminology

Basic arithmetic in COBOL employs the ADD, SUBTRACT, MULTIPLY, and DIVIDE instructions. Data items used in arithmetic, whether numeric literals or numeric fields in file records or working storage, are referred to as operands, and any operand is limited to a size length of 18 digits, whether integers, decimals, or a combination of both. Operands need not be of the same size or have a common decimal point as long as the area in which the result of the arithmetic is placed is large enough to accommodate it; COBOL arithmetic instructions result in object program operations that align integers and decimals according to the data definition requirements in the source program. If all operands are unsigned, all results are treated as positive (even when a number has been subtracted from a smaller one). If one of two or more operands named in an arithmetic instruction is not signed, it will be treated as positive, and the results of the instruction will depend on the signs of the other operands.

When all operands in an instruction are signed, arithmetic takes place following the algebraic sign rules:

• If + and − items are added, the − items are added negatively, and the net result follows the sign of the greater number.

• If + and − items are subtracted from a positive number, − items are actually added and + items subtracted, with the net result following the sign of the net difference.

• Multiplying + by − quantities or − by + quantities will give a negative result.

• Multiplying + by + quantities or − by − quantities will give a positive result.

• Division follows the same rule as multiplication.

Form of Simple Arithmetic Statements

In their simplest form, COBOL arithmetic instructions have a common pattern, expressed as follows, with the operand names being indicated by . . . . :

ADD . . . . TO . . . .
SUBTRACT . . . . FROM . . . .
MULTIPLY . . . . BY . . . .
DIVIDE . . . . INTO . . . .

In each of the above statements, the operand named at the left may be either a numeric literal or the data-name of a stored field; the operand named at the right *must* be the data-name of a stored field. The reason for this is that in the above basic statement form, the result of the operation is transferred to the stored-field area named as the operand at the right; the naming of a literal does not refer to a stored data field.

It should be understood that the arithmetic does not take place in the rightmost operand area. The COBOL arithmetic statement results in the compiler setting aside a large enough work area in which to execute the arithmetic for the object program so that correct results are provided. This area may be considerably larger than the rightmost operand area. When the arithmetic is completed, results are moved from the work area to the result operand field based on the actual or implied decimal points in the operand fields. Either high- or low-order truncation can occur if the rightmost operand does not have enough integer or decimal positions to accept the entire result from the work area.

ADD and SUBTRACT Statements

The ADD and SUBTRACT statements differ from the MULTIPLY and DIVIDE statements in one important respect: we can ADD or SUBTRACT several data items as operands at the left in a single statement, whereas a MULTIPLY or DIVIDE statement can have only one operand following the verb and one following the connecting word. We can say ADD FIELDA, 300, FIELDB TO FIELDC, and the entire sum will be stored in FIELDC if it is large enough to hold the result; but a statement such as MULTIPLY FIELDX, FIELDY BY FIELDZ will be diagnosed as an error by the COBOL compiler. The effect of a simple ADD statement (ADD FIELDA FIELDB TO FIELDC) on the contents of the operand at the right is shown below:

Notice that we made no mention of contents "before and after" statement execution for the operands following the ADD. As is true in all the arithmetic statements, the contents of operand data fields following the verb (and preceding the connector words) are left unchanged by execution of the arithmetic. Only the rightmost operand has its contents changed. This means that the contents of all but the rightmost operand can be used again unchanged until replaced by new data. If the rightmost operand is an input record field, it should be used as a result area only while the one record is being processed, since its contents will be replaced if data from the next record is read in. Normally, working-storage areas should be employed as operands and used to accumulate results of arithmetic operations that extend beyond the processing of a single record.

Other conditions which should be carefully noted are the facts that (*a*) combinations of signed and unsigned fields can produce misleading effects, (*b*) decimal areas to the right of the decimal point will be correctly aligned by an arithmetic statement (though they will be truncated to the number of decimal places in the result field if the result field contains fewer decimal positions than one or more of the operands), and (*c*) a result field not large enough to hold the results of the arithmetic will cause high-order (leftmost) digits to be lost even though all operands are properly signed (see example below). We will see a little later that optional clauses in the arithmetic statements can provide reasonable accuracy in decimal truncation and test for results of arithmetic which may cause the result-field capacity to be exceeded.

No examples of the use of numeric literals appear in the table below. Their use in all arithmetic statements is permitted with two already-indicated restrictions: they cannot be used as the rightmost operand (result field), and they cannot end with a decimal point expressed as part of the literal. Care must be taken, however, to express an internal decimal at the proper

FIELDA		FIELDB		FIELDC		
PICTURE	*Contents*	*PICTURE*	*Contents*	*PICTURE*	*Contents*	
					Before	*After*
9999	1234	999	535	9999	0000	1769
9999	1234	999	535	9999	4321	6090
9999	1234	999	535	S9999	4321	2552
9999	1234	S999	535	9999	0000	0699
S9999	5678	999	535	9999	0000	5143
S9999	5678	999	535	S9999	0123	5020
999V99	12345	9V999	1236	9999V99	000000	012468 truncated right
999V99	12345	999	321	9999V99	000000	044445
S9999	1234	S999	535	S9999	0000	0699
S9999	9468	S999	535	S9999	0000	0003 truncated left

place in the numeric literal, and to use no other special characters. For example, if we wish to ADD $12.50 to another operand, we must specify ADD 12.50 . . .; we cannot ADD $12.50 or specify ADD 1250. Similarly, in multiplying by a fixed percentage, such as 5.85%, we must specify MULTIPLY .0585 BY . . .; we cannot use 5.85 or 5.85% or specify MULTIPLY FIELDX BY .0585.

In a SUBTRACT FIELDA FIELDB FROM FIELDC statement, the following results would be developed from the contents given for the three fields:

when signed fields are used, the following simple rules apply:

- When both fields are signed: If the original contents of the two fields have unlike signs, the result is negative; if the original contents of the two fields have like signs, the result is positive.
- When the result (rightmost) field is unsigned, the result will be regarded as positive regardless of the other field's sign.
- When the leftmost (multiplicand or divisor)

FIELDA		FIELDB		FIELDC		
PICTURE	Contents	PICTURE	Contents	PICTURE	Contents Before	After
9999	1234	999	535	9999	0321	1448
9999	1234	999	535	9999	4321	2552
9999	1234	999	535	S9999	4321̄	6090̄
9999	1234	S999	535̄	9999	0000	0699
S9999	5678̄	999	535	9999	0000	5143
S9999	5678̄	999	535	S9999	0123̇	5266̇
999V99	12345	999	321	9999V99	050000	005555
999V99	12345	9V999	1234	9999V99	050000	037531 truncated right
S9999	1234̇	S999	535̄	S9999	3000̇	2301̇
S9999	9468̇	S999	535̇	S9999	0000	0003̄ truncated left

Note that the same problems and conditioned results are obtained as with addition in connection with mixing of signed and unsigned fields, aligning and truncating decimal positions, and having the rightmost operand too small to contain the complete results.

The ADD and SUBTRACT statement formats used in the above examples are available in *all* ANSI-based COBOL compilers. Lower-level compilers, however, may not have the following capability: If we wish to add the contents of FIELDX, FIELDY, and FIELDZ to *both* FIELDA and FIELDB, higher-level compilers will handle the statement (ADD FIELDX FIELDY FIELDZ TO FIELDA FIELDB), and permit subtraction from two different fields in the same way. In the lower-level compilers, two statements (one each for FIELDA and FIELDB) would be required.

field is unsigned, the result will have the same sign as the original contents of the result (rightmost) field.

The tables (top, p. 103) show some fairly typical examples of simple MULTIPLY and DIVIDE statements. In any of the cases given, a numeric literal could have been substituted for FIELDA (but, of course, *not* for FIELDB). Note that in simple multiplication and division statements the likelihood of truncation, particularly where decimalized results are sure to occur, seems much greater than in addition or subtraction. There are three options, available in even the lower-level ANSI-based COBOL compilers, which make it easier to avoid some of these hazards. These are the GIVING, ROUNDED, and SIZE ERROR options.

MULTIPLY and DIVIDE Statements

If we write statements such as MULTIPLY FIELDA BY FIELDB or DIVIDE FIELDA INTO FIELDB, we know that the contents of FIELDA will be left unchanged and that the multiplier or dividend in FIELDB will be replaced by the product or quotient. Care should be taken, then, to make sure that fields used as multipliers or dividends are also large enough to contain the product or quotient. It should also be kept in mind that

The GIVING Option

This option requires the use of an additional field beyond the operands included in the simplest form of arithmetic statement. Frequently this means creation of a working-storage area as the additional field, although sometimes an output record field is the ultimate result field of input record fields used as arithmetic operands. In these cases, the output record field may be used as the result field named when the GIVING option is used.

	FIELDA		FIELDB			
	PICTURE	Contents	PICTURE	Original Contents	Result	
MULTIPLY	999	021	9(6)	000456	009576	
BY	S999	021	S9(6)	000456	009576	
	S999	021	S9(6)	000456	009576	
	S999	021	S9(6)	000456	009576	
	S999	502	S9(6)	600008	204016	truncated left
	V9999	0500	999V99	31760	01588	truncated right
	V9999	0585	999V99	31760	01857	truncated right
DIVIDE	999	021	9(5)	00462	00022	
INTO	V999	021	9(5)	00462	22000	
	V999	021	9999	0462	2000	truncated left
	999	021	9(5)	00479	00022	truncated right
	999	021	999V99	47900	02280	truncated right

In the illustrations used above for addition and subtraction, we would make the following changes when using the GIVING option:

Instead of: ADD FIELDA FIELDB TO FIELDC
we would say: ADD FIELDA FIELDB FIELDC GIVING FIELDD

Notice that the connector TO, a key word in the simplest ADD format, is not used with the GIVING option:

Instead of: SUBTRACT FIELDA FIELDB FROM FIELDC
we would say: SUBTRACT FIELDA FIELDB FROM FIELDC
                 GIVING FIELDD

Notice that in this case we have not eliminated any words from the simple statement; we have simply added GIVING and the result-operand-name.

When the GIVING option is used for any arithmetic operation, the contents of the operand to the right of GIVING are not included in the arithmetic; the results of the arithmetic done solely on the operands to the left of GIVING are entered in the rightmost operand, clearing out its previous contents. This means that the operand following GIVING cannot be used as an accumulating field. If the GIVING result-field is to be accumulated, the accumulation must be done in another stored field. The use of the GIVING option, however, releases the programmer from operating within the limits of the largest of the original operands. In the cases of truncated results in the ADD and SUBTRACT statements on pages 101 and 102, the GIVING option enables the programmer to set up a working-storage area with enough additional integer or decimal digits to accept the maximum results.

The GIVING option adds flexibility to the MULTIPLY statement; instead of MULTIPLY FIELDA BY FIELDB, we substitute MULTIPLY FIELDA BY FIELDB GIVING FIELDC. Seemingly this is no great advantage; but whereas before we could use only one numeric literal, and then only as the first operand, it is now permissible to say MULTIPLY FIELDX BY .0585 GIVING FIELDZ. In addition, the result-field length is no longer restricted to the length of the operand following BY.

Even greater flexibility is created by the two GIVING options of the DIVIDE statement. Instead of DIVIDE FIELDA INTO FIELDB, we may say either DIVIDE FIELDA INTO FIELDB GIVING FIELDC or DIVIDE FIELDB BY FIELDA GIVING FIELDC. In other words, the forced assumption in the basic DIVIDE, that the number of digits in the dividend field is always larger than the divisor, no longer limits us. We can state the dividend first, followed by BY; or the divisor first, followed by INTO. Mathematical grammarians who find the term DIVIDE . . . INTO a logical monstrosity may prefer the correct grammar of DIVIDE . . . BY. In any event, the operand following GIVING can be set up within the 18-digit limitation, and numeric literals can be used as either dividend or divisor.

As mentioned earlier (see page 78), the GIVING option, since it embraces a computation and a MOVE, has the added advantage of permitting the programmer to specify an edited field as the operand following GIVING.

In the tabular examples given for the four basic arithmetic statements, truncations at the left because of insufficient integer positions were shown. Either with or without the GIVING option, these truncations can be avoided by making sure that the result-field operand is large enough to accommodate the number of integers in the answer. Decimal amounts, however, particularly those resulting from a MULTIPLY or DIVIDE operation, are usually desired to be truncated—but in a logical manner. If a result is to be limited to two places beyond the decimal point, the addition of a 5 in the third place beyond the decimal point will add 1 to the second—if the digit in the third place is greater than 4. This process is sometimes referred to as "half-adjusting," but is more commonly referred to as "rounding." ANSI-based COBOL compilers contain the ROUNDED option.

The ROUNDED Option

With or without the GIVING option, the addition of the word ROUNDED following the last operand in an arithmetic statement will improve the accuracy of a truncated decimal value in the result. Let us look at the right-truncated items in the arithmetic examples and see what improvement the ROUNDED option would make:

ADD FIELDA FIELDB TO FIELDC ROUNDED would produce:
```
    123V45   (Field A)
    1V236    (Field B)
        5 rounding
   0124V69   (Field C)
```
—more correct than the truncated 0124V68.

SUBTRACT FIELDA FIELDB FROM FIELDC ROUNDED would produce:

	0500V00	(Field C)
minus Field A:	123V45 =	0376V55
minus Field B:		1V234
		0375V316
Rounding:		5
Result shown as field C:		0375V32

—again more correct than the truncated 0375V31.

MULTIPLY FIELDA BY FIELDB: The first truncation did no harm, since V0500 multiplied by 317V00 is 015V880000 anyway, and the rounding of $\dfrac{5}{015V88}$ causes the answer of 015V88 to be moved to FIELDB. But the second example is different:

	FIELDA	V0585
	FIELDB	317V60
		V 35100
		V4095
		0V585
		17V55
		018V579600
Rounding		5
Result to Field C		018V58

—the correct figure.

DIVIDE FIELDA INTO FIELDB: The result of dividing 479 by 22 (22 "into" 479) carried to four decimal places is 22.8095. If we DIVIDE FIELDA INTO FIELDB ROUNDED, the rounding before the result is placed in FIELDB is as follows:

First example: 00022V8095   Second example: 022V8095

V5		V 5
00023	—Result in FIELDB—	022V81

The advantages of the ROUNDED option are fairly obvious; however, it need not be used in every arithmetic instruction that involves fields with decimals. A few practical guidelines follow.

For addition and subtraction, use ROUNDED when the operands have decimal areas of differing lengths, and the result has fewer decimal places than the operand with the greatest number of decimal places. Example: ADD FIELDA FIELDB TO FIELDC.

Use ROUNDED where the respective PICTURES are:	99V999	999V9	9999V99
ROUNDED not needed where the PICTURES are:	99V99	999V99	9999V99

For multiplication, use ROUNDED when the number of decimal places in the product is less than the *sum* of the decimal places in the multiplier and multiplicand. MULTIPLY FIELDA BY FIELDB GIVING FIELDC is sufficient if the respective PICTURES

MULTIPLY FIELDA BY FIELDB GIVING FIELDC is sufficient if the respective PICTURES are: 999V99   99   and 9(5)V99, but when they are: 999V99   V99   and 999V99 ROUNDED is needed because two decimal places are being dropped.

For division, no all-inclusive rule can be stated, except possibly that any DIVIDE statement should include the ROUNDED option. As indicated in the example where the quotient contained no decimals at all, absence of the ROUNDED option could lead even to inaccurate integer results.

The SIZE ERROR Option

It has been indicated that care should be taken to see that result fields are large enough to accommodate the product of the arithmetic statement. Nevertheless, there are some conditions in which it is expectable that data errors or other circumstances will cause an arithmetic result to exceed the size of the field set up to receive it. For example, an instruction to MULTIPLY RATE BY HOURS GIVING GROSSPAY ROUNDED, where the respective PICTURES are 99V99, 99V9, and 999V99, can result in four-digit result integers. Presumably GROSSPAY's size limit was based on knowledge that correct hourly payroll data should not result in a figure higher than $999.99. The SIZE ERROR option can be used to identify the limit-exceeding condition and initiate a programmed course of action when it occurs.

The words SIZE ERROR or ON SIZE ERROR, followed by some imperative statement, can be appended to an arithmetic statement (following either the last operand-name or ROUNDED). In the above case, our statement could be either MULTIPLY RATE BY HOURS GIVING GROSSPAY ROUNDED ON SIZE ERROR GO TO ERROR-ROUTINE or MULTIPLY RATE BY HOURS GIVING GROSS-PAY ROUNDED SIZE ERROR GO TO ERROR-ROUTINE. ERROR-ROUTINE might consist of printing an input record-image and error-message and a return to the input-file reading routine.

The SIZE ERROR option can be used with any of the four arithmetic operations. With the DIVIDE statement, it provides the additional features of detecting division by zero as a SIZE ERROR.

FLOWCHART AND PROGRAM

We now return to the task of programming the report specified on page 96. The print layout (Figure 9–1) shows us that no printing of individual records is required; double-spaced total lines, with an extra double space following region totals, are specified. Since there will presumably be numerous salesman total lines preceding each region total line, the extra double space will help to make the report easier to read by providing more unprinted space between regions, as well as between the last region total line and the final total line. No headings are specified, nor is page-numbering or number of lines per page. Accepting this literally, we will omit any instructions to advance to a new page, except when starting the report.

The flowchart shown in Figure 9–2 is relatively simple. Once we have opened the one input file and read a record, we must consider what the AT END condition requires. Obviously final totals must be printed before closing the files and STOP RUN. But if there are no more records to be read, we must also at this point print the last salesman totals and the last region totals; our routine for an AT END—yes condition therefore calls for performing region total routines (which include salesman total routines as an initial step) before printing final totals.

If we are not AT END, there is a record to be processed and we test first whether the just-read record has a region number higher than the preceding record. If so, this means that totals must be printed for not only the region represented by the preceding record

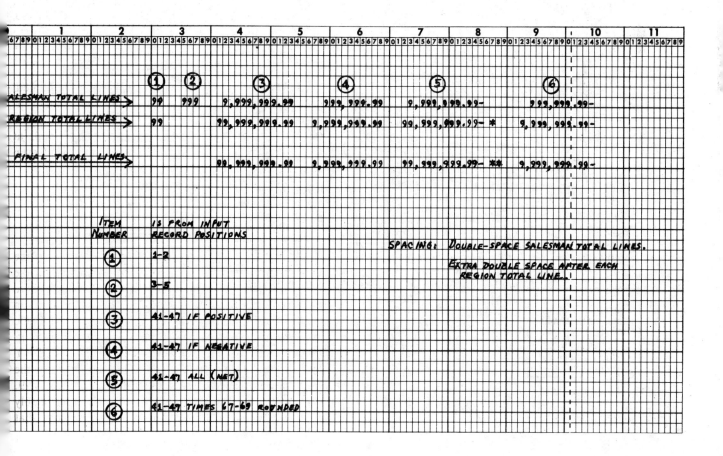

but (prior to the region totals) the salesman represented by that record. On a YES condition, we perform the region total routines, which initially include performing salesman total routines; after these routines are executed, we must process the record just read, which is for the first salesman in the next region.

If a newly-read record does not contain a higher region number than the preceding record, we need test only for whether its salesman number is higher than that in the preceding record. If it is, totals for the pre-

ceding record's salesman number must be printed before we process the record just read, which we have just established is for another salesman within the same region as the preceding record.

If the salesman number in the record just read is the same as in the preceding record, we need only to accumulate sales and return data, and calculate and accumulate commission data, for salesman totals and GO TO read the next record.

The source program is also quite simple (see

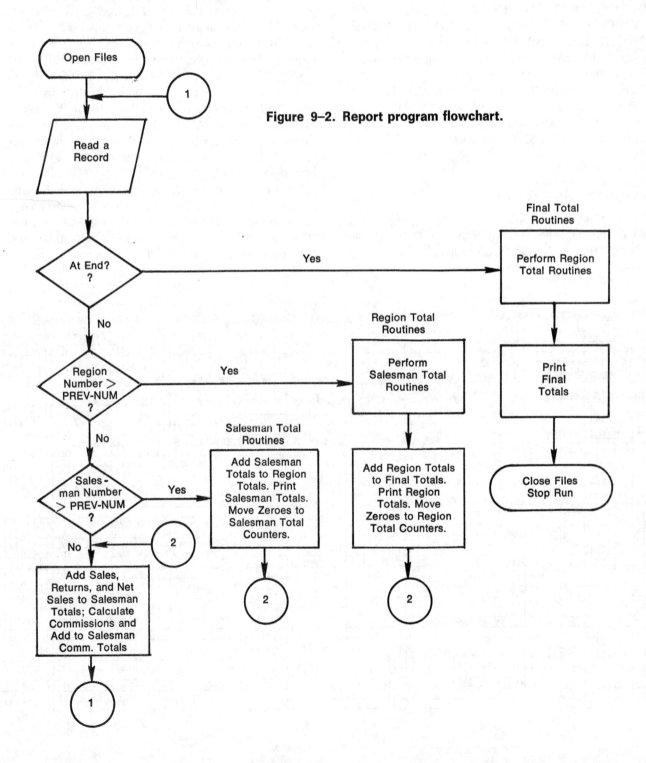

Figure 9–2. Report program flowchart.

Figure 9–3). For the one input file, only four actual data fields are used, permitting the remaining areas to be defined as FILLER. Note that since the sales amount field may be either positive (sale) or negative (return), it has been signed; its PICTURE shows that it is a seven-position field, since neither the S nor the V is included as an actual character in the record area. For correct multiplication, the commission-rate field has been indicated as containing only decimal positions. Count the PICTURE characters (excluding the S and V's) to make sure that the total agrees with the RECORD CONTAINS count.

The simplicity of report layout permits us to set up the print file with a single record. While salesman totals may frequently contain fewer digits than region totals or final totals, all information on each of the three types of lines can be placed in the same alignment based on the maximum requirements of each printed field. In the four money fields, zero suppression replacing with spaces has been used to permit printing of small dollar amounts without leading zeroes or unnecessary commas made available by simple insertion. Zeroes to the right of the decimal point will print. Net sales and commissions have been edited with a fixed rightmost minus to identify the remote possibility of totals for a salesman or region being negative. Since the separate sales and return totals columns will each contain figures with a constant sign condition, no edit sign is needed for either. A three-position area (FLAG) to the right of net sales has been provided to accommodate a single asterisk for region totals and a double asterisk for final totals. Check the PICTURE position counts, including all edit characters; you will find that they total 132. (One additional position would be needed in the first FILLER on some computers because the AFTER ADVANCING option is used in the procedure division.)

The WORKING-STORAGE SECTION contains the two "previous-number" areas required to make the tests for change of salesman and region number, and an area (COMMCALC) where commission amount can be calculated for each record before being accumulated in a counter area with commission totals of other records. Based on the number of integers in the SLS-RET-AMT field, it is possible that the commission amount could have the same number; COMMCALC has accordingly been assigned the same size field. It does not require an initial VALUE of zero, because as the result of a MULTIPLY routine that will necessarily include the GIVING option, any prior contents will be ignored in the arithmetic and will be replaced by the arithmetic result. The other twelve areas in working-storage are for the three levels (salesman, region, final)

for which totals of each of the four report amounts must be accumulated. All have initial zero VALUEs to avoid inclusion of data left in storage areas from execution of a prior program.

The procedure division follows the flowchart precisely; sequence in branching to and performing the three total routines has already been discussed. However, reasons underlying some of the specific instructions should be noted.

In the 02-READ paragraph, the WRITE TOTALINES AFTER ADVANCING NEXTPAGE presupposes a SPECIAL-NAMES entry in the environment division identifying a hardware device as NEXT-PAGE. The MOVE SPACES TO TOTALINES statement before the WRITE assures printing a blank line when paper movement takes place at the beginning of object program execution. The same statement after the WRITE clears the other print buffer area, from which the first salesman total line will be printed. The first printed line on the first page of the report will be two lines below the point where the blank line is "printed." This could cause a slight lack of uniformity with the top line of subsequent pages if we were advancing the paper to the NEXTPAGE line after printing each line-counted page. Since we are not doing this (the report is a continuing double-spaced line stream), it will cause no problem.

Why do we state two IF conditions for both PREV-REGION and PREV-SLSMAN? Both of these working-storage fields have initial values of zero. If we merely tested each of these fields for being less than their corresponding file-section input record fields, the test condition would be met when the first record is read, and both salesman and region total routines would be executed. This would produce three more double-spaced lines (note the last statements in paragraph 05-REGIONTOTALS). The first and third of these would be completely blank; the second would contain only the single asterisk generated as a nonnumeric literal to identify region totals! This printing oddity is prevented by inserting the requirement that each field be greater than zero, as well as less than its corresponding input record field, before initiating total routines.

Reading of the first record results in accumulating and calculation routines as soon as paper movement has taken place. Note the treatment of the field (SLS-RET-AMTS) containing either positive or negative data. Positive data will be added in a sales area and negative data will be subtracted from a returns area; these areas are unsigned since neither will contain data with more than one sign. Since the net sales area, S-NET, represents sales minus returns, the ADD SLS-RET-AMTS TO S-NET will add sales positively and returns negatively. Since both fields named in this instruction are signed, the contents of each carries the operational sign in its rightmost position—the first field from the individual input record, and S-NET the + or − "bit" identifying the condition of the accumulated total in the area at any time.

Note that the COMMCALC is ROUNDED in the MULTIPLY instruction. If negative commission is calculated on a return, the ROUNDED option does not interfere with the negative sign; it is placed in the result (COMMCALC) field, and when a negative COMMCALC is added to the S-COMM field, it will

Figure 9–3. Data and procedure divisions for a report program containing three levels of totals.

```
002010 DATA DIVISION.
002020 FILE SECTION.
002030 FD    RECORDFILE
002040        RECORD CONTAINS 100 CHARACTERS BLOCK CONTAINS 30 RECORDS
002050        LABEL RECORDS ARE OMITTED  DATA RECORD IS SALESREC.
002060 01    SALESREC.
002070        02   REGION          PIC 99.
002080        02   SALESMAN        PIC 999.
002090        02   FILLER          PIC X(35).
002100        02   SLS-RET-AMTS    PIC S9(5)V99.
002110        02   FILLER          PIC X(19).
002120        02   COMMRATE        PIC V999.
002130        02   FILLER          PIC X(31).
002140 FD    PRINTFILE  RECORD CONTAINS 133 CHARACTERS
002150        LABEL RECORDS ARE OMITTED DATA RECORD IS TOTALINES.
002160 01    TOTALINES.
002165        02   FILLER          PIC X(29).
002170        02   T-REGION        PIC 99.
002180        02   FILLER          PIC XXX.
002190        02   T-SALESMN       PIC 999.
002200        02   FILLER          PIC XXX.
002210        02   SALESTOT        PIC ZZ,ZZZ,ZZZ.99.
002220        02   FILLER          PIC XXX.
002230        02   RETNTOT         PIC Z,ZZZ,ZZZ.99.
002240        02   FILLER          PIC XXX.
003010        02   NETSALES        PIC ZZ,ZZZ,ZZZ.99-.
003020        02   FLAG            PIC XXX.
003030        02   FILLER          PIC XXX.
003046        02   COMMISSIONS     PIC Z,ZZZ,ZZZ.99-.
003050        02   FILLER          PIC X(29).
003060 WORKING-STORAGE SECTION.
003070 77    PREV-REGION      PIC 99 VALUE ZERO.
003080 77    PREV-SLSMAN      PIC 999 VALUE ZERO.
003090 77    S-SALES          PIC 9(7)V99 VALUE ZERO.
003100 77    S-RETURNS        PIC 9(6)V99 VALUE ZERO.
003110 77    S-NET            PIC S9(7)V99 VALUE ZERO.
003120 77    S-COMM           PIC S9(6)V99 VALUE ZERO.
003130 77    R-SALES          PIC 9(8)V99 VALUE ZERO.
003140 77    R-RETURNS        PIC 9(7)V99 VALUE ZERO.
```

```
003150 77    R-NET                 PIC S9(8)V99 VALUE ZERO.
003160 77    R-COMM                PIC S9(7)V99 VALUE ZERO.
003170 77    F-SALES               PIC 9(8)V99 VALUE ZERO.
003180 77    F-RETURNS             PIC 9(7)V99 VALUE ZERO.
003190 77    F-NET                 PIC S9(8)V99 VALUE ZERO.
003200 77    F-COMM                PIC S9(7)V99 VALUE ZERO.
003210 77    COMMCALC              PIC S9(5)V99.
004010 PROCEDURE DIVISION.
004020 01-OPEN.
004030     OPEN INPUT RECORDFILE OUTPUT PRINTFILE.
004032     MOVE SPACES TO TOTALINES. WRITE TOTALINES AFTER ADVANCING
004034     NEXT-PAGE. MOVE SPACES TO TOTALINES.
004040 02-READ.
004050     READ RECORDFILE AT END GO TO 06-FINALTOTALS.
004080     IF PREV-REGION > ZERO AND < REGION PERFORM 05-REGIONTOTALS
004085         GO TO 03-ADD.
004090     IF PREV-SLSMAN > ZERO AND < SALESMAN PERFORM 04-SLSMNTOTALS.
004100 03-ADD.
004110     ADD SLS-RET-AMTS TO S-NET.
004120     IF SLS-RET-AMTS POSITIVE ADD SLS-RET-AMTS TO S-SALES ELSE
004130     SUBTRACT SLS-RET-AMTS FROM S-RETURNS.
004140     MULTIPLY SLS-RET-AMTS BY COMMRATE GIVING COMMCALC ROUNDED.
004150     ADD COMMCALC TO S-COMM. MOVE REGION TO PREV-REGION. MOVE
004160     SALESMAN TO PREV-SLSMAN. GO TO 02-READ.
004170 04-SLSMNTOTALS.
004180     ADD S-SALES TO R-SALES. ADD S-RETURNS TO R-RETURNS.
004190     ADD S-NET TO R-NET. ADD S-COMM TO R-COMM.
004200     MOVE PREV-REGION TO T-REGION. MOVE PREV-SLSMAN TO T-SALESMN.
004210     MOVE S-SALES TO SALESTOT. MOVE S-RETURNS TO RETNTOT.
004220     MOVE S-NET TO NETSALES. MOVE SPACES TO FLAG. MOVE S-COMM TO
004230     COMMISSIONS. MOVE ZEROES TO S-SALES S-RETURNS S-NET S-COMM.
004240     WRITE TOTALINES AFTER ADVANCING 2 LINES. MOVE SPACES TO
004250     TOTALINES.
005010 05-REGIONTOTALS. PERFORM 04-SLSMNTOTALS.
005020     ADD R-SALES TO F-SALES. ADD R-RETURNS TO F-RETURNS. ADD
005030     R-NET TO F-NET. ADD R-COMM TO F-COMM.
005040     MOVE PREV-REGION TO T-REGION. MOVE R-SALES TO SALESTOT. MOVE
005050     R-RETURNS TO RETNTOT. MOVE R-NET TO NETSALES. MOVE " * " TO
005060     FLAG. MOVE R-COMM TO COMMISSIONS. MOVE ZEROES TO R-SALES
005070     R-RETURNS R-NET R-COMM. WRITE TOTALINES AFTER ADVANCING 2
005080     LINES. MOVE SPACES TO TOTALINES. WRITE TOTALINES AFTER
005090     ADVANCING 2 LINES.
005100 06-FINALTOTALS.
005110     PERFORM 05-REGIONTOTALS.
005120     MOVE F-SALES TO SALESTOT. MOVE F-RETURNS TO RETNTOT. MOVE
005130     F-NET TO NETSALES. MOVE " **" TO FLAG. MOVE F-COMM TO
005140     COMMISSIONS. WRITE TOTALINES AFTER ADVANCING 2 LINES.
005150     CLOSE RECORDFILE PRINTFILE. STOP RUN.
```

be added negatively. Note also that when all MULTI-PLY and ADD routines are executed, the input record's salesman and region code numbers are moved to their corresponding "previous-number" areas before reading the next record.

Two other techniques in the salesman and region total paragraphs (04 and 05) deserve attention. We are adding salesman totals to region totals only when executing the salesman-total routines, and region totals to final totals only when executing the region-total routines. It is not absolutely necessary that this technique be used; we could, for example, have omitted all ADD instructions in paragraphs 04 and 05 and formulated all ADD instructions in the 03 paragraph along the lines of ADD SLS-RET-AMTS TO S-NET R-NET F-NET. All other parts of the coding would be unaffected by this change. In processing a large file, however, the execution time could be lengthened by this second technique. How? Assume a file of 200,000 records involving 500 salesmen and 20 regions. By the method we have used, the basic four ADD instructions will cause:

> 800,000 ADDS at record processing time
> 2,000 ADDS at salesman total time
> 80 ADDS at region total time
> a total of 802,080 executed instructions

This compares to 200,000 × 12 ADDS for each RECORD processed, a total of 2,400,000 executed instructions. The method we have chosen, usually referred to as *rolling totals* because of the transfer addition from one level of total areas to another during total routines, is obviously less time-consuming. It should be kept in mind, however, that the method chosen saves time in this case because we are not printing or punching out a card for each record read. If we were doing either, the speed of the printer or punch, not that of the vastly faster internal computer processing, would determine total execution time; and the additional ADD routines for each record would make no difference. While the situation just described is relatively simple to evaluate for a small computer, the use of an "operating system" with a large computer may either reduce or magnify the proportionate time differences, leaving unchallenged the validity of the more economical programming method.

The other technique to be observed is the MOVE ZEROES to the total-level accumulating areas during the related total routines. Note that in paragraph 04 the salesman totals are MOVEd to print areas and ADDed to region-level total areas before zeroes are MOVEd to the salesman total areas in working-storage. Zeroes must be moved in so that the accumulation for the next salesman will not include those just processed; but the MOVE ZEROES must follow the printing and adding instruction. If it precedes either, nothing may be printed or added. Paragraph 05 illustrates the same principle in connection with printing region totals and adding them to final total areas.

One other item might be noted: the printing of salesman or region numbers is done following a MOVE of PREV-SLSMAN or PREV-REGION to the related print area. Why use these fields instead of the SALESMAN or REGION field from the input record area? The answer is that at the time totals are to be printed, the record for the *next* salesman or region has been read (and is awaiting processing), and if we used these fields, we would be printing code numbers applicable to the *next* set of totals. The code numbers in the "previous-number" areas are the ones that relate to the current totals being printed.

REVIEW MATERIAL

Terms

Editing (of numeric data)	Algebraic sign rules	High-order digits
Insertion characters	Simple insertion	Rounding
Replacement characters	Special insertion	Print layout
Check-protecting asterisk	Fixed insertion	Final totals
	Floating insertion	Total routines

Questions

In an application involving the printing of group totals, what is the relationship between the levels of totals and the sequence of the input file?

What is the function of the symbol V in the PICTURE clause?

How is a negative quantity keypunched?

What are the algebraic rules which the computer follows in doing arithmetic operations?

What are the four methods of insertion that can be used in editing numeric fields for printing? What are the two types of zero suppression? Review the details of the editing techniques.

How many operands can be used in ADD and SUBTRACT statements? MULTIPLY and DIVIDE?

What effect does the statement, ADD A B TO C, have on the original values of the A and B fields?

What is the function of the GIVING option? In what ways can the operand to the right of GIVING differ from the other operands?

Why is the SIZE ERROR option particularly useful in the DIVIDE statement?

In an application involving group totals, why does the printing of intermediate level totals involve the printing of minor totals?

In the program discussed in this chapter, how are "previous-number" areas used? When is a new "previous number" moved into an area?

True-or-False Statements

A signed field is always treated as if positive.

A decimal point occupies no character position in a numeric field.

A minus sign occupies one character position in a numeric field.

When the period is used as an editing symbol, a decimal point will be inserted into the edited field in a spot corresponding to the location of the V in the field that is being edited.

Zero suppression refers to the replacing of all zeroes in a field with spaces.

Multiplication or division of two quantities of like sign yields a positive result; if the signs are unlike, the result is negative.

Only the result field is changed as a result of the execution of an arithmetic statement; all other fields appearing in the statement have the same value after execution as before.

None of the fields appearing in an arithmetic statement can be edited.

Fields used as total accumulation areas should be set to a value of zero before any accumulation takes place.

Programming

9–1: Weekly pay data cards come to the computer area in ascending sequence on column 1–7, containing the keypunched data shown below. For convenience, the data PICTURE is given for each field.

Columns		
1–2	Department number	99
3–7	Employee number	9(5)
8–30	Employee name	X(23)
31	Rate class	A (either H or W)
32–36	Rate	999V99
37–39	Regular time	99V9
40–42	Overtime	99V9
43–80	Not punched	X(38)

There is one card for each employee. The program is to calculate regular pay, overtime pay, and total gross pay for each employee; print a line showing the data indicated in the report specifications below; and accumulate and print department totals and final totals. Each department begins a new page, and the final totals are to be printed on a separate page.

1. Calculation requirements

There is a 5-day, 40-hour week. H (hourly) employee rates are rates per hour; W (weekly) employee rates are the weekly salary. H regular time and overtime are in hours and tenths; W regular time is in days and tenths; W overtime is in hours and tenths. Therefore:

H regular pay = rate × regular time

H overtime pay = rate × overtime × 1.5

W regular pay = rate × regular time, divided by 5

W overtime pay = rate × overtime × 1.5, divided by 40.

If rate class is not H or W, print WRONG PAY CODE and do not calculate.

In calculating regular, overtime, and total gross pays, use a field of 999V99 in each case, and on any SIZE ERROR, print WRONG PAY DATA in the error message area and do not add or print the calculated pay data for the employee.

In all cases, regular pay plus overtime pay = total gross pay.

Use the ROUNDED option in all cases where it appears to be needed. Where there is more than one multiplication/division step, it is preferable to make the DIVIDE step the last to avoid dropping pennies on rounding. Make some sample manual calculations with a rate like 2.25 to prove this to yourself.

You will need a minimum of three working-storage areas at each level (employee, department-total, and final-total) for the pay fields. It is permissible, though not absolutely necessary, to create additional working-storage areas at employee level for intermediate steps in the calculations.

2. Print requirements

Data Item	Print PICTURE		Print Positions
Department number	99		3–4
Employee number	9(5)		7–11
Employee name	X(23)		14–36
Rate class	A		39
Rate	ZZ9.99		42–47
Regular time	ZZ,ZZ9.9	*	50–57
Overtime hours	Z,ZZ9.9	*	60–66
Regular pay	ZZZ,ZZZ.99	*	69–78
Overtime pay	ZZ,ZZZ.99	*	81–89
Total gross pay	ZZZ,ZZZ.99	*	92–101
Error message	X(14)		104–117

The five fields marked with asterisks are those for which department and final totals are to be accumulated. The print pictures shown are for final totals. Working-storage areas for department totals should be one integer digit smaller; for example, department total gross pay can be defined as 9(5)V99. Size of the individual employee time and pay fields has already been indicated.

Headings are optional. Single-space the report. Maximum number of lines per page is 54.

10

MORE ARITHMETIC AND NEAR-ARITHMETIC

COBOL was developed as a language to handle common business problems with simplicity and efficiency; it is general-business-oriented rather than mathematically oriented, as are such "problem-oriented" languages as FORTRAN and ALGOL. Nevertheless, COBOL contains some instruction formats related to handling of arithmetic and numerically coded data that are intended to reduce programmer coding time and source-program bulk. The instructions discussed in this chapter are examples of this type of technique. It should be emphasized, however, that in saving programmer effort in writing the source program, particular techniques that save *coding* instructions and programmer time are used. Sometimes this may cause the compiler to generate more object-program instructions than there would have been had the programmer used more basic techniques requiring the writing of a larger number of source program statements. This is particularly true of the use of the COMPUTE statement, which may replace three or four basic arithmetic statements yet quite frequently generates more object-program instructions than would have been generated by the three or four basic arithmetic statements.

THE COMPUTE STATEMENT

Available only in higher-level COBOL compilers, the COMPUTE statement may vary from the equivalent of a MOVE of data from one area to another to a fairly complex set of arithmetic instructions. ANSI specifications prescribe the format of the statement but leave the techniques in handling arithmetic expressions to the "implementor." Consequently, the COBOL manual for the specific compiler must be consulted to make sure of the particular relative priorities of arithmetic symbols and internal reading-sequence assigned by the compiler to particular operations in the COMPUTE statement. The standard format of the statement is:

COMPUTE identifier-1 [ROUNDED] =

$$\left\{ \begin{array}{l} \text{identifier-2} \\ \text{literal-1} \\ \text{arithmetic-expression} \end{array} \right\} \left[\begin{array}{l} \text{ON SIZE ERROR} \\ \text{imperative statement} \end{array} \right]$$

Identifier-1, the result field, is followed by the ROUNDED option if required. The result field may contain editing symbols. As in ordinary arithmetic statements, the SIZE ERROR option, if used, is followed by an imperative statement to end the instruction series. The operand or combination of operands immediately following the = presents possibilities that must be examined separately; but one general rule can be stated regardless of differences in implementor techniques: any operands to the right of the = that are stored fields do *not* have their contents changed by the COMPUTE statement operations. Only the result field (to the left of the =) has its contents changed by execution of the statement's operations.

In its simplest form, the COMPUTE statement can be used essentially as a MOVE; COMPUTE FIELDA = FIELDB could have the following results:

| | FIELDA | | FIELDB | |
PICTURE	Contents Before	Contents After	PICTURE	Contents Before and After
999V99	12345	65432	999V99	65432
999V99	67890	01034	99V9999	103486

The second case would be better served by COMPUTE FIELDA ROUNDED = FIELDB, producing

999V99	67890	01035	99V9999	103486

If we wished to replace FIELDA's contents by a literal, the statement COMPUTE FIELDA = 350.00 would result in 35000 replacing the prior contents of FIELDA.

The use of two or more operands to the right of the = will involve use of the arithmetic signs for add, subtract, multiply, divide, and exponentiate. In general, implementor techniques permit the use of parentheses in the normal algebraic manner to assure proper sequence of arithmetic operations. Variations between different implementors' compilers are usually in techniques developed to aid the programmer in avoiding misstatements of the problem or failure to use parentheses in the proper place. Proper use of parentheses in connection with a recognition of priority levels of arithmetic should enable the programmer to write COMPUTE statements that will function properly regardless of differences from one implementor's techniques to another's. The signs used for each type of arithmetic and the operations they represent are:

- ** for exponentiation (followed by the necessary exponent, such as 2 for square, 3 for cube, etc.)
- * for multiply
- / for divide
- + for add
- — for subtract

From a strictly arithmetic viewpoint, three operational levels can be identified.[1] These operations, being performed from left to right at each level in the order named, are: (*a*) exponentiation, (*b*) multiplication and division, and (*c*) addition and subtraction. Usually, it is necessary to use parentheses to set off operations in separate groups only where a COMPUTE statement contains operations at mixed levels, although occasionally a series of * and / operations may require grouping in parentheses to make them both readable

---

1. Actually, the unary operator (—), a minus sign placed immediately before an operand, is given priority over all of the other three levels of arithmetic. An operand such as —A or —(X + Y) results in multiplying the operand by —1 before any other COMPUTE arithmetic takes place.

and arithmetically correct. In a simple series such as: COMPUTE FIELDZ = R + S — T — U + V — W, the presence of parentheses would not alter the result. A simple averaging operation, however, would be vastly different in result if parentheses were omitted. Suppose A, B, and C represent bowling scores of 170, 181 and 153, and we wish to COMPUTE the average score. If we say COMPUTE AVERAGE = A + B + C / 3, the statement could be interpreted as $170 + 181 + \frac{153}{3}$ and *would be* so interpreted by most compilers. The result would be 170 + 181 + 51 = 402, neither an average nor a total. Obviously, we should say: COMPUTE AVERAGE = (A + B + C) / 3, which any COBOL compiler would interpret as $\frac{170 + 181 + 153}{3}$ and give us $\frac{504}{3} = 168$.

Notice that each of the arithmetic signs requires a space before and after, while a parenthesis has no space between it and the expression it encloses, but does require a space between it and any external part of the statement.

Even a simple COMPUTE statement may require both the ROUNDED and SIZE ERROR options. If A, B, and C have PICTUREs of 999V99, 999V9, and 9V99 respectively, and our equation is basically A = B times C, we would need to say COMPUTE A ROUNDED = B * C ON SIZE ERROR GO TO ERR-RTN, since such simple combinations of B and C as 00154 and 233, or 50000 and 600 would cause respectively a slight understatement of A and a loss of significant high-order data.

While COBOL is not intended to be primarily mathematical, the exponentiation feature makes possible more complex algebraic calculations than are possible without the COMPUTE feature. For example, since the mathematical equivalent of a square root is raising a number to its ½ power (the square root of $16 = 16^{1/2}$), obtaining a square root is the same as raising a number to its .5 power ($16^{1/2} = 16^{.5} = 4$). If A = square root of B, we can express this as: COMPUTE A = B ** .5.

If we have the simple formulation that $Z = \sqrt{x^2 + y^2}$, it can be expressed as: COMPUTE Z ROUNDED = (X ** 2 + Y ** 2) ** .5.

In this last instance parentheses should be used for clarity of reference even if not required by the specific compiler.

Since the COMPUTE statement permits the result field to contain edit symbols, it frequently provides considerable convenience in division and percentaging operations. Suppose that we have fields identified as PROFIT and SALES, each a six-digit integer, and wish to compute MARGIN (percentage of profit on sales) as a four-digit figure, which we have specified in a print-record PICTURE as ZZ.99. Since we must divide PROFIT by SALES, and the latter is always the larger figure, our initial answer, even if ROUNDED, can never contain an integer—it will always be preceded by a decimal. If, however, we multiply it by 100 before moving it to MARGIN, whole percentages will appear as if integers in MARGIN, and tenths and hundredths of a percent will appear as decimals. The statement, COMPUTE MARGIN ROUNDED = (PROFIT / SALES) * 100 will serve the purpose. A PROFIT of 024000 on SALES of 200000 will result in a MARGIN of 12.00. The use of separate MULTIPLY and DIVIDE statements would necessitate having available an intermediate field, whose PICTURE contained a V in the decimal point location required by the MARGIN print picture.[2]

THE EXAMINE STATEMENT

The EXAMINE statement provides a scanning operation; its use results in checking each character in a data field, from left to right, "looking" for a specific character named (as a literal) in the statement, and either (a) replacing it with another specified character, (b) counting (TALLYING) it, or (c) both counting and replacing it. The field EXAMINEd may be either numeric or nonnumeric; if numeric and signed, the sign is ignored by the EXAMINE operation—the character is scanned as if the sign were not present.

In its replacement function, the EXAMINE statement format is:

$$\underline{\text{EXAMINE}} \text{ identifier} \left\{ \begin{array}{l} \underline{\text{ALL}} \\ \underline{\text{LEADING}} \\ [\underline{\text{UNTIL}}] \text{ } \underline{\text{FIRST}} \end{array} \right\} \begin{array}{l} \text{literal-1} \\ \underline{\text{BY}} \text{ literal-2.} \end{array}$$

The literals used may be numeric, nonnumeric, or any of the figurative constants except ALL. Any literal used must be consistent with the identifier PICTURE; for example, if the identifier PICTURE were numeric, a numeric literal or ZERO would be permissible, but a nonnumeric literal or SPACES would not. Uses of this EXAMINE statement format are rather miscellaneous: it is sometimes of value in editing a file of data for certain types of inconsistencies or errors in

data preparation; in rather limited circumstances it may be of some aid in recoding file data; and it is a convenient way of editing file data for use between computers whose character sets interpret a given bit configuration as a different special character or vice versa. An actual example of the last-named situation occurred in converting an inventory master file created on one computer for regular use on another of a different manufacture. The stock-item description field contained numerous hyphens, usually where the description contained a size. These hyphens were keypunched and converted to magnetic tape readably enough on the first computer as 2-½, 6-¼, etc. On the second computer, however, the bit configuration for the hyphen was equivalent to an exclamation point. To avoid printing reports and invoices with such odd-looking sizes as 2!½, 6!¼, and the like, the statement, EXAMINE ITEMNAME REPLACING ALL "!" BY "-", served as an instruction in a file-copying program on the second computer to correct the descriptions to readable ones. ITEMNAME, of course, had an alphanumeric PICTURE.

Occasionally, a stored file will be created with a consistent error of failing to punch leading zeroes in a field intended as numeric. One way to correct this situation is through a file-copying program containing the statement, EXAMINE FIELDX REPLACING LEADING SPACES BY ZERO, which scans FIELDX from leftmost to rightmost character and, until a significant digit is encountered, replaces each space in the storage area for the field with a zero. It should be noted that any field containing both spaces and numeric characters must be defined as alphanumeric. While SPACES cannot be moved to a numeric field, a move of ZERO to an alphanumeric field is permissible. Using b to indicate a space, the following indicates the before-and-after condition of a six-digit FIELDX EXAMINEd as above:

Before	After
bbbb76	000076
b82005	082005

The EXAMINE . . . LEADING option is less comprehensive than it looks; to be effective, it must be used with caution. For example, suppose a file of account numbers has been set up with a range of 001–699. It has now become overloaded in the 400–699 range, and to create more space we wish to change the 400 series to 500–599, the 500's to 700's, and the 600's to 900's.[3] It is permissible to use a series of EXAMINE statements for the same field; we *could* say:

---

2. The REDEFINES clause, described in chapter 11, is an interesting device available in the data division which can sometimes be used for a purpose of this type without using additional storage to create an intermediate working area.

---

3. This is normally another situation in which use REDEFINES may be helpful, as will be discussed in Chapter 11.

```
EXAMINE ACCTNO REPLACING LEADING 4 BY 5
EXAMINE ACCTNO REPLACING LEADING 5 BY 7
EXAMINE ACCTNO REPLACING LEADING 6 BY 9
```

But suppose we had such account numbers as 550 and 570 in the original file. Both would now be changed to the same new number—770!

An EXAMINE statement using the REPLACING FIRST option would be no improvement! EXAMINE ACCTNO REPLACING FIRST 4 BY 5 would result in changing account 140 to 150 and leaving an original number 150 the same.

Actually, many of the formats and combinations of formats of the EXAMINE statement have little *general* business use. Their chief value lies in rather special uses connected with statistical data, in which the effects of substituting one type or range of data for another would be the subject of an analysis following the substitution. The UNTIL FIRST variation of the REPLACING format is one whose use seems obscure. If we use the statement, EXAMINE FIELDZ REPLACING UNTIL FIRST 6 BY 2, and the original contents of FIELDZ is 021634, the changed contents will be 222634. The purpose of such an operation would appear logical only in rather limited statistical contexts.

The application of the EXAMINE . . . TALLYING format options is considerably wider in tabulating the results of questionnaires used in various types of survey studies. Frequently data files are created in which each record is a complete set of answers to a questionnaire. A data field may consist of several card columns or tape positions, each column or position containing a numeric digit representing one of a number of possible answers to a question. A six-column data field may contain answers to six interrelated questions, with possible numeric answer codes from 1 to 4 in each case and a zero indicating no answer. One of the three variations of the simple EXAMINE . . . TALLYING format can be used to make various types of counts, accumulate them as report or output file data, and make further analyses from them. The basic TALLYING format is:

		UNTIL FIRST	
EXAMINE identifier	TALLYING	ALL	literal-1
		LEADING	

The TALLYING statement itself (without any programmer effort on data division entries) makes available a five-position special register (counter) called TALLY, in which the TALLYING operation counts are accumulated. In subsequent statements, the source program can use TALLY, which is a reserved word, as if it were the name of some working-storage elementary item, and make use of its contents accordingly. The TALLYING statement itself moves zeroes to TALLY

before beginning any counting, so any instructions for use of TALLY's contents must precede the next TALLYING statement.

Assuming the kind of six-column data field described above, let us call it FIELDY and attempt to accumulate totals of the following:

1. All questions left unanswered (six zeroes). If at least one question was answered, the pattern of occurrence of answer number 2, as follows:

2. No occurrence of answer number 2.

3. One or two occurrences of answer number 2.

4. Three, four, or five occurrences of answer number 2.

5. Answer number 2 to all six questions.

Two EXAMINE . . . TALLYING statements and a distribution of the contents of TALLY to various working-storage counter areas should suffice:

```
EXAMINE FIELDY TALLYING ALL 0.
IF TALLY = 6 ADD 1 TO CTR-NOANSWERS ELSE
EXAMINE FIELDY TALLYING ALL 2
IF TALLY = 0 ADD 1 TO CTR-NOTWOS ELSE
IF TALLY = 1 OR 2 ADD 1 TO CTR-SOME2 ELSE
IF TALLY > 2 and < 6 ADD 1 TO CTR-MOSTLY2 ELSE
IF TALLY = 6 ADD 1 to CTR-ALL2.
```

In the cases where we made use of a numeric zero, use in its place of the figurative constant ZERO would also be permissible. The above indicates that we can (*a*) EXAMINE the same field more than once, (*b*) make use of the contents of TALLY elsewhere as long as we do it before clearing TALLY with another TALLYING statement, and (*c*) address TALLY in the same way as we would any other numeric data area.

When the LEADING or UNTIL FIRST variation of the TALLYING statement is used, the counting will take place under the same conditions as specified for the corresponding variations of the REPLACING clause.

It should also be noted that the REPLACING clause can be appended to a TALLYING, with the REPLACING following the conditions specified for TALLYING. For example, if we had said in the above illustration: EXAMINE FIELDY TALLYING ALL 2 REPLACING BY 7, the counts of the digit 2 would have taken place in the same manner, but contents of 213224 would be replaced by 713774. With the same original contents, if we had said: EXAMINE FIELDY TALLYING LEADING 2 REPLACING BY 7, TALLY would contain a count of 1 and the changed FIELDY contents would be 713224. If FIELDY had original contents of 143022 and our statement had been: EXAMINE FIELDY TALLYING UNTIL FIRST 2 REPLACING BY 7, the count in TALLY would be 4 and the changed FIELDY contents would be 777722.

THE GO TO . . . DEPENDING ON STATEMENT

Within a restricted number of conditions, this format of the GO TO statement may be used instead of a series of IF . . . GO TO instructions. The possibilities of this substitution depend on the existence or creation of a series of consecutive numeric codes in some data area, with each code in the series requiring a branch to a different procedure division paragraph. Under these circumstances, we may be able to make use of the format:

GO TO procedure-name-1 [procedure-name-2] . . .
procedure-name-n DEPENDING ON identifier

Suppose that in a file-updating program, instead of using the codes A, C, and D, we used update-card code 1 to represent an addition, code 2 to represent a change, and code 3 to represent deletion. The instruction GO TO ADD-RTN CHANGE-RTN DELETE-RTN DEPENDING ON CARDCODE would supply the procedure alternatives that otherwise would require three IF . . . GO TO statements. Absence of any of the conditions implicit in the DEPENDING ON statement would result in control passing to the next statement, which might logically be an unconditional GO TO ERROR-ROUTINE.

The DEPENDING ON format requires that the code series depended on be numeric,[4] consecutive,[5] either positive or unsigned, and begin with the digit 1. A code field that included a possible zero could not be used as the identifier for a GO TO . . . DEPENDING ON statement. Nor could a code field which included negative numbers. On the other hand, any code field with inherent possibilities of conversion to consecutive numbers beginning with 1 can be used as an identifier if some statement producing the conversion precedes the GO TO . . . DEPENDING ON. If, for example, the identifier field is always an even number successively incremented by 2 (such as 2, 4, 6, 8), an instruction to DIVIDE 2 INTO CODEFIELD would effectively reduce the code possibilities to 1, 2, 3, and 4, and permit the instruction: GO TO RTNW, RTNX, RTNY, RTNZ DEPENDING ON CODEFIELD. Sim-

ilarly, if a code field contained the possibility of digits 1, 2, 3, 8, or 9, a preliminary IF CODEFIELD > 7 SUBTRACT 4 FROM CODEFIELD would effectively provide a consecutive series possibility of 1 through 5 and make it available as the identifier in a GO TO . . . DEPENDING ON instruction.

Irregularly assigned numeric codes can be subjected to use of the GO TO . . . DEPENDING ON, but with some degree of awkwardness. If a field contained codes of 2, 5, and 7, the following *could* be used: GO TO BADCODE RTN2 BADCODE BADCODE RTN5 BADCODE RTN7 DEPENDING ON TRANSACTIONCODE. Three IF statements and a GO TO BADCODE achieve the same results with little, if any, additional effort.

Individual COBOL compilers may vary as to the maximum number of procedure-names usable in the GO TO . . . DEPENDING ON format. The manual for the subset being used should be consulted to determine the individual compiler's limitation.

REVIEW MATERIAL

Terms

Arithmetic-expression	Power	Significant
Exponentiation	Leading zeroes	digit

Questions

In a COMPUTE statement, how is the sequence of operations determined if there are no parentheses? How are parentheses used?

What is the significance of ** .5 in an arithmetic expression?

What are the two major functions of the EXAMINE statement? Can they be combined in one statement?

How is TALLY affected by the EXAMINE statement? How can it be used by other statements?

What would be the result of executing a GO TO . . . DEPENDING ON statement if there were five procedure-names and the value of the identifier were 3? 6?

True-or-False Statements

If the value of X is 6, then the value of X / 2 + 1 is 4.

If the value of A is 2, then the value of 2 ** A + 1 is 8.

---

4. At the risk of overselling the uses of REDEFINES, it can be noted that with its aid, an alphabetic code field employing the A through I range of letters can be made a base for a GO TO . . . DEPENDING ON statement (see Chapter 11).

5. As indicated in the immediately following examples, the actual codes need not be consecutive, since there are various ways of filling even irregular gaps.

(A — B) (C — D) is a valid arithmetic expression.

When using an EXAMINE statement with the TALLYING option, TALLY need not be entered in the data division.

The identifier in the GO TO . . . DEPENDING ON statement must be a positive or unsigned integer.

Programming

10–1: Modify the pay data program of the preceding chapter by substituting COMPUTE instructions wherever possible for the simple arithmetic instructions used. You may be able to COMPUTE some print-record fields. Consider whether this would be feasible if you were writing the same COMPUTEd data as output tape or disk- record fields as well as printed report fields.

10–2: Write routines to add the following to the sales analysis program illustrated in the preceding chapter: Assume that we wish to calculate and print, at all total levels, the average commission percentage, printed out as two integers and two decimals, using a PICTURE of Z9.99. Total commissions are to be divided by net sales and the result multiplied by 100 to achieve this percentage, which must be ROUNDED. It is suggested that for purposes of comparing the programming effort involved, the alternatives of simple arithmetic and COMPUTE both be exercised.

11

DATA DIVISION PROGRAMMING AIDS

Technically, the procedure division of a COBOL program supplies the instructions which result in actual computer operations; but the instructions must be made effective by the organization of the data division. Conditions in the data division can:

1. Render a procedure division instruction invalid —a statement will be diagnosed as an error if it refers to a data field not a literal and not defined in the data division.

2. Cause the result of an instruction to be unpredictable, such as a MOVE of an alphanumeric item to a numeric field.

3. Modify the form of the results of an instruction—the editing function and numeric sign control determine the form *and* numeric content of arithmetic statement results.

4. Provide means of identifying different types and conditions of data which enable the source program to indicate different courses of action.

The last-named function of the data division suggests that we are referring to *contents* of data division fields which furnish bases for comparison, testing for presence of specific digits, etc., rather than to *techniques* made available through data division reserved-word uses. While it is true that data division contents provide the operands for procedure division instructions, it is also true that certain data division clauses provide means of procedure division handling of data that can minimize both use of data storage area and number of instructions, at least in the source program and sometimes in the object program as well. The manner in which one or more of these advantages can be obtained will appear in the discussion of each specific clause which follows.

THE REDEFINES CLAUSE

When an input file is described, it may have more than one record (01-level) description. A card file, for example, may contain cards of two or more different layouts, and an 01-level record description will be required for each different layout. When any one card is READ, the eighty columns of data are temporarily stored in one specific area regardless of which layout format is present in the card. There may be four 01-level records described, but each of these simply provides a different way of interpreting the eighty-position area where the data is temporarily stored. In a sense, the second, third, and fourth 01-level record descriptions redefine the first. Since the availability of multiple 01-level descriptions in the file section makes possible redefinitions of an entire record area, the REDEFINES clause need not be used at an 01-level in the file section; in fact, such use is not permitted. It is permissible, however, to use REDEFINES at an 01-level in the working-storage section.

Primarily, the function of REDEFINES is to permit

the storage area for a group item or elementary item to be interpreted in more than one way. The clause format is: level-number data-name-1 <u>REDEFINES</u> data-name-2. The level-number in the REDEFINES clause must be the same as that for data-name-2 (the item being redefined); the entry containing the clause must immediately follow the entries redefining the area being redefined; the clause must immediately follow data-name-1; and the storage area occupied by data-name-1 must be defined as the same *size* as that for data-name-2. ANSI COBOL specifications rule that multiple redefinitions must all use the data-name of the entry originally defining the area; for example:

```
03  FIELD-A                     PIC 9(4).
03  FIELD-B REDEFINES FIELD-A   PIC 99V99.
03  FIELD-C REDEFINES FIELD-A   PIC 999V9.
```

Some COBOL compilers, however, permit the preceding redefined field to be referred to as data-name-2; these would permit the third line above to be:

```
03  FIELD-C REDEFINES FIELD-B   PIC 999V9.
```

When a group item area is being redefined, the first redefinition follows the last elementary item completing the original definition:

```
02  FIELDJ.
03  ITEMR                     PIC 9(2).
03  ITEMT                     PIC 9(5).
02  FIELDQ REDEFINES FIELDJ.
03  ITEMV                     PIC 9(4).
03  ITEMW                     PIC XXX.
```

If, in the above illustration, FIELDQ had been a single data field, it would have been permissible for the re-definition to be expressed as:

```
02  FIELDQ REDEFINES FIELDJ   PIC 9(5)V99.
```

Probably the most uniform use of REDEFINES is in connection with table-handling procedures, discussed in Chapter 13; its other uses are quite miscellaneous. Let us examine first the three possibilities footnoted in our preceding chapter.

In our first example, we use the COMPUTE statement to divide and convert an all-decimal result to a four-digit figure, which would be printed as two integer and two decimal positions. Thus, both a multiplication and a division operation were required to make the four-digit field, MARGIN, available for printing in the form desired. Using a REDEFINES, we could have eliminated the multiplication:

```
03  MARGIN                      PIC V9999.
03  PROFITRATE REDEFINES MARGIN PIC 99V99.
```

This would have enabled us to say:

```
    COMPUTE MARGIN ROUNDED = PROFIT / SALES
or  DIVIDE PROFIT BY SALES GIVING MARGIN ROUNDED
```

And, instead of using MARGIN on the MOVE to a print area defined as ZZ.99 (which would print as two blanks followed by .12), we would MOVE PROFIT-RATE (enabling us to print the 12.00 as desired). In all probability, the most economical use of object instructions and storage areas would be the DIVIDE instruction and the REDEFINES.

In the second case, we found the use of the EXAMINE . . . REPLACING LEADING format subject to the risk, under certain conditions, of converting some numbers that should not be converted. If we are concerned with changing only certain first digits in a three-digit account number, we have two alternatives in the data division field definition:

1. Define the field as both group and elementary items:

```
02  ACCTNO.
03  GROUPNO     PIC 9.
03  DETAILNO    PIC 99.
```

2. If for some reason 1. is undesirable, use RE-DEFINES as follows:

```
02  ACCTNO               PIC 999.
02  ACCT REDEFINES ACCTNO.
03  GROUPNO              PIC 9.
03  DETAILNO             PIC 99.
```

In either case, a series of IF statements, such as IF GROUPNO = 4 MOVE 5 TO GROUPNO, can be used to make the desired change without affecting the second or third digits of the field.

The third example cited, this time in connection with GO TO . . . DEPENDING ON, suggested that it would be possible to use alphabetic codes as a base for the DEPENDING ON clause. In most current computers, the configuration of letters A through I is the same as the positively signed numbers 1 through 9. If a code field contained only a possibility of letters A through I, it would be redefinable as follows:

```
02  ALPHACODE                PIC X.
02  NUMCODE REDEFINES ALPHACODE   PIC S9.
```

Our procedure division instruction could be GO TO PARA1 PARA2 . . . DEPENDING ON NUMCODE.

From the foregoing examples, the following rules should be evident:

• The redefinition must immediately follow the complete definition of data-name-2 (the area originally defined).

• The word REDEFINES must immediately follow data-name-1 (the redefined name of the area).

• The redefinition must account for the same area size as accounted for in the original definition of data-name-2.

In addition, the following restrictions apply:

• Neither a 66-level nor 88-level data area can be redefined.

• The area as redefined (data-name-1) must not contain a VALUE clause—REDEFINES cannot change *contents* of an area; it can only change the manner of *interpreting* the contents.

Data-name-2 cannot contain a REDEFINES or OCCURS clause, or be subordinate to an entry which does contain a REDEFINES or OCCURS clause. (As previously suggested, this is an ANSI rule which may be modified in some current compilers).

As already indicated, aside from rather specific uses in table handling operations, REDEFINES serves rather miscellaneous purposes and should be used with care. In some instances appearing to require its use, an original definition combining group and elementary items is sufficient without a REDEFINES, a possibility in one of the examples discussed. Such possibilities should be considered to avoid unnecessary use of REDEFINES where appearances at first seem to require it.

THE JUSTIFIED CLAUSE

The printing composition term "justified" means the arrangement of type character lines so that they will begin or end at the same vertical margin. Computer-processed numeric data is normally both prepared as input and internally processed so that it is "right-justified"—all amounts, large or small, having the units position of an integer in the same right-hand position for vertical alignment. Alphabetic and alphanumeric data, on the other hand, are normally left-justified; the first data character is always given the leftmost position and unused positions at the right are left blank in data preparation or filled with spaces by internal moves of the data to a designated area in computer storage. Contemplated need for right-justifying alphanumeric or alphabetic field contents caused one computer manufacturer in the late 1950s to provide rather complete ability to realign such field contents so that on a move of data originally left-justified, the last character not a space would become the rightmost character in the receiving field. In the CODASYL conferences that developed COBOL, this technique did not meet with majority acceptance; the resulting compromise was the requirement of a JUSTIFIED RIGHT clause applicable to receiving field data definitions, which has a limited range of utility.

The JUSTIFIED RIGHT clause (JUST RIGHT is a shorter acceptable form) following the PICTURE specification for a receiving field will permit a sending field to be moved in from right to left, space-filling or truncating the sending field data (depending on the comparative size of the sending and receiving fields). Note in the examples below that this does *not* justify the *contents* of the sending field; it justifies the field itself. For example, if the receiving field is 02 LAST-NAME PIC X(15) JUSTIFIED RIGHT, and we are moving contents of a sending field defined as 02 NAME PIC X(12), whose contents are WASHINGTONbb, the result of the MOVE will be contents in LAST-NAME of bbbWASHINGTONbb. Conversely, if we were moving the contents of NAME to a field 02 ABBREV PIC X(10) JUST RIGHT, the contents of ABBREV after the MOVE would be SHINGTONbb.

Despite the seeming lack of utility indicated by the above examples, JUSTIFIED RIGHT may occasionally have marginal convenience, such as in the setting up of print heading lines which are largely blank areas. Suppose, for example, that the sole contents of a report heading line are PAYROLL REGISTER (to be centered in positions 51–66), PAGE (to print in positions 124–127), and a page number to print in positions 129–132. We might find it convenient to define in the file section:

```
01  REPORT-HEADING
    02  REPORTNAME    PIC X(66) JUST RIGHT.
    02  PAGENUM       PIC X(62) JUST RIGHT.
    02  PAGECOUNT     PIC ZZZ9.
```

Our routine to print the report heading line on each page would then include the following:

```
MOVE "PAYROLL REGISTER" TO REPORTNAME
MOVE "PAGE " TO PAGENUM
MOVE PAGECTR TO PAGECOUNT
```

This is perhaps a slight gain in convenience over setting up a report heading line with three FILLER areas or a 128-position nonnumeric literal. Note that the blank position 128 is taken care of in the second nonnumeric literal.

CONDITION-NAMES; THE 88-LEVEL

When a program must be involved with a rather large number of codes for the data to be processed, and there is frequent communication required between programmer and user, it is often easier for both to talk in terms of the conditions themselves that are identified by codes instead of the codes. Hence, if the condition-names are incorporated into the source program, communication is improved and the programmer finds it easier to locate data for writing of related procedure division statements. The 88-level of data-names is used to identify conditions of the contents of an elementary item whose definition precedes the 88-level condition-name. A series of 88-level condition-names can follow a single elementary item. Since any 88-level condition-name refers to the item preceding it, a procedure division instruction involving the condition-name refers only to the condition-name, not to the item. The simplest condition-name format is: 88 condition-name VALUE IS literal. It should be noted that lower-level ANSI subsets frequently do not have the condition-name clause available, even in the simple format above. Its availability, however, is an exception to the general rule that VALUE clauses must not be used in the data division file section. Use of the 88-level, whether in the file section or working-storage, requires the VALUE clause. An illustration might be:

```
02  SEXCODES              PIC 9.
88  MALE VALUE IS 1.
88  FEMALE VALUE IS 4.
```

A related set of procedure division instructions might be:

```
IF MALE GO TO RTN-X.
IF FEMALE GO TO RTN-Y ELSE GO TO BADCODERTN.
```

A somewhat more elaborate format of the 88-level is:

```
88 condition-name VALUES ARE literal-1 [THRU literal-2]
                  [literal-3 [THRU literal-4]]
```

Without making the maximum use of the above format, an illustration might be:

```
02  SEXCODES              PIC 9.
88  MALE VALUES ARE 1 THRU 3.
88  FEMALE VALUES ARE 4 THRU 6.
```

This permits the procedure division instructions given above to cover a range of code number possibilities; however, any instruction confined to a single MALE or FEMALE VALUE would now have to be based on an IF statement referring to SEXCODES, such as IF SEX-CODES = 2 GO TO RTN-M. In addition, the source program now has no reference to what the three condition-values in each range represent. Depending on the requirements of the application, and in any event, providing greater readability to the source program, a more detailed use of the simpler format might be practical:

```
02  SEXCODES              PIC 9.
88  SINGLE-MALE VALUE 1.
88  MARRIEDMALE VALUE 2.
88  DIVORCEDMALE VALUE 3.
88  SINGLEFEMALE VALUE 4.
88  MARRIEDFEMALE VALUE 5.
88  DIVORCEDFEMALE VALUE 6.
```

Condition-name entries are not permitted with the following types of data items:

1. Those containing a JUSTIFIED clause.
2. Those containing descriptions involving such terms (not covered in this text) as SYNCHRONIZED.
3. 66-level items (also not dealt with in this text).
4. Items with other USAGE than DISPLAY (see discussion of COMPUTATIONAL below).
5. Index data items (involved in advanced table-handling techniques not covered in this text).

SPECIAL USAGES OF NUMERIC DATA: COMPUTATIONAL

Up to this point, any data division PICTURE has been specified without any USAGE clause. When *no* USAGE clause is present, the data is stored for internal operations just as described in the PICTURE—one character per storage location. Computers making use of binary or hexadecimal arithmetic formats can store numeric data in a more compact manner. As indicated in our first chapter, the hexadecimal format permits storing of two numeric characters per location, except in the numeric field's rightmost position, where the positive or negative sign must be stored, as well as the units digit of the field. *Maximum* storage efficiency in the binary format is theoretically slightly greater than two characters per location. When it is desired to use the special storage format available, a USAGE clause so specifying must follow either the group-item data-name or the elementary item PICTURE, depending on the extent of the special USAGE. Although it is normally not essential to indicate when the standard data format of one character per location is being used, the USAGE clause permits this identification as DISPLAY. When there is no USAGE clause for a numeric data item, it is said that USAGE DISPLAY is implicit—the compiler will assume that the data are to be stored in the standard one-character-per-location format.

The format of the USAGE clause is:

$$[\text{USAGE IS}] \left\{ \begin{array}{l} \underline{\text{COMPUTATIONAL}} \\ \underline{\text{COMP}} \\ \underline{\text{DISPLAY}} \end{array} \right\}$$

COMP, of course, is the abbreviated manner of identifying COMPUTATIONAL.

The variation in use of the clause for group and elementary items can be simply illustrated by the following:

```
02  PAYDATA USAGE COMP.
    03  GROSSPAY              PIC S9999V99.
    03  NETPAY                PIC S9999V99.
02  DEDUCTIONS.
    03  FICA                  PIC S999V99.
    03  INCOMETAX             PIC S999V99 USAGE COMP.
```

Note that:

    1. All fields are signed.

    2. The PICTURE for any field is in the standard (DISPLAY) format of one character per storage location.

    3. When USAGE COMP is appended to a group item definition, it will apply to all elementary items within the group.

    4. If no USAGE is explicitly specified for the group item, an elementary item within it may be identified as USAGE COMP; however, it is not permissible to *specify* USAGE DISPLAY for a group item and USAGE COMP for an elementary item within it, or vice versa.

The two advantages that *may* be gained by COMPUTATIONAL usage are saving in use of internal storage areas during program execution and reduction of program execution time. The processes of converting input data from implicit DISPLAY to COMP formats and COMP format results of arithmetic back to DISPLAY for writing output records, however, require processing time. No categorical statement can be made that COMP usage will reduce processing time; in fact, injudicious application of USAGE COMP to numeric data fields with little or no involvement in arithmetic operations may even prolong processing time since the time for format conversion may possibly exceed the time saved in the arithmetic operations. Obviously, the greater the number of arithmetic operations required for specific data fields the greater the likelihood of reducing processing time.

The techniques of COMPUTATIONAL applications depend on the hardware and compilers. For example, Burroughs or CDC techniques differ from IBM, whose 360 and 370 compilers make available such a variety as COMP, COMP-1, COMP-2, and COMP-3. And for some computers, such as Honeywell's 200 family, the method of storing data precludes the availability of COMPUTATIONAL formats altogether. Where the nature of required program arithmetic suggests both possible storage-saving and time-reduction, the availability and techniques of the COMPUTATIONAL clause in the compiler and hardware must be carefully reviewed by the programmer considering its use.

MISCELLANEOUS EDITING CONSIDERATIONS

In Chapter 9, the most frequently used editing characters were discussed in connection with presentation of various conditions of numeric data in printed reports. Since there are (a) certain restrictions on the use of edited data items and (b) PICTURE characters other than A, X, and 9 that are *not* considered edit characters, and (c) one or two miscellaneous editing means, a few paragraphs clarifying the situation are in order.

ANSI COBOL specifications distinguish among five categories of data that can be described by a PICTURE clause. The distinction is based on the allowable characters in the data item's PICTURE and contents, as follows:

Data Item	PICTURE	Contents
Alphabetic	Only A	Any of the 26 alphabetic characters and the space.
Numeric	9, P, S, and V	Numerals 0 through 9 and an operational sign.
Alphanumeric	X, A, and 9 (but not all A or all 9)	Any of the characters in the character set available on the object computer.
Alphanumeric edited	X, A, 9, B, zero (but see note 1)	Any of the characters in the character set available on the object computer.
Numeric edited	B, P, V, Z, zero, 9, comma, period, *, +, −, CR, DB, currency sign ($) (see note 2)	Numerals 0 through 9 and an operational sign.

Note 1. To be considered edited, the PICTURE must contain at least one of the following combinations: X and B, X and zero, or A and zero.

Note 2. Combinations of these characters are subject to the editing rules discussed in Chapter 9; the maximum number of *digit* positions that may be represented in the character string is 18.

It is important to notice that the characters P, S, and V are *not* considered edit characters. The warning against using numeric edited fields for performing arithmetic does *not* apply to numeric items whose PICTUREs contain nothing beyond 9, P, S, and V. We are already familiar with the 9, which represents a numeric character position in the data, and S and V, which do not. The PICTURE character P needs further consideration.

Input data records designed for keypunching economy sometimes contain data fields that exclude a constant known number of leading or trailing zeroes. For example, a field of four digits representing minute quantities of chemicals may require a decimal point and three zeroes preceding the four significant digits; or a six-position dollar amount field may represent thousands of dollars and require three trailing zeroes as integers.

If output records must be written reflecting the full amounts, the character P is ordinarily used in input data definitions so that internal transfers of data provide the necessary zeroes.

Like the S and V, the P occupies no storage character space and is not counted in determining the data-name field size. Each leading P represents an implied decimal zero; each trailing P represents an implied integer zero. When the character P is used at the left of a field, the implied decimal point precedes the first P; when it is used at the right, the implied decimal point follows the last P. The use of P for this purpose thus provides implied decimal-point location and renders the use of V unnecessary in the data PICTURE. In the above examples, with card input, we would use the following PICTURES of the input record fields:

```
02  FIELDA      PIC PPP9999.
02  FIELDB      PIC 9(6)PPP.
```

The input field sizes would still be counted as four- and six-character positions respectively, but calculations would be made assuming seven decimal and nine integer positions and the results positioned accordingly.

For supplying additional zeroes in print output, the zero (0) is used as a simple insertion character, and can be used as many times as needed internally or at the beginning or end of a data field. For example, the addition of three zeroes at the right of a six-position integer field simply requires the otherwise-desired print editing of the six integers followed by three zeroes.

Two other editing techniques have occasional use. Because the comma is more readily suppressed than the period, cases may arise where it is convenient to exchange these two characters. This can be done by use of the SPECIAL-NAMES paragraph in the environment division, followed by the clause DECIMAL-POINT IS COMMA, and by the use of the two characters in the edit positions desired, but under each other's rules. While these instances are rather rare, they do supply some flexibility of use.

A final editing feature with quite limited, but specific, use is the BLANK WHEN ZERO clause, which may be appended following the PICTURE character-string. It serves a purpose only when zero suppression, replacing with spaces or floating symbols, terminates with a decimal point followed by numeric digits; for example:

```
PICTURE ZZZ,ZZZ.99 BLANK WHEN ZERO.
PICTURE $$$,$$$.99 BLANK WHEN ZERO.
PICTURE +++,+++.99 BLANK WHEN ZERO.
PICTURE ———,———.99 BLANK WHEN ZERO.
```

In all of the cases above, the object is to print amounts smaller than 1.00. If BLANK WHEN ZERO were *not* used, zero amounts would be represented by seven blank spaces (or six blank spaces and the edit character) and .00, which is sometimes desired by users of reports as assurance that no failure of print mechanism occurred at that point. Use of BLANK WHEN ZERO will result in the entire ten-position item appearing as spaces. Two other conditions involving BLANK WHEN ZERO should be considered:

1. When the asterisk (*) is used as the zero-suppression symbol, use of BLANK WHEN ZERO has no effect. The reason is clear: the asterisk is used as a check-protecting symbol and its purpose would be destroyed by substitution of blank spaces that would permit manual insertion of figures.

2. For the same reason, BLANK WHEN ZERO should not be used when the floating dollar sign (second example above) is used for check protection. BLANK WHEN ZERO *will* operate when the floating dollar sign is used, so it is possible for the programmer to make the mistake of negating the floating dollar sign in its check-protecting function.

It should be clear from the editing examples given in Chapter 9 that the use of Z or the floating edit characters as the only symbol other than the comma and/or period will result in complete printout of blank spaces under zero data-contents conditions; thus BLANK WHEN ZERO is superfluous if used with, for example, ZZZ,ZZZ.ZZ or +++,+++.++.

REVIEW MATERIAL

Terms

Redefinition area	Condition-name	Format conversion
Justifying	Hexadecimal format	

Questions

What is the function of the REDEFINES clause? How is this function carried out in the case of records in the file section?

Must a redefinition area be the same size as the original area? If a redefinition area is a group item, must it have the same number of elementary items as the original area?

A payroll record has a six-position area that can be either of two things: (*a*) a single-position alphanumeric union code, followed by an hourly rate consisting of two integer and three decimal positions, or (*b*) an annual salary area of six integer positions. How would you define this data area using REDEFINES?

What is normal justifying for numeric data? For alphabetic or alphanumeric data?

What is the advantage of using condition-names?

What is the advantage of using USAGE COMPUTATIONAL on appropriate hardware?

How may proper use of the picture symbol P affect keypunching and the layout of the card record?

True-or-False Statements

REDEFINES can appear in the file section or in working-storage.

REDEFINES cannot appear at the 01-level.

The use of the JUSTIFIED RIGHT clause assures that the rightmost character of the field will not be a space.

Condition-names can appear in the file section or in working-storage.

The VALUE clause in an 88-level item must contain one, and only one, literal.

The USAGE clause refers to the form a number is stored in.

The picture symbol P stands for implied significant zeroes.

12

MISCELLANEOUS PROCEDURE DIVISION STATEMENTS

It is the purpose of this book, as described in the Introduction and specifically limited in the early pages of Chapter 3, to provide a working knowledge of the COBOL programming techniques made available in the basic compilers, through the three modules common to them. A brief reference to the COBOL reserved word list as analyzed by module will indicate that at this point almost all of the reserved words in the nucleus module's identification, environment, and data division groupings have been discussed. A few basic procedure division verbs with a variety of specific, and somewhat incidental, uses remain to be considered, since occasion for their use did not arise in any of the typical programming situations so far encountered. Several have frequent enough use to justify discussion here: of these, four (ACCEPT, DISPLAY, ENTER, and some uses of STOP) are partly hardware- or operating-system-dependent; two (ALTER and EXIT) are concerned with transfer of logic control within the program; one (NOTE) supplies information about the function of procedure division routines but is not itself an instruction, and one (nested conditional) is a means of telescoping IF statement conditions to permit several conditions to be dealt with in one sentence. In addition, some aspects of the PERFORM instruction will be discussed at this point.

ACCEPT AND DISPLAY STATEMENTS

ACCEPT and DISPLAY statements, though usable independently, often supplement each other in connection with low-data-volume operations or steps, usually at the beginning of program execution, which require the computer operator to check for the presence of specific input-output conditions or data. Either or both may require a SPECIAL-NAMES statement in the environment division assigning a mnemonic-name to a hardware device whose use is required by the ACCEPT or DISPLAY instruction, which then refers to the hardware device by the mnemonic-name assigned by the programmer.

The ACCEPT statement transfers input data to internal processing areas from such hardware devices as the reader, the console keyboard, or special reading devices; the DISPLAY statement transfers data-name fields already in storage and/or literals supplied in the DISPLAY statement itself to output devices such as the printer, the punch unit, or the console typewriter. The formats of the two statements are:

ACCEPT identifier [FROM mnemonic-name]

$$\text{and DISPLAY} \begin{Bmatrix} \text{literal-1} \\ \text{identifier-1} \end{Bmatrix} \begin{bmatrix} \begin{Bmatrix} \text{literal-2} \\ \text{identifier-2} \end{Bmatrix} \cdots \end{bmatrix}$$

[UPON mnemonic-name]

ANSI COBOL specifications permit the computer manufacturer (implementor) to designate its standard input device for the ACCEPT statement and standard output device for the display statement. When these devices are employed in the program, the programmer need not use the FROM or UPON clauses. Typically, the card reader is the standard device for ACCEPT and the printer is the standard device for DISPLAY. For other available devices, the implementor's compiler contains a reserved word for each, such as CONSOLE, SYSPUNCH, etc. If one of these devices is to be involved in an ACCEPT or DISPLAY statement, a mnemonic-name must be assigned to it as indicated, for example: SPECIAL-NAMES. CONSOLE IS TYPER. The statements would then be worded as: ACCEPT . . . FROM TYPER or DISPLAY . . . UPON TYPER.

Also left to the implementor, subject to its hardware capacities, is the definition of the size of the data transfer. In the ACCEPT statement, the identifier is usually some field in working-storage. The implementor's compiler will specify the maximum number of card columns, cards, or console typewriter character positions of data to be ACCEPTed, and when the data is entered by a card fed into the reader or by keying in console characters, the transfer is made beginning at the left of both the ACCEPTed data and the identifier field. A typical use of the ACCEPT statement is to provide data at the beginning of a computer run that must vary each time for purposes of identifying an otherwise standard report, such as a report date or number. REPORT-DATE may be the name of an 02-level field in working-storage; a mere ACCEPT REPORTDATE will transfer the data punched into a card to the identifier field. No file or record definition for the ACCEPTed card is needed; but the limited amount of data transferable and the slowness of execution time make the ACCEPT instruction impractical as a substitute for a READ instruction for handling entire input data files.

DISPLAY has a slightly more flexible application, since it cannot only be used to identify error conditions during processing without interrupting the run, but also to set up conditions (usually by providing an ACCEPT statement) that will permit the computer operator to correct input data errors and continue processing. Uses of this sort for DISPLAY are generally to be avoided whenever possible, since repeated stoppages for error correction normally waste more computer time than they save; but on smaller computers with only sequentially accessible storage devices, occasions do arise when the only method of input data validation involves processing against a massive master file, and the likely number of stoppages for error correction may take considerably less time than a second processing against the master file.

Probably the most frequent use of DISPLAY is to generate some message printout at the beginning of program execution that will remind the computer operator to supply specific data before actual processing can be begun. This may also require an ACCEPT statement in the program to enable the computer operator to supply the data on a punched card in the reader or key in data on the console. In a well-organized system, the card or other information to be ACCEPTed has already been supplied to the computer operator; the DISPLAY and ACCEPT instructions in the program create a momentary stoppage during which the operator is expected to check the data supplied and assure himself that it is correct and applicable for the processing at hand. The programming routines that include DISPLAY and ACCEPT can frequently contain a limited number of validation tests of the data to be ACCEPTed; but seldom is it possible to anticipate all possibilities of error in (a) the user's furnishing of the data, (b) the keying of the data, and (c) the computer operator's checking of the data. Though these statements are quite often well-nigh unavoidable, they are inadvisable if some alternative not so dependent on human accuracy, type of hardware, or compiler characteristics, can be found. A prohibitive amount of space would be required to list the variations of compiler and hardware in connection with DISPLAY and ACCEPT statements. Different programming conditions will be created by the nature of the card-reading and punching devices alone; some compilers will not permit DISPLAY or ACCEPT to be used on a device performing its normal function during program execution, while some others will. For example, it may or may not be permissible, depending on compiler and hardware, to use DISPLAY on the printer during a program that provides for report printing, or on a card-punch during a program whose function includes punching of an output file of cards; and ACCEPT is sometimes prohibited for the card reader when the regular input file consists of cards to be read.

In general, the uses of DISPLAY and ACCEPT are aimed toward aiding the computer operator to process data efficiently and correctly and to provide a limited check on the accuracy of the data and the operator's use of it, usually at the beginning of program execution. Ordinarily, these statements should not be employed as error display and correction techniques in editing entire data files; file-editing and validation programs with error-message printouts or error-card punchouts usually are faster and more efficient means of serving this purpose. In a program involving batched data likely to contain a dozen or so error conditions per batch, the requirement of using DISPLAY and ACCEPT will waste enough computer time to make the practice prohibitive.

THE ALTER INSTRUCTION

Unlike the DISPLAY and ACCEPT statements, which require computer-operator activity in direct response to program-generated instructions, the ALTER statement enables the programmer to incorporate within the program itself changes in the program's own sequence of instructions. This not only sounds more impressive than it is, but the ALTER statement is probably used (*a*) rather sparingly and (*b*) somewhat less than it could be, even in its fairly-limited application. In its simplest form, it is: <u>ALTER</u> procedure-name-1 <u>TO [PROCEED TO]</u> procedure-name-2, and in higher-level compilers a single ALTER statement may change multiple procedures by appending [procedure-name-3 <u>TO [PROCEED TO]</u> procedure-name-4] . . . . When the ALTER statement is used, procedure-name-1, -3, etc., must be paragraphs whose only instruction is a single unconditional GO TO statement. Procedure-name-2, -4, etc., must be paragraph-names or section-names. Once the ALTER statement has taken effect, and procedure-name-2 has replaced procedure-name-1 and the program routines it calls for, the sequence of instructions originally called for by procedure-name-1 will not be executed again during the program unless another ALTER statement (changing procedure-name-1 to its original state) restores them.

Typically, ALTER *may* be useful in rerouting program logic shortly after the beginning of a program so that routines used only once need not be referred to or tested for again. Conversely, routines used throughout the program may be ALTERed when an end-of-file condition produces a need for introducing a different program path. Usually, however, either necessity or convenience causes some other arrangement of program logic techniques than use of the ALTER statement. A third possible use for ALTER is the rather rare occasion when more than one type of data input must be processed by a single program. The two or more types of data are separated into intact groups, and substantially different program logic applies for each group. Conceptually, the use of ALTER to shift to a new sequence of routines for each distinct data group could avoid a considerable number of IF statements and might improve program execution speed.

Without any claim of practicality or relevance to reality, the following paragraphs demonstrate the logic-substitution achieved by the ALTER statement:

```
010-STEPA.
    GO TO 011-STEPB.
011-STEPB.
    MOVE FIELDX TO FIELDY.
    MOVE 1 TO FIELDZ.
    ALTER 010-STEPA TO PROCEED TO 012-STEPC.
012-STEPC.
    MOVE GROUPDATAIN TO GROUPDATAOUT.
    COMPUTE XCALC ROUNDED = A + B — DEDUCTIONS.
```

In the case above, 011-STEPB will be executed only once; the ALTER has the effect of making the lone GO TO in 010-STEPA an instruction to GO TO 012-STEPC. The program sequence will now be from 010-STEPA to 012-STEPC. The original sequence can be restored, if it is desired and feasible to do so, by inserting at the proper point in the program a statement to: ALTER 010-STEPA TO PROCEED TO 011-STEPB.

THE ENTER STATEMENT

A rather widely ignored ANSI COBOL specification is one that provides for the ability to introduce an implementor's programming language into a COBOL program. The introduction can be made by the simple statement, <u>ENTER</u> language-name. Statements in the implementor-provided "other language" follow, preceding the statement ENTER COBOL, from which point statements are once again written in COBOL.

Although the ANSI specifications include the ENTER statement in both low- and high-level nucleus modules, it is not available in at least one major compiler.

STOP STATEMENTS

Typically, the last instruction to be executed by a program (but not necessarily the last instruction in the source program) is STOP RUN, which terminates the program's control and makes the computer hardware devices available for control by the next program, whether supplied by operator action or called in through the stored program control exercised by an "operating system."

The other format, <u>STOP</u> literal, communicates a message to the computer operator through some output device as provided for in the implementor's compiler. Typically, the device is the console typewriter or, on a smaller computer, one of the console registers. Continuation of the program depends on operator action, which is, in turn, dependent on the nature of the message represented by the literal, usually numeric if a console register is involved, and nonnumeric if transmitted through the typewriter. In either case, the literal often refers the operator to the "run book" containing instructions on the handling of the condition indicated. The instructions will enable the operator to determine whether to terminate or continue the job. Continuation will begin with execution of the statement immediately following the STOP statement, so the routine in which the STOP statement occurs must be planned to permit the operator to do what is necessary based on this continuation sequence. Consider the following:

```
CARD-READING.
  READ DATACARD AT END GO TO EOCARD.
  IF CARDCODE = PREVCODE GO TO SAMECODERTN.
  IF CARDCODE > PREVCODE AND CARDNUM = 1 GO
    TO FIRSTCARDRTN.
  STOP "CARDNUM NOT 1".
  GO TO CARD-READING.
```

Note that if the program is to continue, a card with the digit 1 in a field called CARDNUM must be read. On any card reader, there is a runout key, which permits the operator to eject any cards in the input feed stations without disturbing the execution of the program. The operator will be able to remove these cards, and examine them for a possible mispunch, out-of-sequence condition, or missing card. If he determines from run-book instructions that he can continue by correcting the card sequence, correcting a mispunched card, or holding a mispunched card or card set out of the processing, he will make sure that the first card returned to the input feed correctly contains a CARDNUM of 1, and resume operation by pressing the start key on the reader. The statement following the STOP will cause a branch back to the beginning of the paragraph. A proper card will be read, and the IF statement will cause a branch to the required processing routine.

As suggested by the above description of operator activity, the STOP routines of this sort should be used as sparingly as the DISPLAY and ACCEPT combination. Techniques that require operator activity in addition to interruptions of processing can be highly wasteful of computer time. Printout of error messages, writing of error tapes, or, where feasible, punchout of error cards as a last choice, involve far less computer and operator time, and are preferable to the type of interruptions described. Like the DISPLAY and ACCEPT combination, the STOP literal option should be restricted, if at all possible, to single-occurrence tests, such as checking for presence and accuracy of a leader card which may be required to precede an input file.

THE NOTE SENTENCE

Earlier we described the REMARKS paragraph of the identification division (see Chapter 4), which served an information-providing purpose concerning the nature of the program, but generated no program instructions. The NOTE sentence in the procedure division serves the same function for a routine or set of routines. Because it must be inserted somewhere between instructions or

paragraphs, however, there are specific rules that must be followed to enable the compiler to distinguish between a NOTE, which is explanatory commentary, and actual instructions. The NOTE sentence format is: NOTE character-string. Any characters in the computer's character set may be used in the NOTE. Two simple restrictions govern the NOTE sentence usage:

1. If a NOTE sentence is the *first* sentence in a paragraph, the entire *paragraph* is regarded as a note. In effect, this restriction may be an aid to the programmer if comment requiring two or more sentences is involved. Any sentence following the NOTE sentence in the same paragraph will not be compiled even though intended as program instructions.

2. If a NOTE sentence is *not* the first sentence of a paragraph, the compiler treats the NOTE commentary as ending with the first period followed by a space, and the next sentence in the paragraph will be compiled as an instruction if validly written.

The NOTE sentence must otherwise conform to the rules of format for paragraph structure. While the NOTE contains no instructions that will be compiled, the NOTE comments will print out, just as keypunched, on the source program listing that accompanies the compilation attempt. Particularly for programs which may, by the nature of the application, require frequent change, well-planned and carefully worded NOTEs may save hours of program checking and analysis for the programmer undertaking the change. A source program containing clear, concise, and comprehensive NOTEs in areas subject to change is far more likely to continue as an effective program after change, with much less time and cost in changes, than is the same program with no NOTEs whatsoever.

A possible use of a NOTE in a payroll calculation program might be as follows:

```
PENSION-CALCS.
  GO TO EXECPEN ADMINPEN UNIONPEN NOPLAN MISC-
  DEDUCT DEPENDING ON PENCODE. NOTE EXECPEN IS
  NONCONTRIBUTORY, OTHERS CONTRIBUTORY; IF PEN-
  DATE IS BLANK EMPDATE IS BASIS; PENCODE 4 IS NO
  PLAN.
MISCDEDUCT.
  . . . . . .
```

Notice that the NOTE is not the first sentence in a paragraph, but consists of only one sentence, followed by a new paragraph. What would be the effect on compilation of the program if periods were keypunched instead of the two semicolons?

THE EXIT STATEMENT

The EXIT statement is perhaps the only COBOL instruction that performs a highly useful operating function by performing no operation at all. Its specified function is to provide, in ANSI words, a common endpoint for a series of procedures. It does this by appearing as a one-word sentence in a paragraph where it is the only sentence. Its typical function is brought about by the necessity of using a GO TO within a statement being PERFORMed, and involves the PERFORM format that includes the THRU option: PERFORM procedure-name-1 THRU procedure-name-2. This option permits a PERFORM statement to require execution of two or more paragraphs, which are consecutive within the program, in their successive order, and to return program control to the sentence following the PERFORM. We might say:

```
PERFORM PARAGRAPH5 THRU PARAGRAPH8.
MOVE X TO Y . . .
```

Suppose it became necessary to deal with a condition in PARAGRAPH7 that would not permit completion of that paragraph; for example:

```
PARAGRAPH7.
    ADD A TO B.
    SUBTRACT B FROM C.
    IF C = D GO TO PARAGRAPH11.
    COMPUTE X ROUNDED = (C + E) * F.
    MOVE F TO PRINTF.
```

According to ANSI COBOL rules, a GO TO within a statement being PERFORMed is permissible only if control remains within the series of statements being PERFORMed. Clearly, if C = D, control will not remain within PARAGRAPH7. However, PARAGRAPH11 may have as its last instruction GO TO PARAGRAPH8, and that paragraph may be:

```
PARAGRAPH8.
    EXIT.
```

In this case control *does* remain within the series of statements to be PERFORMed. PARAGRAPH11 will be executed, and the GO TO PARAGRAPH8 at its end will cause the last two instructions in PARAGRAPH7 to be omitted; control will be reestablished at PARAGRAPH8, which does nothing except "provide the common exit" to the next paragraph (presumably 9) for both PARAGRAPH7 and PARAGRAPH11.

An important distinction must be made here between the use of a GO TO within a PERFORM and a PERFORM within a PERFORM. In the above case, the last two steps in PARAGRAPH7 would be executed only if C did not equal D; and PARAGRAPH11 would be executed only if C did equal D. While ANSI specifications permit the use of a PERFORM within a PERFORM, two conditions must exist to permit it:

1. The "included" PERFORM's associated instructions must be either totally included in or totally excluded from the sequence of instructions called for by the first PERFORM.

2. The two PERFORM statements may not have a common exit.

These two conditions indicate that we could *not* have written a valid instruction which said IF C = D PERFORM PARAGRAPH11, first because PARAGRAPH11 is partially excluded from the logic of PARAGRAPH7 (it is an alternative to the last two statements of PARAGRAPH7), and second because PARAGRAPH11 ends with a GO TO PARAGRAPH8, which is a common exit for both paragraphs 7 and 11.

Had the conditions been such that if C = D, PARAGRAPH11 were to be executed, followed by execution of the last two statements in PARAGRAPH7, the instruction IF C = D PERFORM PARAGRAPH11 would be valid. PARAGRAPH11 (*a*) would then be totally included in or totally excluded from PARAGRAPH7 and (*b*) should not include GO TO PARAGRAPH8 as a last statement. Under these conditions, no common exit would be needed; PARAGRAPH8 would not only be superfluous, but violate the second condition stated for a PERFORM within a PERFORM. The PERFORM . . . THRU statement, of course, would then be PERFORM PARAGRAPH5 THRU PARAGRAPH7.

THE "NESTED CONDITIONAL"

Higher-level COBOL compilers contain the capability of interpreting IF statements within IF statements. The basic IF statement format contains the following possibilities:

IF condition	statement-1	ELSE statement-2
	NEXT SENTENCE	ELSE NEXT SENTENCE[1]

A simple condition presents a single choice between two alternatives, such as: IF AMOUNT GREATER THAN MINIMUM GO TO TAXCALC ELSE GO TO NOTAXRTN. The choice is simple to flowchart:

---

1. In this format, statement-1 and statement-2 can each be more than one statement.

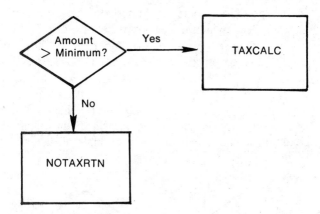

Suppose, however, there are two possible tax calculations which might be made, each different from and excluding the other. Once the taxable condition exists, a tax code 1 or 2 will determine whether a TAXCALC1 or TAXCALC2 routine applies. A flowcharted course of possible actions might be:

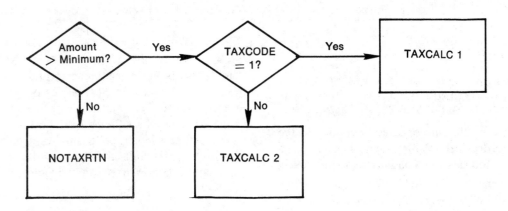

Since statement-1 and statement-2 are permitted to contain an IF condition, we can "nest" the second alternative in either of two ways:

> IF AMOUNT GREATER THAN MINIMUM IF TAXCODE = 1 GO TO TAXCALC1 ELSE GO TO TAXCALC2 ELSE GO TO NOTAXRTN.
>
> *or* IF AMOUNT NOT GREATER THAN MINIMUM GO TO NOTAXRTN ELSE IF TAXCODE = 1 GO TO TAXCALC1 ELSE GO TO TAXCALC2.

Each of the above statements "nests" the IF TAXCODE = 1 condition within the AMOUNT GREATER THAN MINIMUM condition. Each does exactly the same set of operations. Each follows the flowchart; but perhaps it is more readily apparent that the second statement does so. The second statement appears easier to read; it disposes of the basic negative (or neutral) condition first, as does the flowchart, then makes the decision, under the positive condition, as to which of the two tax calculations to execute.

Conditional statements are compiler-read from left to right. Each IF and ELSE combination is considered a pair, and if more than one IF precedes an ELSE, the ELSE is considered as applying to the immediately preceding IF that has not already been paired with an ELSE. Each version of the above "nested conditional" statement, if analyzed, will be found to satisfy this rule.

Although it would seem that the second version of the statement is not only easier to read but corresponds more clearly to the flowchart, there apparently is a tendency for programmers to use the first style, leading to consecutive IFs followed by consecutive ELSEs.

Since this makes for difficulty in interpretation, some implementors have extended their compilers to permit the insertion of THEN immediately preceding sentence-1 and allow either ELSE or OTHERWISE to precede statement-2. It should be noted that THEN and OTHERWISE are not reserved words in the basic ANSI COBOL vocabulary.

The observing student may have already noticed the possibility of an unattended-to condition in the above-described programming situation. There is an assumption that TAXCODE will always be either 1 or 2; if we can rely on this, we are safe in executing TAX-CALC2 if TAXCODE is not 1. But suppose TAXCODE is a 3 or a blank; is this an error condition, or does it simply mean that tax is not applicable and that NOTAXRTN should be executed? If the latter, a slight change in the flowchart and statement makes the nested conditional still useful:

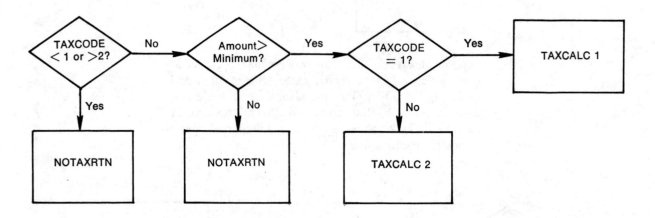

Our statement can then be written:

IF TAXCODE < 1 OR > 2 GO TO NOTAXRTN. IF AMOUNT NOT GREATER THAN MINIMUM GO TO NOTAXRTN ELSE IF TAXCODE = 1 GO TO TAXCALC1 ELSE GO TO TAXCALC2.

Notice that there is still only one nested condition, the same one as before. All we have done is to make a preliminary test for the one condition not previously considered. Everything else in the statement, including the nested conditional, is intact.

If, however, the presence of a TAXCODE other than 1 or 2 is not a legitimate condition, and we now face, in addition to the possibilities of tax calculations or a no-tax routine, a possible error routine, the nested conditional may be either no solution at all or one so involved that simpler programming choices would be preferable. Assuming that only codes 1 and 2 are legitimate, our flowchart would require:

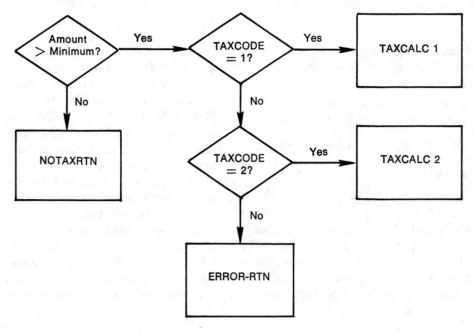

Probably the simplest sequence of statements to execute the above possibilities would be:

```
IF AMOUNT NOT GREATER THAN MINIMUM GO TO
    NOTAXRTN.
IF TAXCODE = 1 GO TO TAXCALC1.
IF TAXCODE = 2 GO TO TAXCALC2 ELSE GO TO
    ERROR-RTN.
```

The use of nested conditionals should be restricted to cases where the number of statements can be reduced while preserving the programming logic and maintaining clear readability of the source program listing. Nested conditionals that fail to do even one of these things should be avoided. The three simple IF statements above, properly sequenced, are certainly no more difficult to read or follow than either of the original statements containing the nested conditional; yet they cover one additional situation with no greater verbiage. No test is made for tax codes unless the taxable condition, AMOUNT GREATER THAN MINIMUM, occurs. TAXCALC1 will be executed only if TAXCODE = 1; if not, and TAXCODE = 2, TAXCALC2 will be executed. Only when TAXCODE is neither 1 nor 2 for an otherwise taxable amount will ERROR-RTN be executed.

REVIEW MATERIAL

Terms

Console typewriter	Program logic	Common exit
Sequence (of instructions)	Run book	Nested conditional

Questions

In what ways are the ACCEPT and DISPLAY statements simpler to use than the READ and WRITE? What are their disadvantages?

What are the limitations on a GO TO that is being ALTERed?

What is the function of the ENTER statement?

How can STOP literal be used to signal the operator to take corrective action during the execution of a program?

What is the result of executing an EXIT statement?

When using nested conditionals why is it desirable to follow the pattern IF . . . ELSE . . . IF . . . ELSE . . . IF . . . ELSE rather than IF . . IF . . . IF . . . ELSE . . . ELSE . . . ELSE . . .?

True-or-False Statements

Normally data is ACCEPTed from the card reader and DISPLAYed on the printer.

When DISPLAYing error information to the operator the programmer should insure that the data is printed at the top of a page.

The ALTER statement allows us to modify data fields in the memory of the computer.

STOP RUN terminates program execution, but STOP literal, on some computers, allows for the resumption of execution at the operator's discretion.

13

TABLE-HANDLING

THE TABULAR CONCEPT

A table can be defined as one or more sets of a finite number of data items placed in specific and orderly relationship to each other. The table can be *one-dimensional*, such as a table of twenty-five pay rates. The one dimension in this case is pay rate. If, however, the rates are accompanied by a corresponding list of pay codes, and the rate for every pay code were increased in ten successive steps after specific periods of service, a *two-dimensional* table would be required, the dimensions being rate and period of service. If there were eight different regions, in each of which the pay-rate codes carried different rates, a *three-dimensional* table would be required to present complete data in the three dimensions of pay rate, period of service, and region. In appearance as organized data, a one-dimensional table simply appears as a list of related items; tables of more than one dimension appear in a rectangular presentation of multiple lines of data related to multiple columns of data. This rectangular presentation is often referred to in other terms, such as matrix or grid.

From the standpoint of computer usage, tables fall into two broad categories: (*a*) input data accumulated and stored during execution of the program in format for printout as a report, and (*b*) data stored either as part of the program or as special input data to be available for reference during execution of the program on the regular input data. The first category includes many types of sales analysis and various types of count or experience data, such as for insurance experience purposes or general business purposes; for example, a business might desire a count of employees in each service-period bracket in each pay code. The second category of tables is comprised of those that are referenced during program execution to obtain data for coding or computation. Probably the most frequently used table of this type for general business purposes is the Federal income-tax deduction table used in computing income-tax deductions in payroll programs. Although these two categories of tables seem vastly different, the COBOL techniques of handling them are essentially the same—definition of the table in the data division and either accumulation or referencing in the procedure division. The COBOL table-handling techniques reduce the number of data division entries and avoid the use of multiple IF statements and other repetition of instructions in the procedure division; the programming economy of these techniques has resulted in the use of table handling for a variety of miscellaneous purposes not covered by these two categories. For example, mailing labels using three- or four-line addresses and printed three at a time side-by-side from tape- or disk-stored name-and-address records are often printed by use of programs which set up the three-by-three or four-by-three format as if it were a table. Conditions frequently occur in programming where material that is not actually in table form can be handled logically as if it were, with considerably less programming effort than in some other manner. The table-handling programming technique can, then, be applied to material that is not necessarily tabular in nature. We might say that the table-handling technique is applicable to two general types of actual tables, and to material that is not tabular but lends itself to handling for programming purposes as if it were logically a table.

ANSI COBOL specifications provide for three levels of table-handling modules. At the lowest level there is capability for accessing only one-dimensional fixed-length tables; at the second level, up to three-dimensional fixed-length tables; at the highest level, three-dimensional variable-length tables. It should be pointed out, however, that the limitation at the lowest level is not as serious as it might first appear, since it is possible for certain types of two-dimensional tables to handle each dimension as if it were a one-dimensional table with moderate extra effort over that used for a two-dimensional table treated as such.

ONE-DIMENSIONAL TABLES

As already indicated, a one-dimensional table is really a list of related items. Each item in the list is usually related to a corresponding list of names for the items. Using the example given in the first paragraph of this chapter, but reducing the number of pay codes to nine for convenience in program illustration, let us assume the following: A company's mass-storage file of 200-position master payroll records contains a pay code in position 6, in the range of digits 1 through 9. The basic nine rates associated with these digits are $2.50, $2.75, $3.00, $3.50, $4.00, $4.50, $5.00, $5.50, and $6.00. A count of the number of employees at each of these rates is desired, with the printout showing actual base rate and number of employees at that base rate. If we were to program this specification without the use of table-handling techniques, we would require not only the entries for nine literals for the rates, but data definitions of the nine rate codes individually and the setting up of nine counter areas individually, as well as a series of IF statements to govern addition in each of the nine counters. Using table-handling techniques, detailed entries can be replaced by much shorter data definitions and procedure division routines for all except the definitions of the literals. Our data division file-section records would be normal in appearance:

```
FD   MASTERFILE . . .   . . . .
01   MASTERREC.
     02   FILLER          PIC X(5).
     02   PAYCODE         PIC 9.
     02   FILLER          PIC X(194).
FD   PRINTFILE . . . . . . .
01   PRINTREC.
     02   FILLER          PIC X(10).
```

```
     02   PAYRATE         PIC X(5).
     02   FILLER          PIC XXX.
     02   RATECOUNT       PIC ZZZ9.
     02   FILLER          PIC X(110).
```

In working-storage we would set up the following:

```
WORKING-STORAGE SECTION.
77   SUBS               PIC 9 VALUE ZERO
01   RATECOUNTERS.
     02   RATETALLY      PIC 9999 OCCURS 9 TIMES.
01   RATERECORD.
     02   RATENAMES
     03   FILLER         PIC X(5) VALUE "$2.50".
     03   FILLER         PIC X(5) VALUE "$2.75".
     03   FILLER         PIC X(5) VALUE "$3.00".
     03   FILLER         PIC X(5) VALUE "$3.50".
     03   FILLER         PIC X(5) VALUE "$4.00".
     03   FILLER         PIC X(5) VALUE "$4.50".
     03   FILLER         PIC X(5) VALUE "$5.00".
     03   FILLER         PIC X(5) VALUE "$5.50".
     03   FILLER         PIC X(5) VALUE "$6.00".
     02   RATETABLE REDEFINES RATENAMES.
     03   RATE           PIC X(5) OCCURS 9 TIMES.
```

The procedure division can be brief:

```
PROCEDURE DIVISION.
   OPEN INPUT MASTERFILE OUTPUT PRINTFILE.
   MOVE ZEROES TO RATECOUNTERS.
READ-MASTER.
   READ MASTERFILE AT END GO TO PRINT-ANALYSIS.
   ADD 1 TO RATETALLY (PAYCODE).
   GO TO READ-MASTER.
PRINT-ANALYSIS.
   PERFORM MOVE-TO-PRINT UNTIL SUBS = 9.
   CLOSE MASTERFILE PRINTFILE.
   STOP RUN.
MOVE-TO-PRINT.
   ADD 1 TO SUBS.
   MOVE SPACES TO PRINTREC.
   MOVE RATE (SUBS) TO PAYRATE.
   MOVE RATETALLY (SUBS) TO RATECOUNT.
   WRITE PRINTREC AFTER ADVANCING 2 LINES.
```

The following new techniques should be noted in order:

1. In the working-storage section, nine counters have been set up by the entry for RATETALLY, using an OCCURS clause immediately following the RATETALLY picture. RATETALLY is defined at an 02 level because the OCCURS clause cannot be used at either an 01 or 77 level. The basic OCCURS clause format is: OCCURS integer TIMES. Since TIMES is optional, we could have written it, in this instance, OCCURS 9. By defining one counter area, we have allocated nine (as many as there are pay codes) through use of the OCCURS clause. The next question is: how do we add in a specific counter area?

2. Since the PAYCODE input data field indicates the specific counter to be added into, when we wish to add in the proper RATETALLY counter we *subscript* the counter reference in the ADD instruction

with the name of the field (PAYCODE) containing the counter number.[1] This is done by enclosing the subscript field name in parentheses, as is done in the READ-MASTER paragraph's ADD instruction. If PAYCODE contains a 2, addition will take place in the second of the nine RATETALLY counters, if a 5, in the fifth, and so on. When an OCCURS clause is used to set up a data-name field numerous times, any reference to that data-name *must* be subscripted,[2] since only one of the numerous areas is being referenced. The absence of the subscript in the reference instruction will cause a diagnostic indicating that the instruction is incomplete.

3. Note that the effect of using the OCCURS clause and the subscripting technique has been to provide a two-line entry to set up nine counter areas and a one-line instruction that both determines which counter is to be used and does the adding into it. Since the entire program is strictly an accumulation of count data from a file and the printout of the results, the only remaining consideration is how to print the data in a sequential format after the file has been completely processed. Use of OCCURS and subscripting enables us to keep the end-of-job print routine to a minimum of instructions.

4. We cannot escape specifying the nine rates individually, since they are not in the file data and each must be supplied as a literal to identify each of the nine lines of printed-out counts. To avoid nine separate MOVEs to the PRINTREC area, the following devices are used:

a. The literals for the nine rate identifications are listed in sequence in the working-storage section as elementary items within an 02-level group item called RATENAMES. To permit referring to these by subscripting (since an OCCURS clause cannot be used with data division entries containing a VALUE clause), we set up another 02-level entry—RATE-TABLE REDEFINES RATENAMES—and indicate by an 03-level entry within it that RATE . . . OCCURS 9 TIMES.

b. A subscript field, SUBS, is made available as a 77-level item and assigned an initial VALUE of ZERO.

c. Now, if we are careful in incrementing the value of SUBS by 1, we can replace nine sets of rate-name and rate-count MOVEs and nine WRITE instructions with one rather compact print routine.

5. The READ-MASTER paragraph indicates that the program is to GO TO PRINT-ANALYSIS at the end of file-reading. The first instruction in PRINT-ANALYSIS is PERFORM MOVE-TO-PRINT UNTIL SUBS = 9. This is a new format of the PERFORM statement: PERFORM procedure-name-1 [THRU procedure-name-2] UNTIL condition-1, which may not be available on some lower-level COBOL compilers. This is no insurmountable obstacle, however; an available format on all COBOL compilers is:

PERFORM procedure-name-1 [THRU procedure-name-2]
$$\left\{ \begin{matrix} \text{identifier-1} \\ \text{integer-1} \end{matrix} \right\} \underline{\text{TIMES}}$$

In this case, the statement would be: PERFORM MOVE-TO-PRINT 9 TIMES.

Note that the MOVE-TO-PRINT routine first adds 1 to SUBS and, before moving any data to the print record area, moves spaces to it. The MOVE RATE instruction will, for the first print line, move the first (SUBS = 1) rate of $2.50 to printing position, and MOVE RATETALLY (SUBS) will move the contents of the corresponding counter to its print area. The WRITE instruction will cause printing to take place, and the MOVE-TO-PRINT routine will be repeated eight times, each time producing the next matched pair of rate and count as SUBS is increased by 1 at the beginning of the routine. It is clear that if the PERFORM . . . 9 TIMES format is used, the files will be closed after the ninth execution of MOVE-TO-PRINT. It should also be clear that this will occur if the PERFORM . . . UNTIL . . . format is used, since after eight printouts, SUBS will contain a count of 8, MOVE-TO-PRINT will be executed the ninth time, and only then will the PERFORM . . . UNTIL . . . show that SUBS now contains 9 and the file-closing is to take place.

One comment should be made concerning tabular *printout* presentations: when a mass-storage file is in a particular sequence which does *not* correspond to the sequence of the table presentation, table-handling techniques provide a similar processing advantage to that supplied by random-access techniques. Accumulation of data in tabular form for printout is independent of the sequence of the file being processed. No file-sorting to achieve a particular sequence need be performed prior to processing for table accumulation, and the processing itself will take place at speeds limited only by the complexity of the table-processing routines themselves.

An additional comment to avoid misunderstanding should be made. In the table described, counts were

---

1. In the illustrations in this chapter, and probably for the great majority of subscripting uses, the subscript is a parenthesized data name. The subscript can also be a parenthesized *integer* which is (*a*) itself a data-name or (*b*) the number of an item's place in a table. For example, if we have a table of 100 NAMEs, we might have reason to MOVE NAME (35) to FIELDX.

2. Or indexed. The indexing technique is computer-dependent and, primarily for this reason, is not discussed in this text.

employed rather than data accumulation. This should not be taken to indicate a necessary characteristic of table-handling. If, for example, year-to-date earnings were a part of the master-file records in the case just described, and we had wished to accumulate earnings totals by pay rate, we would have specified dollar-and-cent amount fields instead of the RATECOUNT and RATETALLY fields, defined the input data fields accordingly—possibly as EARNINGS—and instead of an ADD 1 in the READ-MASTER paragraph, specified ADD EARNINGS.

TWO-DIMENSIONAL TABLES

The handling of a two-dimensional table basically requires the same techniques as a one-dimensional table with a minimum of two new devices—double subscripting and the . . . VARYING . . . format of the PER-FORM instruction. Let us assume an additional data item in the master record file used in the one-dimensional example, and a second dimension to the report form: the seventh position in the master record file is a length-of-service code, and the digits range from 1 to 6; and the count requirement is that within each basic pay code, the number of employees in each length-of-service code be shown.

Let us make the following changes.

1) In the MASTERREC, add the entry, 02 SVC-CODE PIC 9. following PAYCODE, and change the last FILLER picture to X(193).

2) Revise the contents of PRINT-REC to:

```
02  FILLER          PIC X(10).
02  PAYRATE         PIC X(5).
02  RATECOUNTS      PIC ZZZZZZZ9 OCCURS 6 TIMES.
02  FILLER          PIC X(69).
```

As we shall see shortly, the RATECOUNTS fields are not expected to contain eight digits each; the leftmost four positions are to provide spacing preceding each printed count for a length-of-service code within a rate.

3) In the working-storage section, the first 01-level entry and its contents will appear as follows:

```
01  RATECOUNTERS.
    02  RATETALLY     OCCURS 9 TIMES.
    03  SVCETALLY     PIC 9999 OCCURS 6 TIMES.
```

Note that although the OCCURS clause can be used for a group item, only the basic data item is provided with a PICTURE. We are defining the two-dimensional table structure here, in effect saying that there are nine rates, and for each rate, counts are taken in six groups. We have a nine-by-six table of 54 counts.

4) The READ-MASTER paragraph requires modification of one instruction. Since the elementary counter areas are now SVCETALLY, we must add in them. Now, however, we require two identifications to locate the proper counter: first, the pay code, to locate the correct main grouping, then the service code to identify the correct counter within the correct main grouping. Our double-subscripted ADD instruction will now be: ADD 1 TO SVCETALLY (PAYCODE SVC-CODE).

5) The remaining changes (including an additional 77-level item in working-storage) are concerned with assembling the accumulations and printout of them in the nine-by-six matrix or grid required. Since we have six service-code counts for each pay rate, we will need an additional counter area, used as a subscript in a manner similar to SUBS, to aid in controlling movement of each set of six service-code counts to their related pay-rate print line. We will add to working storage (preceding the first 01-level record, of course) an entry: 77 SUB2 PIC 9. For a reason which will be evident shortly, there is no need to assign a VALUE to SUB2.

The MOVE-TO-PRINT paragraph will require expansion, though the first three instructions will be retained intact. It will now appear as:

```
MOVE-TO-PRINT.
   ADD 1 TO SUBS. MOVE SPACES TO PRINTREC.
   MOVE RATE (SUBS) TO PAYRATE.
   PERFORM SERVICE-MOVE VARYING SUB2 FROM 1 BY 1
       UNTIL SUB2>6.
   WRITE PRINTREC AFTER ADVANCING 2 LINES.
SERVICE-MOVE.
   MOVE SVCETALLY (SUBS SUB2) TO RATECOUNTS
       (SUB2).
```

The PERFORM . . . VARYING statement used here is an abbreviated version of a format so lengthy that its full statement (including numerous unused portions) would only be confusing. The applicable format of the VARYING clause is:

$$\underline{\text{VARYING}} \text{ identifier-1 } \underline{\text{FROM}} \begin{array}{l} \text{literal-1} \\ \text{identifier-2} \end{array}$$

$$\underline{\text{BY}} \begin{array}{l} \text{literal-2} \\ \text{identifier-3} \end{array} \underline{\text{UNTIL}} \text{ condition.}$$

The effect of this PERFORM format is to move an amount to an area being used as a subscript, have the instruction called for PERFORMed, increment the area by another specified amount, and continue to perform the called-for instruction until the named condition is fulfilled. Note that the specified amounts used need not be literals; they can be data fields that contain numeric digits.

Step by step, the effect of the first execution of this PERFORM instruction is first to move a 1 to SUB2 (the FROM provides the 1 for the first execution only), then (since at this point SUBS contains a 1) move the first service-code count for the first pay rate to the first (leftmost) print area for a count. When this has been done, the VARYING . . . BY 1 adds another 1 to SUB2, and since SUB2 is not greater than 6, the contents of the *second* SVCETALLY within the first pay rate is moved. This cycle continues until after the sixth SVCETALLY for the first pay rate is moved, the VARYING . . . BY 1 causes SUB2 to read 7, which causes the PERFORM to terminate the WRITE PRINTREC to print the six counts for the first pay rate. Since MOVE-TO-PRINT is being performed nine times, this routine is returned to, a 1 is added to SUBS (providing a subscript for the second pay rate), and the SERVICE-MOVE cycle is performed the required six times for the second pay rate.

It should be pointed out here that the PERFORM . . . VARYING instruction is used here only for illustrative purposes of its basic function; its use here was not absolutely essential. The VARYING option is not available on some lower-level COBOL compilers; and if programming a two-dimensional table under such conditions, the following alternative is available: since SUB2 must be available for subscripting, but not necessarily to limit the number of service-move performances, we can substitute for the PERFORM . . . VARYING the simple statement PERFORM SERV-ICE-MOVE 6 TIMES. We can make SUB2 an effective subscripting item by assigning it a VALUE of ZERO following its 77-level picture, and inserting as the first instruction in the SERVICE-MOVE paragraph, ADD 1 TO SUB2, in effect doing the same thing for SUB2 as the first MOVE-TO-PRINT instruction does for SUBS. SUB2 must be returned to zero after every sixth performance of SERVICE-MOVE. We can do this by inserting a MOVE ZERO TO SUB2 instruction either just before or just after the WRITE PRINTREC . . . instruction in the MOVE-TO-PRINT paragraph.

Since the printout will occupy only one page, and there are six columns of data in addition to the pay-rate column, a single heading can readily be provided by a few entries: one SPECIAL-NAMES entry in the environment division to designate a top-of-page name, and three entries at the end of the first paragraph of the procedure division. These should, respectively, move spaces to PRINTREC, move an appropriate non-numeric literal containing spaces and properly positioned column headings to PRINTREC, and write the PRINTREC after advancing to the top-of-page name.

STORED TABLES AS REFERENCE FOR PROCESSING INSTRUCTIONS

The one- and two-dimensional tables just described are examples of the use of tables stored during program

execution and printed out as reports. The storing of tables for *reference* during program execution is also a frequent use of table-handling techniques. One of the most universal of stored-table referencing involves the Federal income-tax deduction tables in computing income taxes to be withheld based on amount of gross pay, marital status, and number of withholding allowances. The Internal Revenue Service has set up tax tables for payroll periods of different lengths, which it assumes will be used in processing of computerized payrolls. The 1973 table for a weekly payroll period is given below to illustrate the format of one complete table. Note that it is really two tables, one for taxpayers classified as single and one for taxpayers classified as married. The amount-of-wages columns represent the *taxable* pay, which is determined by multiplying the number of withholding allowances by the exemption for each allowance and subtracting it from gross pay. Since one exemption is $14.40 per week, in COBOL terms, COMPUTE TAXABLE = GROSS — (14.40 * ALLOWANCES).

	IF AMOUNT OF WAGES		AMOUNT OF INCOME TO BE WITHHELD		
		but not			of excess
	is over	over	shall be	plus	over
Single	0	$ 11	0	0	
person:	$ 11	$ 35	0	14%	$ 11
	$ 35	$ 73	$ 3.36	18%	$ 35
	$ 73	$202	$10.20	21%	$ 73
	$202	$231	$37.29	23%	$202
	$231	$269	$43.96	27%	$231
	$269	$333	$54.22	31%	$269
	$333	$999[3]	$74.06	39%	$333
Married	0	$ 11	0	0	
person:	$ 11	$ 39	0	14%	$ 11
	$ 39	$167	$ 3.92	16%	$ 39
	$167	$207	$24.40	20%	$167
	$207	$324	$32.40	24%	$207
	$324	$409	$60.48	28%	$324
	$409	$486	$84.28	32%	$409
	$486	$999[3]	$108.92	36%	$486

As with many types of tables stored for reference during program execution, the choice of storage techniques arises with the tax table. Should it be stored during compilation by use of the VALUE clause in conjunction with the table-defining entries, or should the table data

---

3. The figure of $999 is shown here to provide a specific figure in the storage area defined as MAX to be compared with the three integers in TAXABLE. The Internal Revenue Service tax table sets no limit in the top tax rate brackets.

be punched on cards to be read in as special input preceding the regular input data for program execution? If the former, the table data cannot be as readily tampered with or subjected to change by careless card handling, unless the object program is on cards; but to reflect a change in the table, the source program must be updated and recompiled. If read in as special input data, a change in the table data will not require recompilation as long as the number of table items remains the same, but there is somewhat more exposure to card-handling errors. For purposes of illustration, we will assume read-in of special input cards containing tax-table data prior to reading of the payroll data record file.

Within either option of tax-table storage, numerous ways of storing and referencing are available. The illustrations below are based on the assumption that the table data will be on sixteen cards in the sequence listed above. We will use PERFORM options and COMPUTE statements, which are available only on higher-level COBOL compilers; but lower-level PERFORM options and simple arithmetic statements can be substituted with the same results.[4] We will also assume that reading of the sixteen table cards precedes reading of the pay data input file, whose records contain, among other fields, the following:

```
02   NO-OF-ALLOWANCES      PIC 99.
02   MARITAL               PIC X.
02   GROSSPAY              PIC 999V99.
```

MARITAL, we will assume, is either S (single) or M (married).

The sixteen tax-table cards will be identified as TAXFILE and have the following record layout:

```
01   TAXCARD.
     02   S-OR-M      PIC X.
     02   TAXES       PIC 9(13).
     02   FILLER      PIC X(66).
```

The S-OR-M column will not be needed for program reference, but should be punched in each card to identify the card for visual reference when required. Notice that the tax table is *not* defined here. We will define it in working-storage.

The following working-storage entries will be needed for tax computations:

---

4. Lower-level PERFORM options such as PERFORM . . . integer TIMES and the related ADD 1 TO (subscript area) have already been illustrated in the preceding table-handling routines.

```
77   CTR              PIC 99.
77   TAXABLE          PIC 999V99 VALUE ZEROES.
77   INCOME-TAX       PIC 999V99 VALUE ZEROES.
01   TAXWEEKLY.
     02   TAXTABLE OCCURS 16 TIMES.
     03   MIN          PIC 999.
     03   MAX          PIC 999.
     03   BASE-TAX     PIC 999V99.
     03   TAXRATE      PIC V99.
```

CTR will be used for subscripting. TAXABLE will be computed by subtracting the result of NO-OF-ALLOWANCES times $14.40 from GROSSPAY. INCOME-TAX will be computed by the routine illustrated below. The four elementary items in TAXABLE are the first four columns of the weekly-payroll tax table printed above, in exact order. Note that the first two items are in whole dollars, BASE-TAX is in dollars and cents, and TAXRATE (a percentage less than 100) is stated as a decimal figure.

Concerning ourselves only with entries related to the tax-table cards and the pay data file, our opening procedure division entries could be as follows:

```
PROCEDURE DIVISION.
  OPEN INPUT TAXFILE.
  PERFORM READ1 VARYING CTR FROM 1 BY 1 UNTIL CTR
     > 16.
  CLOSE TAXFILE. OPEN INPUT PAYDATAFILE. GO TO
     READ2.
READ1.
  READ TAXFILE AT END GO TO EOJ.
  MOVE TAXES TO TAXTABLE (CTR).
READ2.
  READ PAYDATAFILE AT END GO TO EOJ.
  · · · ·
  · · · ·
  COMPUTE TAXABLE = GROSSPAY − (14.40 * NO-OF-
     ALLOWANCES).
  IF MARITAL = "M" MOVE 09 TO CTR ELSE MOVE 01 TO
     CTR.
TAX-RTN.
  IF TAXABLE IS NOT < MAX (CTR) ADD 1 TO CTR GO TO
     TAX-RTN.
  COMPUTE INCOME-TAX ROUNDED = TAXRATE (CTR) *
     (TAXABLE − MIN (CTR)) + BASE-TAX (CTR).
```

Note the following:

1. The tax-table cards are treated as a file that is opened, read, and closed prior to opening of the pay data file. The READ1 statement, which actually creates the table, is performed as many times as there are tax-table cards, each READ1 performance adding a line of data to the table. After sixteen cards are read, the TAXFILE will be closed and the pay data record file will be opened. READ2 will then become the repetitive reading operation.

2. Once a pay-data record has been read, taxable *pay* is computed by the COMPUTE TAXABLE in-

struction. Since marital status determines whether the top or bottom half of the tax table is to be accessed, the IF MARITAL = "M" statement will provide the proper subscript data in CTR to access (at the beginning of TAX-RTN) the ninth line of table data which begins the "if married" half of the tax table. If the employee's marital status is S, 01 will be moved to CTR and the "if single" half of the table will be accessed in TAX-RTN.

3. The object of IF TAXABLE . . . is to locate the tax-table line on which taxable pay is greater than MIN but less than MAX. If taxable pay for a married employee is $167.60, three comparisons will be made before going to the COMPUTE instruction, since each time TAXABLE is greater than MAX, TAX-RTN will be started again. The fourth time around, TAXABLE will be less than MAX, and the COMPUTE instruction will take place.

4. Since, in the instance just cited, three comparisons will have been made, 1 will have been added to 09 in CTR three times, which now will contain the figure 12. The table's twelfth line is the one which has a taxable pay range from $167 to $207. The tax computation is then made, using the other three items on the twelfth line, as subscripted by CTR. Note that the enclosure of a parenthesized subscript within algebraic parentheses is permissible.

ADVANCED TABLE-HANDLING TECHNIQUES

Numerous other facets of table-handling must be left untouched here because of the necessarily limited scope of an introductory textbook. *Three-dimensional tables* are not so serious an omission; they are a logical extension of the two-dimensional variety. *Binary search* is a valuable technique for referencing bulky tables that must be stored for use during program execution. However, although binary search reduces substantially the computer-processing time required for accessing locations of table data, it is not necessarily the most effective time-saver for referencing specific types of tables. Many types of tables can be organized so that even if the number of table items runs into many hundreds, specific workable small segments of the table can be quickly located by use of input data coding and procedure instruction techniques similar to those which enabled us to locate the desired half of the tax table as just illustrated. Failure to use binary search or comparably efficient techniques in large-table handling can sometimes slow down internal processing to less than input-output processing speeds. More often than not, the applicability of tables and table-handling techniques to computer programming for business purposes depends upon the ability of the systems analyst or programmer to recognize the situation where their application would be significantly helpful.

REVIEW MATERIAL

Terms

Table	Subscript	Two-dimensional table

Questions

How do one-dimensional tables differ from two-dimensional tables?

What two broad categories do tables fall into?

How many dimensions can be handled in a COBOL table?

What is the function of the OCCURS clause?

Why is a subscript necessary when referencing a table entry?

When defining a two-dimensional table, how many OCCURS clauses are required? how many PICTURE clauses?

In the PERFORM . . . VARYING . . . statement, what is the use of the data item following VARYING? FROM? BY?

Why might it be desirable to read a reference table in from cards rather than storing it as part of the program during compilation?

True-or-False Statements

Use of tables in a COBOL program can result in the saving of considerable effort on the part of the programmer.

The OCCURS clause can be used with any data item.

A subscript must be a numeric data item.

Use of the UNTIL, TIMES, or VARYING options of the PERFORM statement allows a procedure to be executed a number of times.

When referencing a table in the procedure division, one subscript is required for each dimension of the table.

A subscript can only be modified by a PERFORM . . . VARYING . . . statement.

Programming

13–1: A company has a deck of sales cards containing one card for each sale made during the year. The card format includes the following fields:

Columns 1–7   Sales amount — dollars and cents
        8–9   Month number (from 01 for January to 12 for December)

Write a program to produce a monthly sales analysis for the company. The printed output should be a twelve-line table in this form:

JANUARY	$999,999.99
FEBRUARY	$999,999.99
. . .	. . .
. . .	. . .
DECEMBER	$999,999.99

13–2: The company described in the preceding specification has six divisions. The division number (1 through 6) is punched in column 10 of each sales card. Write a program to produce a sales analysis in two-dimensional form for the company. The printed output should be in a twelve-line format containing six columns of numbers, with maximum print areas as shown below:

	1	2	3	4	5	6
JANUARY	$99,999.999	$99,999.99	$99,999.99	$99,999.99	$99,999.99	$99,999.99
FEBRUARY						
. . .						
. . .						
DECEMBER						

PART D

Some Additional
Perspectives

14

SYSTEMS AND PROGRAMMING CONTROLS

One of the chief advantages of computerized data-processing systems is that a limited variety of checking against human error or mechanical error is possible at high speeds within the computer, a practice not feasible manually because of the amount of human time and cost involved. No computer program can set up means of detecting all types of errors in input data, but careful validation techniques used in a computer program, or even at preprogramming stages in a computer area, can detect many types of errors which can be referred to the error source or elsewhere for correction. For example, a system of coding that includes the principle known as the self-checking digit can be used to detect *invalid* account code numbers by using validation techniques in programming at the computer processing stage; such a technique, however, will not detect the error of recording customer A's account number on invoice data for customer B as long as all digits in customer A's number were correctly recorded in proper sequence.

In computerized systems, the computer processing and the programming of it cannot and should not be the only areas of reliance for control of accuracy and detection of errors in data processing. The manual time saved, by incorporating high-speed computer data-checking to replace manual review, can be partially used in (*a*) providing controls over data input so that the computer area will have means of checking to determine accuracy of its own output results and (*b*) follow-up in use and routing of computer-produced reports so that their function is properly fulfilled in the data-

processing system as a whole. In relationship to actual computer processing, data-processing controls are sometimes classified as being in three phases:

1. Preprocessing controls, which are developed by the user's data-preparation personnel and normally attached to batch data forwarded to the computer area. An example would be an adding machine tape of amounts of checks received from customers, forwarded by an accounts receivable department to the computer area with data regarding the invoices paid. Most preprocessing controls contain totals that execution of the first program processing the data will produce in printout form. If the computer-generated totals are the same as the control totals, processing through the computerized cycle will continue; if not, the differences must be resolved before being processed further. In general, preprocessing controls initiated by the user's data-preparation personnel must be followed up by programming routines which provide the means of checking the data to the controls on the first computer processing.

2. Processing controls. From the standpoint of responsibility, processing controls *within the computer area* can also be classified in the same three phases as data-processing controls generally:

a. Preprocessing controls: Controls in data-preparation stages, such as clerical control to make sure that all batches of data listed by the user on a transmittal sheet have been received, and keypunch area controls of key verification.

b. Processing controls: These are largely controls of two types. (*1*) Some controls are initiated in the computer programming, based on the nature of the data, checking for specific types of error conditions. The data-validation techniques described in connection with file-updating are examples of such controls. (*2*) More positive types of processing controls are those which are developed as part of the computerized portion of the system, normally by requiring totals or counts to be reported as output from one program in a series and substantiated by requiring a subsequent program making use of the output to report the same totals or counts. In this way, accuracy of output data from one processing to the next in a series is verified by the computer's execution of each program.

c. Postprocessing controls: Within the computer area, clerical audit must take place to check first computer processing (balancing and editing stage) of input data to assure agreement to user's controls before processing further; in addition, after completion of all computer processing of a series of reports, continuity of control figures through the series must be clerically checked, and in many cases, figures must be logged in the computer data control area that will serve as cumulative controls for the next computer processing of periodic reports using as input data the output files created by the current computer processing. When these clerical operations have been done, input documents and computer reports are ready for return to the user area.

3. Postprocessing controls. In the user area these may include:

a. Some repetition of control-figure checking from input to output already done in the computer area.

b. Followup for correction, in accordance with agreed-upon procedures, of any unprocessable data returned by the computer area.

c. Distribution of reports to concerned personnel in the user area and elsewhere.

d. Using the data, as furnished by the computer area, in ways which by their nature will confirm validity or detect errors in the data furnished.

The concern of the programmer with specific phases in the cycle of controls centers around (*a*) implementing the user's preprocessing controls by providing logically accurate means of substantiating them in the execution of his computer programs, and (*b*) supplying data-validation techniques in computer programs which the user cannot possibly or practically supply manually through its preprocessing controls. If the programmer is required to do his own systems work, he must familiarize himself with the nature of the entire cycle of controls needed within the system; if he is assigned only programming responsibility, his obligation is to develop in his programs the techniques called for in the systems analyst's program specifications and, at most, to suggest and, if approved, incorporate in the programs such data-validation techniques as appear to him to be inherent in the nature of the programs themselves.

PROGRAM IMPLEMENTATION OF USER'S PREPROCESSING CONTROLS

Numerous data-processing control techniques, either inherent in manual accounting processes or developed as pre-computer or computer-mechanized systems aids, are available for implementation by computer programming. Among these are control listings with totals, batch controls, and hash totals.

Control listings with totals: Lists, usually adding machine tapes, of totaled amounts representing data on batches of input documents, are ordinarily transmitted by the user area to the computer area. The grand total of this quantitative data is normally expected to appear on some computer-produced report, either as the exact figure supplied by the user or as adjusted by user-approved corrections, additions, and/or deletions made in connection with some initial computer processing done specifically for the purpose of assuring input data accuracy. The program for this initial processing should not only provide a printout of the computer's version of the user's control totals, but also the listing of control tape detail constituting the totals (preferably in the same sequence as the user's control tape), to permit rapid manual checking of tape-versus-printout for location of the errors, which may have originated in either user's or computer center's data-preparation area.

Batch controls: Individual batches of data will ordinarily be transmitted with control tape listings as just described; but batch controls have two auxiliary purposes. One is to break up large volumes of data into groups small enough to provide ease of handling and efficiency in checking for errors. A thousand or more input documents in one group is not only awkward to control in the user's data-preparation area, but equally awkward in processing through keypunching and verification. Equally important is the time advantage gained in error-checking between user's control totals and initial computer-processing totals. A single difference between these totals for a thousand items may consist of one or more errors in the last hundred items. Ten batches of approximately 100 items each, with a control listing and total for each batch, matched by batch listings and totals on the computer printout, supply the ability for a quick visual check that shows nine totals are correct; a search for the error can be confined to the one batch of data for which totals do not agree.

To give effect to these economies and provide what accountants call an *audit trail*, a batch-numbering system is used. Each batch of data is assigned a consecutive number, which is made a field in each data-record keypunched. This makes it possible for the computer program for initial processing to include totaling routines by batch number, and for any subsequent programs listing the data records to print the batch number related to each record so that processing dates and location of documents can be readily traced. In addition, documents coming into the computer center's data-preparation area can be checked out by consecutive batch number to make sure that no batches are missing and to provide more controllable assignment of work to keypunch personnel to produce punched and verified data sooner.

Hash totals: Listings and totals of quantitative data supply some, but not all, controls over data accuracy. Many code fields are equally important for assuring that the amounts found correct by proving to control totals are charged or credited to the proper customer, supplier, employee, salesman, account number, or stock item, to mention only a few possibilities. Users may fear the possibility of code numbers properly marked on data by their own personnel being keypunched incorrectly and the errors not being detected or corrected through key verification. To protect against this possibility, user data-preparation personnel may run an adding machine tape for each batch of data listing such relevant codes as employee numbers on payroll data, adding the code numbers as if they were quantities. The total of such a control tape is referred to as a "hash" total since it represents no real amount. When "hash" control tapes are supplied, however, the computer program for the initial processing of data must supply a printout that lists the code numbers and their batch totals. This permits checking in the same manner as when proving to control totals of quantitative data.

THE SELF-CHECKING NUMBER

Rather obviously, users who are concerned with the possibility of errors in code numbers occurring only at the keypunching and verifying stage can easily be ignoring the most frequent source of error—their own data-preparation personnel. Only two types of computer-input source documents are not subject to coding errors made by users' data-preparation personnel. These are (*a*) the prepunched cards supplied as "turnaround documents" by the computer area from computer output, which already contain code numbers and require only a minimum of data-writing (usually on the cards themselves) by user data-preparation personnel prior to return to the computer area for keypunching on the cards of the data supplied; and (*b*) other forms of documents that will be keypunched as complete input records but already have code numbers imprinted on them. Examples of these are sales slips which bear a customer account number imprinted from a plastic credit card being registered through an inked mechanism on each slip; or an accounts payable or receivable open-item listing prepared on a computer and returned by the user with settlement data notations.

In other cases, perhaps more typical, user data-preparation personnel supplies code numbers on documents by the rather tedious method of looking up the item to be coded on a master list of some type, such as an employee roster, a chart of accounts, or a coded list of customers or suppliers. In most cases, these are computer-generated listings with enough open spaces (sometimes with unused code numbers shown) provided to permit user personnel to write in additional names on the list, allocating an unused code number to each new name.

Two types of error-creating possibilities are immediately suggested. First, the user's personnel may find the name being looked up, and write on the document the code number for the name on the line above or below the one intended. No method of checking, except the rather impractical one of two completely independent lookups and codings is likely to detect this type of error. A complaining customer, supplier, employee, or salesman is usually the result of this type of undetected error. Only if (*a*) there is an additional code number in the data which must be matched to some computer-file record related to a specific customer or code number or (*b*) user personnel has made a detectable error in transcribing the wrong number is there a possibility that computer processing will expose this type of error.

Another source of error is that user personnel may transcribe the proper code number incorrectly, or form digits in such a manner that keypunch and verifier operators interpret the number the same way but differently than intended. The self-checking number can be used advantageously to detect more than 95% of such errors.

The self-checking number is a device that can be,

and is, used independently of computers; its effectiveness can be aided by computer generating of self-checking numbers for setting up master codes and by incorporating in programs for initial input processing the routines required for verifying the correctness of the number.

Essentially, any self-checking number is a series of digits in which the last (rightmost) digit is a result of prescribed mathematical manipulation of the other digits. In a six-digit self-checking number, applying specified arithmetic to the first five digits would determine what the sixth should be. For any given sequence of five digits, only one specific digit could be a correct sixth. Thus the last digit in a self-checking number is referred to as the *check digit*. Anyone might construct his own arithmetic formula for generating check digits; however, any self-checking number formula contains the possibility that in a very small percentage of cases an error in recording a self-checking number could result in the same check digit as for the correct number. Two self-checking number formulas in current use, the Modulus 10 and Modulus 11, can be calculated by special devices attachable to IBM's 24, 26, and 29 keypunches. These devices perform the required arithmetic as soon as the operator punches each digit, and immediately after the one preceding the check digit, which is then calculated by the device and punched. Most large-volume credit-card systems use one or the other of these two formulas for generating credit-card identification numbers. Availability of computers has probably reduced the usage of the keypunch attachments. Computer programs can be written to produce master lists of available account numbers, each number complete with its self-checking digit. Since the check digit is made part of the number, accuracy of keypunching of the number can be verified by a program routine for the initial computer processing, which calculates the check digit and compares it to the one keypunched, using the error-message technique to flag the error.

Descriptions and examples of the Modulus 10 and Modulus 11 formulas follow:[1]

Modulus 10: 1. Multiply the units position and every alternate position of the basic code number by 2.
2. Add the *digits* of the products above to the code number digits *not* multiplied.
3. Subtract the sum of the above from the next-higher number ending in zero.
4. The difference is the check digit.

---

1. Based on descriptions in IBM's publication GC20–1649–06, *Introduction to IBM Direct-Access Storage Devices and Organization Methods*, in turn based on IBM's publications G24–1057, *Self-Checking Number Feature*, and G24–1022, *Self-Checking Number Feature, Modulus 11, and Its Associated Self-Checking-Number Generator, Modulus 11.*

As an example, let us use the seven-digit code number 4821736:

Basic code number:

4	8		2	1		7	3		6
$\times$ 2			$\times$ 2			$\times$ 2			$\times$ 2
8			4			14			12

2. $8 + 8 + 4 + 1 + 1 + 4 + 3 + 1 + 2$
$$= 32$$

3. From the next-higher zero-ending number, 40, subtract 32, giving 8.
4. The check digit is 8. The self-checking code number is 48217368.

Modulus 11: Each digit position in the code number is assigned a "weight," beginning with 2 in the units position and increasing by 1 with each digit to the left, starting again with 2 after a weight of 7 has been reached. The check digit is calculated as follows:
1. Multiply each digit by its "weight" factor.
2. Add the products.
3. Divide the sum by 11.
4. Subtract the remainder from 11.
5. The result is the check digit.

Using the same number as in the Modulus 10 example:
1. Multiply by:

4	8	2	1	7	3	6
2	7	6	5	4	3	2

2. Add the products: $8 + 56 + 12 + 5 + 28 + 9 + 12 = 130$
3. Divide: $130/11 = 11$, with a remainder of 9.
4. Subtract: $11 - 9 = 2$.
5. The check digit is 2. The self-checking number is 48217362.

It would appear that COBOL program routines for Modulus 11 might be easier and shorter to write than for Modulus 10, except for the necessity of completing the arithmetic by use of the division remainder. Lower-level COBOL compilers may not provide a convenient means of handling this; in the higher-level compilers, a REMAINDER clause option is available with either of the DIVIDE . . . GIVING formats (DIVIDE BY or DIVIDE INTO), which permits storing the REMAINDER in a named data field (presumably defined as a working-storage area). The related portion of a Modulus 11 routine for this purpose, using the full REMAINDER option format, might be:

```
DIVIDE MODSUM BY 11 GIVING AMOUNT ROUNDED RE-
   MAINDER LEFTOVER ON SIZE ERROR GO TO ERROR-
   RTN.
SUBTRACT LEFTOVER FROM 11 GIVING CHECKDIGIT.
```

ROUNDED and ON SIZE ERROR are included in the DIVIDE routine above only to show the positioning of the REMAINDER option clause. The words REMAINDER LEFTOVER compile as an instruction to move the remainder to the area called LEFTOVER.

PROCESSING CONTROLS IN COMPUTER PROGRAMS

As indicated in our classification of controls, those originated in the computer programs themselves are either error-checking (data-validation) techniques or the generation of totals or counts by one program carried forward in some output form to be verified in subsequent processing. The latter technique involves no special routines in programming; its use is normally decided by the systems personnel; and the programmer may not even be aware that the technique is being used unless he is assigned all the programs of a series. The data-validation techniques, on the other hand, although they should be called for in systems specifications to initiate a programming requirement, are rather standardized tests occasioning a specific type of programming instruction or routine. A programmer should be familiar with both the terminology and type of program instructions involved in these data-validation techniques.

Although most of the data-validation techniques appear in programs for first processing of input data, many (particularly those having to do with the size of computed amounts) must be developed in programs for subsequent processing. As pointed out in Chapter 1,[2] one of the first considerations of a programmer in reading program specifications is to determine what, if any, checks are to be made for error detection. Such checks or tests are rather numerous.

Sequence checks: Except for planned random-access processing, or random-order card-to-tape (or disk) processing prior to sorting and validation processing, input data is normally in some stated sequence, usually in an ascending order. The "previous-number" technique for sequence-checking and controlling totals on printouts has already been described. What is not standardized is any basis for operating instructions regarding the degree to which an input file may contain sequence errors before stopping the job for a re-sort. The programmer would often be wise to raise this question, and get a decision on what number to put in the blank space in statements such as those below:

```
IF CURRENTNUMBER < PREVIOUSNUMBER ADD 1 TO
    SEQERRCTR.
IF SEQERRCTR > __ DISPLAY "SEQUENCE ERRORS
    OVER MAXIMUM; STOP JOB AND RE-SORT INPUT"
    STOP RUN.
```

Character-of-data tests: These are simple checks by use of the "class" test to determine whether a data field is alphabetic or numeric, or the "sign" test to determine whether a numeric field is positive, negative, or zero. Compilers may vary as to the range of application of the class test, which is:

IF identifier IS [NOT] $\begin{Bmatrix} \text{NUMERIC} \\ \text{ALPHABETIC} \end{Bmatrix}$ . . .

While there is some variation among compilers as to the scope of class tests, ANSI specifications assume that a field whose PICTURE is alphabetic cannot be tested for NUMERIC, and vice versa. A summary of the permissible tests is:

IF FIELD PICTURE IS	AN IF STATEMENT CAN TEST FOR	
Alphanumeric	ALPHABETIC	NOT ALPHABETIC
	NUMERIC	NOT NUMERIC
Alphabetic	ALPHABETIC	NOT ALPHABETIC
Numeric	NUMERIC	NOT NUMERIC

Care must be taken in applying tests to numeric fields. If a numeric field carries a possible operational sign, the field's PICTURE must begin with an S; if the PICTURE is unsigned, and the data contains an operational sign, the data will test as not numeric. Presence of the S in the PICTURE means that signed numeric data will test as numeric. In addition, if numeric fields of varying length are keypunched with spaces instead of leading zeroes, they can be numeric-tested only after an instruction (presumably an EXAMINE . . . REPLACING) has been executed replacing the spaces with zeroes. It should be noted also that such fields would have to be initially defined as alphanumeric because of the combination of spaces (alphabetic) with numeric digits; and if the field might carry an operational sign, it would have to be REDEFINEd with an S in its PICTURE in order to be recognized (through use of the redefinition in the test statement) as numeric.

As suggested by the above, the success of a "sign" test will depend on the same careful definition and handling of fields that are necessary for a workable class test. The sign test has three, rather than two, alternatives:

IF $\begin{Bmatrix} \text{identifier} \\ \text{arithmetic-expression} \end{Bmatrix}$ IS [NOT] $\begin{Bmatrix} \underline{\text{POSITIVE}} \\ \underline{\text{NEGATIVE}} \\ \underline{\text{ZERO}} \end{Bmatrix}$ . . .

Before making use of a sign test which involves a zero condition as a possibility distinct from positive and negative data conditions, it is safest to determine (by feeding in signed and unsigned zero input data and creating signed summed internal fields that zero-balance), just how the computer being used evaluates zero conditions. Some computers still current will identify a zero condition as positive or negative, based on the sign of the balance prior to the last operation which brought the field to zero. For example, a field which had a 345 balance before a subtraction of 345 took place would be considered 000. If sign tests must be made to include

---

2. On pages 9–10, in the discussion of the first of seven phases of the programming function.

or exclude zero conditions, it is usually safest to provide specifically for the possibility of zero in the sign test statement—unless, of course, the compiler recognizes such a statement as inconsistent, a rather unlikely possibility. If a particular routine is to be executed when FIELDX is positive but not when it is zero or negative, the statement IF FIELDX POSITIVE AND NOT ZERO GO TO RTNZ should be acceptable, particularly in a computer whose arithmetic may register a positive zero. For other computers, IF FIELDX POSITIVE GO TO RTNZ should be adequate; ANSI COBOL specifications regard zero as a third condition neither positive nor negative.

Class and sign tests for error conditions occur most often in programs for initial processing of new data; they usually require only the printing of some type of error message identifying the occurrence of the condition, and are seldom a stop-the-job type of test. The complete absence of either type of test from program specifications for initial processing should alert the programmer to review the susceptibility of the data to validation tests. This should be done at the first of the seven phases of the programming function.

Completeness checks: These may be necessary in certain types of processing. Unpunched data fields or a missing card in a consecutively coded series may be among the possible subjects of error tests and messages, particularly in programs written to create stored files from original data. For the edit run that is normally the first processing of the data, it may be desirable to set up a list of code letters or numbers that represent specific types of errors (of which a large part is usually the missing data error) and print each error digit, on occurrence of the error condition, in a fixed position at the right margin of the printout page. In this way, the situation of multiple error conditions on one input record can be handled without creating a printout problem; for example, the possibility of eleven errors on one record would present a maximum use of eleven columns and twenty-two printing positions instead of creating the problem of how and where to print eleven possible error messages simultaneously.

Size tests: "Size test" might be an applicable term for three types of quantitative tests of numeric data which overlap each other in scope. From the early days of computers to the present, some of the favorite news stories on "computer errors" have been those which told of computers producing checks for astronomical sums of money to pay a small invoice or a low-paid employee. Yet almost never have any of these situations involved a computer error. In the practical case, such errors occur either because the user or systems personnel failed to specify actual or reasonable limits as the basis for programmer-initiated data tests, or either or both neglected to set up control proofs of arithmetic totals from one program to the next in a series. At the high-order end of fields used to represent results of arithmetic, the SIZE ERROR option based on the number of positions in the numeric data field, is the standard available size test in COBOL. In addition, the user or systems personnel should request the programmer to initiate size tests in the following types of cases where there is any danger of data-preparation personnel (either clerical or keypunch) making errors on input data.

A *limit check* should be made where it is known that specific data fields have an upper or lower numeric limit, beyond which data is erroneous. When the data field has both upper and lower limits, this is referred to as a *range check*. Where there are not specific known limits, the user may be asked to indicate a *reasonableness check*, which is not based on arithmetic inherent in the data, but is to be incorporated in the programming to prevent arithmetically possible errors from causing difficulties. For example, in a weekly payroll, it might be possible that individual gross pay could reach the low six-figure range (including cents), requiring that the data field have a PICTURE of 9999V99; yet it is known that gross pay in the high six-figure range would be erroneous. How high? A reasonableness check might be set to make a gross pay of $2,000 or more subject to an error-message generation.

Once individual data-items have been subjected to some type of size check, and controls set up based on the results as checked, the accumulation of the same data in subsequent processing should check to these controls. For example, initial processing of payroll data to compute individual gross pays should contain the necessary size tests and develop a control total or totals (e.g., departmental and grand) on gross pay. At a subsequent stage, taxes and other deductions may be calculated, and on this processing, gross pay, deductions, and net pay totals are accumulated. Gross pay must agree with the controls already developed. Net pay serves as a control for the processing of pay checks, whose program should carry a routine for printing, following the last pay check, at least the net pay totals as a means of checking to the controls established.

Consistency checks: These are tests which relate two or more conditions of the input data to each other for the purpose of validating the data. In the updating of master-file data, consistency checks include the practice already described of assigning a class-of-data code to update data which must be related to matching another update data code field with a master-file record. Operational signs in amount fields may sometimes be related to other code fields in consistency checks, so that a sign test may be part of a consistency check if a particular transaction code means, for example, that a specified amount field must never be negative. Consistency checks may also involve size tests. If a payroll includes personnel on both daily and hourly rates of pay, there may be tests to make sure that the rate for an employee coded as daily falls within one range and a weekly-coded rate falls within another. Also, if the time is reported in days for daily-rated employees and hours for hourly-rated, the time should be subjected to a range test and consistency with the rate code established.

In a sense, the record counts which should be established in sequential file updatings are consistency checks (as well as control total checks). They relate input master record counts to counts for classes of update data in a way that requires proof to the number of output master records created. In part, however, they belong to another somewhat different category of tests: checks on the computer operation itself.

Checks on the computer operation itself: Various internal hardware techniques or devices have been developed or adopted by computer manufacturers to check accuracy of performance or malfunction of operating devices. Among the more standard of these are the parity check (see Chapter 1) to test for proper internal transfer of data, character by character; the generation of error signals when a disk or tape record surface is in damaged condition so that data cannot be read from it or written on it; error signals generated when input data contains data so mispunched that the bit configuration does not represent for a given position anything in the computer's character set; and error signals or halts when coordination between computer devices is faulty.

The programmer, however, also has some means of checking internal computer performance, which at the same time afford checks on the correctness of his programming logic. Among these are reverse arithmetic tests, crossfooting checks, and record counts.

Reverse arithmetic tests may be desirable, and may be considered necessary wherever sufficient storage capacity permits, to check computations within a program to assure computer operational accuracy. Consider the following statements:

```
COMPUTE FIELDX = (FIELDA * FIELDB) + FIELDC.
COMPUTE RECHECK = (FIELDX − FIELDC) / FIELDA.
IF RECHECK NOT EQUAL TO FIELDB MOVE "BADCALC" TO
    ERRORMESSAGE.
```

Error messages resulting when carefully prepared test data provides seemingly correct answers should be checked to reveal possible logic errors either in the original computation statement or in the reverse arithmetic. If it is necessary to use the ROUNDED option in original arithmetic statements, reverse arithmetic logic should be carefully checked to determine its validity if the REMAINDER option is not available.

Crossfooting checks are also desirable as an internal operation consistency check; in central-processor-bound programs, however, they should be strategically used to avoid creating excessive running time. The example of a payroll preparation is perhaps the most relevant. A typical determination of net pay may involve subtraction of a dozen or more possible deduction fields from the gross pay field. A reverse-arithmetic check would involve adding the net pay and deduction fields to assure agreement with gross pay. Doing this on each employee's current-pay record would present no running-time problem if execution of the program involved printing each employee record on a payroll register, since running time would be paced by the printer's speed. In a "spooled" operation, however, where a formatted report "print file" is written on tape or disk for later processing on the printer, internal processing speed may be the governing factor. In such a case, since the report format should provide group-level (for example, department) totals of all fields involved in the crossfoot, the reverse-arithmetic check may be adequate if done only at the time each group-level set of totals is ready to be formatted for printing. The time-saving principle here is the same as that employed for "rolling totals" (see Chapter 9). In effect, there is a trade-off of calculable computer time saving for each error-free processing when only group-level reverse checking is used, against the unknown and probably very rarely-occurring time which might be used in locating the individual record error on a printout where an error message on a departmental crossfoot failure necessitated manual check of individual employee detail within the department.

Record counts, already illustrated in file-updating, provide a method of verifying using data counts, furnish a recapitulation of the program's results, give totals which can be used as carry-forward controls, and afford an opportunity for the programmer to make sure that end-of-file and other routines in his program are adequate. If properly followed up, record counts are also safeguards against rare but possible read- and write-failures of the computer. This follow-up is related to the use of the record counts as controls. Suppose that the record count on a file-updating shows:

Records read	23,114
Additions	896
Deletions	112
Records written	23,898

This is no proof of correctness until the record count of the last previous processing has been checked. Suppose the previous record count shows 23,117 records written. Were there three write-failures on the last update or three read-failures on the current one? Or is it possible that some unanticipated and untested condition is showing up which renders otherwise adequately tested program routines not quite comprehensive enough? Certainly a "dump" of the input master file from the current processing would be the first step in investigating the trouble, since it could then be determined whether the error occurred on the previous or current processing. The situation, however, points up the importance of processing controls.

POSTPROCESSING CONTROLS

As suggested in our classification of controls, those in the postprocessing category may be the responsibility of clerical personnel in either the computer area or a user department, or in both. Checking to controls between intermediate steps in computer processing may be assigned to either clerical or operating personnel in the computer area, but computer operations management is responsible for its proper exercise. Checking final reports to controls is often considered a double responsibility: the computer area is expected to check them before release of reports to user, and the user department is expected to check them before putting the report data to use. In spite of this double check (or perhaps because of it!), there are instances where the controls, made available by the user and furnished through programming as specified by the systems organization, are not checked at all in the postprocessing stages. While this failure to use the system exists, the controls have fully as much value as if they had never been created, systems-specified, or programmed. If, however, there is adequate systems and programming documentation, internal audit procedures can readily pinpoint responsibility for failure of follow-up; and reinstatement of the required control-checking can be made without additional systems or programming effort.

REVIEW MATERIAL

Terms

Preprocessing controls	Self-checking number	Limit check
Processing controls	Check digit	Consistency check
Batch controls	Class test	Reverse-arithmetic tests
Postprocessing controls	Sign test	Crossfooting checks

Questions

What is the purpose of control listings with totals? What is the advantage of batching input data and using batch control totals?

What is the significance of a "hash" total?

What kinds of errors are detected by use of the self-checking number?

Why are sequence checks often used?

What is the class of a field? What special treatment must be given to numeric fields keypunched with spaces instead of leading zeroes?

What are three types of size checks that may be included in a program? Think of instances in which each may be employed.

What checks can be built into a program to detect hardware malfunctions?

True-or-False Statements

Preprocessing controls, such as control totals, are primarily a check on the hardware.

Large volumes of input data are broken down into smaller batches because the computer can handle the latter more efficiently.

"Hash" totals may be used as a check on the clerical and keypunching transcription of code numbers.

The proper use of the self-checking digit will detect the interchange of two adjacent digits in a code number.

When preparing input data each column of a numeric field must be punched with a numeric character or the card will not be processed.

A size test detects the situation where a number overflows the boundaries of its field on the punched card.

The proper use of record counts can detect input-output malfunctions.

Programming

14–1: CUSTNO is a six-digit numeric field of which the units position is a Modulus 10 self-checking digit. Sales orders are hand-coded; in the first computer processing after keypunching, it is desired that this field be computer-checked to determine the validity of the code number. Set up the necessary data division and procedure division entries for the validation.

14–2: Invoices from suppliers must be hand-coded. The SUPPNO assigned is seven digits, the rightmost being the Modulus 11 check digit. Write the necessary data division and procedure division entries to check the validity of the seven-digit number.

14–3: A field called AMTBILLED is a dollars-and-cents field of eight positions, which a large percentage of the time is only three or four significant positions. Key-punch operators are instructed to punch only the significant figures; consequently, the field contains leading spaces rather than leading zeroes. The field may contain a minus sign in the pennies position. Write the necessary data division entries to replace the spaces with zeroes and test the field to make sure it is numeric, with a GO TO ERR-RTN if it is not.

14–4: Write routines for your payroll program (Chapter 9) that will make the following tests:

1. If rate class is H, regular time must be at least four hours but not more than 40; overtime must not be more than 40 hours.

2. If rate class is W, regular time must be at least 0.5 days but not more than 5; overtime must not be more than 40 hours.

15

CONCEPTS AND TECHNIQUES FOR FURTHER STUDY

AN ASSESSMENT: WHAT HAVE WE COVERED?

If the student will refer to the breakdown of the ANSI reserved word list by module (see Figure 3–3, page 43), the following will be almost immediately evident: almost all of the words occurring in the nucleus module have been illustrated in the course of text discussion, as well as a few in the sequential-access module. Though we have devoted a chapter to basic table-handling, none of the reserved words listed specifically for the table-handling module has been used. A logical question might be put: why the omissions, particularly in the cases of sequential access and table-handling? In ascending order of omission proportions, the answers are:

1. Coverage has not included a small number of items in the nucleus module for a variety of reasons. Rarity of occurrence is one: the SPECIAL-NAMES statement in the environment division, for example, permits designation of a special character in the CO-BOL set to be used to identify reports in foreign currencies, by the entry: CURRENCY SIGN IS special character. Dependence upon implementor hardware is another: the use of the word STATUS is another SPECIAL-NAMES feature typically associated with computers having external, manually-controllable switches for which ON and OFF STATUS conditions are specially-named. The combination of hardware dependence with usage that is infrequent and/or complex rendered discussion of such data division vocabulary

items as SYNCHRONIZED (LEFT) and RENAMES inappropriate in a basic programming text. Lastly, one procedure technique, the (MOVE) CORRESPOND-ING, was omitted for the same reason that use of data-name qualifiers was discouraged—source-program readability and economy of instruction coding can be better served by careful location-prefixing of a data-name occurring in two or more files.

2. While it appears that most of the reserved words associated with the sequential-access module have been ignored, the significance is not what might be expected. The standard minimal environment division statements discussed in Chapter 4 implicitly assume sequential processing. Every program illustrated or assigned is or can be written using these minimal formats for sequential processing, since each program assumes existence of one or more input data files in ascending sequence and production of output in the same manner. While not in the strictest sense completely hardware-dependent, the undiscussed portion of the vocabulary of the sequential-access module is concerned almost exclusively with the handling of hardware devices in the environment used for a given program. In most cases, this has little if any reference to internal logic detail in the program. The environmental framework in which the program is to be used will determine the applicability of specific operations in environment division statements, which in turn may require specific variations in the data division FD

statements, and modifications (in probable descending order of frequency) in CLOSE, OPEN, READ, and WRITE instructions in the procedure division. Perhaps the most basic considerations governing statements in these three areas are:

a. The number of input and output files involved in the program and the number of tape reels or disk units each will occupy. This may involve (1) modifications of the CLOSE statements to allow for a CLOSE REEL or CLOSE UNIT condition where a file occupies more than one tape reel or disk unit; (2) tape- or unit-"swapping" procedures when a limited number of reels or disks are available; (3) relationship of the above to the other two, or additional, considerations.

b. Whether the program runs as an entity or as one of a series of programs called in automatically within an operating system.

c. The possible sharing of hardware facilities in environments having multiprogramming or multiprocessing capabilities.

The ANSI-defined level of a given COBOL compiler, and implementor variations at that level, will also determine the scope and technique of file-labeling procedures, variations from standard buffer use, "rerun" facilities (the writing of output records to be used for "memory dumps"), variable-length records, and error handling procedures, to mention perhaps the most conspicuous additional functions of the sequential-access module.

Probably because of the environmental (as distinguished from internal-logic) nature of both the sequential- and random-access modules of ANSI COBOL, there has been a tendency for implementors to develop "job control language" (JCL) which serves as a bridge between program and its functioning within a given hardware configuration. While it is the responsibility of the programmer to determine (usually from the implementor's COBOL manual for the specific hardware) what environment, data, and procedure division instructions are needed to make his program functional for the given hardware, additional JCL instructions external to the source program may be required to enable compilation and execution to take place. There seems to be no standard definition of responsibility for checking applicability of job control language to program; there is probably an almost equal likelihood of finding it an operations area responsibility as there is a programming responsibility. In either event, to assure the proper functioning of a program whose internal logic is sound, both the JCL and the source program entries required by the specific hardware environment for sequential processing may require close cooperation of programmer and operations personnel, whether at operator or management level. In any event, the pronouncement of any general principles regarding the more specific-hardware-related aspects of sequential processing would probably be of very slight benefit at the introductory stages of learning to program.

3. The table-handling module is perhaps the most specialized of COBOL's eight modules, being basically a technique for statistical analyses and presentations and having a rather restricted area of general business applications, typically confined to lookups of core-stored table data for such purposes as assigning code classifications or computing income-tax deductions on payroll data. However, the basic one- and two-dimensional table techniques already described can often be used in incidental ways in business programming for efficient data manipulation, even though the data itself is not intended to be tabular in the strict sense. For these and any general business applications of tables, the techniques described and illustrated in Chapter 13 are an adequate foundation. The indexing and search techniques associated with more sophisticated forms of table-handling are at least as far outside the scope of an introductory programming textbook as are, for example, somewhat more advanced general business applications involving programs relating to accounts receivable aging, production scheduling, accounting statement preparation, and the like.

FUNCTIONS OF THE OPTIONAL COBOL MODULES

Of the five optional COBOL modules, the inclusion of four is dependent in one way or another on the hardware configuration and the extent to which the options available with it are judged necessary to meet the user's requirements. Although in one sense this is also true of the fifth (random-access module), the choice of disk equipment for file storage is almost always made on the assumption that some random-access processing will be done, necessitating the inclusion of the random-access module in the COBOL compiler. Consequently, some fairly extensive consideration must be given to the characteristics of both disk hardware and random access, to which the latter part of this chapter is devoted.

The Sort Module

This optional module provides certain economies of both processing time and programming by permitting a file sort to be introduced at a particular point in a program and completing execution of the program after the sort. As suggested by the ANSI specifications for this module, the user may apply special processing such as addition, creation, altering, editing, or other modifications of the individual records by input or output procedures, either before or after (or both) the sort takes place. In lower-level compilers, only one sort of one file is permitted by the sort module. In higher-level compilers, more than one sort of more than one file is permitted.

The advantages of the sort module are rather readily evident to a programmer familiar with a specific user's needs. For example, a sales analysis printout may be basically a single format with slight variations in report headings and data fields to be printed in the body of the report. Conceivably, one report might be an analysis with product line as the major grouping, with intermediate totals by region, and minor totals by salesman. Another form of the report might be desired with region as the major grouping, and salesman and product line as the intermediate and minor groupings respectively. Each report would make use of the same file, but in different sort sequence. The basic program instructions would remain the same, but the designation of data fields as keys for minor, intermediate, and major group totals and as printout items would be changed before or after each sort so that the resumption of the program after each sort would produce the report in the format rearrangement for the new file-sequence.

The Report-Writer Module

This is quite possibly the least-used of the options available; if so, it is at least partly because ANSI COBOL nucleus requirements make the setting up of report-heading, page-heading, page-numbering, and related routines relatively simple, and to a somewhat lesser extent because of the availability of implementor-supplied features in ANSI subset compilers which facilitate these routines. These are the essence of the lower-level report-writer modules, in addition to the ability to specify detail group types. The higher-level report-writer module provides either detailed or summarized reporting, and furnishes the ability to specify control group types and automatic summation and resetting of counter areas for specified items. The fact that this module is absent from some compilers of substantial scope suggests that in some implementor and user areas there is a feeling that its functions can be readily fulfilled through use of other COBOL compiler features.

The Library Module

The usefulness of the library module depends on the existence in the user's stored files of a library of program routines. The library material is not restricted to procedure division instructions but may include environment and data division text as well. The lower-level library module enables the programmer to specify environment division paragraph clauses, data division levels, and section or paragraph contents to be copied from the named library text during compilation and have them incorporated into the object program as if they had been part of the programmer's source program. ANSI specifications permit the implementor to determine whether (a) the COPY statement which calls in the library routine or (b) the library routines called in, or (c) both, are to appear on the source program listing accompanying the compilation, but the specifications do require that if both are shown, the relationship between the two must be clearly indicated.

One restriction is placed on the use of the library module: the library routines called in by the COPY statement must not themselves contain any COPY statements. This is true for both levels of the library module, which are exactly the same except for one additional feature provided in the higher-level module. This feature is an optional REPLACING clause in the COPY statement itself, which permits replacement of one or more words in the library text copied by specific words, data-names, or literals identified by the programmer in the REPLACING . . . BY clause.

The primary benefits that can be gained from use of the library modules are programmer time-saving, consultation and review time-saving (depending on the care exercised in the systems function of program specification-writing), and the assurance that routines that must be common to two or more programs will actually be the same or will vary only within the bounds specified in the REPLACING clauses.

The Segmentation Module

Computers of any internal-storage capacity are used under a variety of conditions which create the need for minimizing the amount of internal storage in use during processing. In a small computer, the amount of internal storage required for actual program instructions, input and output file records, buffering, and record-blocking, may tax the computer's capacity during the execution of a single program. In a large computer, multiprogramming or multiprocessing compounds this problem by requiring allocation of storage capacity to different programs and processing on a basis which is for practical purposes simultaneous use. In both theory and fact, if the entire contents of a program need not be available in internal storage at a given stage of execution, parts of it could be placed in external storage and transferred to internal storage for execution as needed. In this way the burden on internal-storage capacity can be substantially reduced. For a small computer, this often means that an object program which requires more total internal-storage capacity than the computer physically has can nevertheless be executed; for a computer sophisticated enough for handling more than one program, it means that a greater variety of combinations of programs and combinations of programs requiring more total capacity can be executed.

The segmentation module provides this capability for COBOL source programs by requiring the programmer to designate all paragraphs or groups of paragraphs in the procedure division as sections and assigning a priority number to each section. Within a specified range of low numbers, the fixed portion—or permanent segments (sections)—of the program is identified; sections containing higher numbers are identified as independent segments. These identifications are carried into the object program with the result that, when the program is made available for execution, the sections identified as permanent segments are made available (along with identification, environment, and data divisions) in internal storage (memory). Those sections identified as independent segments are externally stored on tape or disk. The fixed portion of the program remains in memory during the course of execution; under implementor-supplied controls, such instructions as a PERFORM can call for specific sections or paragraphs within sections that are identified as independent. These are "overlaid" in (read into) internal storage made available for some part of the externally-stored independent segments. As each portion of independent segments is called into internal storage at a given point, it effectively replaces for reference (overlays) any independent segments previously called in.

In the lower-level segmentation module, priority numbers from 0 to 49 identify permanent segments of the program, and numbers from 50 to 99 identify the independent segments. These numbers are made part of the section header, which is in the format: section-name SECTION priority-number. In the higher-level module, a clause in the environment division's OBJECT-COMPUTER paragraph—SEGMENT-LIMIT IS priority-number—permits reducing the maximum priority number for permanent segments below 49. Sections numbered in the range from the segment-limit number through 49 inclusive are considered as overlayable fixed segments.

The segmentation feature places only a moderate burden on the programmer, that of determining priority numbers for the sections in his program, deciding which sections are to be fixed and which independent (based on frequency of use within the program), and making sure that restrictions on use of PERFORM and ALTER statements are observed. Essentially, controls developed by the implementor do the rest. Special COBOL compilers for minicomputers provide a theoretical capability of using segmented programs whose total capacity demands are twenty times as great as the internal-storage capacity of the computer on which to be executed. One note of caution: the use of segmentation, particularly on smaller, slower computers, may slow down execution time because of the transfer of program instructions from external to internal storage. There may be occasions when slight halts in program execution may be physically noticeable while these transfers of segments are taking place.

THE RANDOM-ACCESS MODULE AND DISK-PROCESSING TECHNIQUES

The relationship of random access to disk usage is similar to the relationship of the term "computer" to the actual functions of a computer. A computer is a processor of data in a variety of ways, one of which is computing, though only a rather small fraction of the processing time and subject-matter processed is devoted to computing. Disk-storage devices are the only hardware generally available for random-access operations.[1] However, random-access operations, even though they may be the specific reason for choosing disk hardware in preference or addition to tape hardware, probably constitute a minor rather than major fraction of the processing time for which disk equipment is used. Certainly where disk units are the only external-storage devices, a substantial majority of the processing time is likely to be in the sequential-access mode. Random-access processing is likely to be more efficient than sequential processing in two generic types of applications and is the only practical method in a third; for other, general-purpose uses of disk storage, the sometimes-but-not-always time advantage (such as in sorting) must be weighed against its space-consumption and cost disadvantages as compared to tape. The three types of conditions in which the random-access technique is either definitely more efficient or the only practical technique are:

1. The single-inquiry situation. These are most frequently inquiries concerning availability, the most conspicuous being those referring some type of cus-

---

1. Though other random-access storage devices, such as drums, exist, they are not available from all implementors who provide ANSI COBOL subset compilers.

tomer order inquiry to a computer lookup of availability of an item on some type of stored inventory data file. Airline space reservation systems and some order-processing systems are perhaps the most conspicuous examples. The use of tape hardware is totally inapplicable here, and the possibility of using internal computer storage facilities is normally quite impractical.

2. The low-volume input data processing against a massive stored master file. When frequent low-volume processing is required in this type of situation, and sequential processing would waste a considerable amount of time in comparing input data records against 98% of 99% of unmatched master-file data (for example, input data involving only 500 of 30,000 master-file records), it may be far faster to process the input data (even if it is in the same sequence as the master file) on a random-access basis. Processing to locate only those records in the master file which are related to the input data normally takes far less time under these circumstances than does a comparison of input data with every record in the master file, which is a necessity with sequential-access processing. This type of situation can occur in almost any type of general business application.

3. A third set of conditions which has some of the characteristics of the first two is the case where input data must be related to more than one master file and there is a time and/or cost advantage to processing once against the two or more master files simultaneously (rather than subjecting input data to repeated sorting and subsequent processing against each master file separately). A typical example is processing of customer sales orders against both accounts receivable master records and inventory status master files at the same time. Particularly in low-volume processing, it is usually desirable to access both master files randomly. When remote-terminal operations are involved (see Chapter 1, page 12), this processing may have the characteristics of the single-inquiry method, in which there is no practical substitute for random-access processing.

The nature of random-access processing requires that some description of the generic hardware configuration making it possible be given, so that something more than a theoretical perspective be furnished. Physically, a disk unit, or disk pack, resembles a "juke box," each disk surface being physically accessible by an access arm. There the resemblance ends somewhat sharply; and two essential differences appear. First, the disk tracks for containing data are *not* spiral as they would be on phonograph records; from the outermost

track to the innermost, each track is a concentric ring around the next. A typical disk surface may have 200 such tracks or rings. Second, instead of being equipped with a phonograph "needle," each access arm is equipped with a "read/write head" for each disk surface it contacts (normally two). In this way each access arm is able to write new information on the disk surface or to read information from it. In a typical disk "pack" of six disks, there are five access arms, each positioned to reach between a pair of disk surfaces, the upper surface of the top disk and the lower surface of the bottom one not being available for receiving or supplying data. In the unit just described, ten disk surfaces would be available for processing data. With a 200-track surface per disk and ten surfaces, 2,000 tracks would be available for reading and writing of stored data.

From a processing standpoint, the recording (writing) of data takes place in a typical disk pack beginning at the outermost track of the underside of the topmost surface and proceeding downward on the same track for each of the available surfaces in the pack, creating a cylinder of data, then continuing on the track next inside from top to bottom in the same manner. In the pack described above, implementor location references to data would be by one of 200 possible cylinder numbers and one of ten possible track numbers within that cylinder. Only one read/write head would be engaged in the process of writing at any time.

When data files are stored on disk units, they may be stored sequentially as determined by some code number field common to all the data records, or by some nonsequential pattern. If input data is sequential and is processed against a sequential file on the basis of the common code number by matching pairs of detail and master file records successively, every record on the master file must be read in the process. This is the same process as the typical sequential processing for tape files. No reference to any master-file key data is required other than the code field by which the master file is organized in sequence. In a file-updating operation, the master file in its updated form typically would be a physically new file containing the additions and changes made by applying the updating data. Both old (input) and new (output) master files would exist as in a sequential tape updating operation; for safety in accuracy of data preservation, the "grandfather" principle should be applied in the same way as for tape processing.

When access is not sequential, whether or not the master file is organized sequentially, a typical master file would be organized to permit the addition of new records in some reasonably convenient pattern, but changes in master record data would replace previous data in the applicable record without the writing out of a complete new master file. The master file in an updating process would be *both* an input file and an output file; it would be both read and written on; and it would be identified as an input-output file in the OPEN statement.

Nonsequential access, which essentially is based on locating and reading and/or writing on only those master-file records related to the detail-file records being processed, may be implemented by programmer-generated techniques, implementor hardware techniques, implementor software (compiler-generated) techniques, or (most typically) a combination of these techniques. At the very minimum, the programmer must supply in the environment division file-control section a clause indicating by data-name the code field in the master-record format that is the basis for matching other input data, and a clause indicating that the access mode is random. Procedure division READ and/or SEEK statements are used to serve the function of locating the master-file record for processing in relation to a detail input record. An INVALID KEY condition, set up as a phrase within a READ or WRITE statement and followed by an imperative statement, serves to identify and process the error condition of inability to locate a master-file record which matches the code field number of the input data record being processed. The INVALID KEY has other uses as well, in both sequential and random-access operations; a typical protective use is in connection with master-file creation. When a particular file-limit area (in terms of disk "cylinders") has been assigned in the environment division, an IN-VALID KEY condition can be used to indicate what is to be done if the area limits have been reached at a point when there are still input records to be written on the master file.

Although ANSI specifications for reserved words and statement formats in the random-access module are precise, implementor substitutions seem to be more frequent and varied than in any other phase of ANSI COBOL. In addition, variations of sequential file *organization* (not to be confused with sequential *processing*) such as indexed sequential structures, have been designed to reduce complete rewriting of sequential disk files and conserve disk usage. Not only do space limitations and textual scope of this book prevent detailing of these variations, but two practical considerations make it likely that a detailed discussion at this stage of disk system and other hardware development would be more misleading than useful. First, both type of file organization and method of processing are likely to be determined at the systems, rather than programming, level. The decisions will be based upon type of file, frequency and volume of processing, and relative likely speeds of types of processing and the relationship of disk-processing speeds to other hardware device speeds. This last consideration alone is one in which the answers and decisions have been changing within the last few years because of improvements in disk hardware and techniques. Second, where the programmer has any choice in the matter (or even where programming is being done in a particular way based on a systems decision), he should familiarize himself, before programming, with the various device speeds of the object computer. This, of course, will vary with the programmer's user environment, and must be based on implementor, not textbook, information. Until such time as disk programming techniques come more legitimately within the range of a basic COBOL programming textbook, we must, however regretfully, leave the bulk of this subject to other areas of learning.

REVIEW MATERIAL

Terms

Job control language	Library module	Random-access module
Sort module	Segmentation module	Disk pack
Report-writer module	Overlay	Track
	Priority numbers	Cylinder

Questions

What are the advantages of using the sort feature in a COBOL program?

What type of library material may be copied using the library module? What is the restriction on this material?

What is the advantage of using the segmentation feature? What inefficiency may be introduced?

What are three conditions under which the random-access technique is employed?

How is data recorded on a typical disk pack?

Contrast the updating of sequential disk files with the updating of random-access disk files.

True-or-False Statements

Job control language is separate from and not a part of the COBOL language.

The sort module allows the programmer to rearrange a series of numbers stored in memory.

The report-writer feature is relatively seldom used because its functions can be achieved by using other ANSI COBOL nucleus features.

Use of the library module saves programmer time and insures consistency of common routines.

The segmentation feature allows the splitting of a program into two or more segments for separate execution.

Random-access processing permits updating records on a master file without rewriting the entire file.

INDEX OF SYSTEMS, PROGRAMMING, AND "HARDWARE" TERMS

INDEX OF RESERVED WORD USAGE

Page references are to text discussion; examples will also be found in the program coding illustrations related to the text page references. Please note that references are largely to key word usage; usage as an optional word is identified by *.